Lecture Notes in Economics and Mathematical Systems

439

Springer-Verlag Berlin Heidelberg GmbH

Learning to Become Rational in Self-Referential Autoregressive and Non-Stationary Models

Inaugural-Dissertation
zur Erlangung des Grades eines Doktors
der Wirtschafts- und Gesellschaftswissenschaften
durch die
Rechts- und Staatswissenschaftliche Fakultät
der
Rheinischen Friedrich-Wilhelms-Universität
Bonn

vorgelegt von
Diplom-Mathematiker
Markus Zenner
aus
Marburg/Lahn

Angefertigt mit Genehmigung der Recht- und Staatswissenschaftlichen Fakultät
der Rheinischen Friedrich-Wilhelms-Universität Bonn

Dekan:	Prof. Dr. U. Schweizer
Erstreferent:	Prof. Dr. P. Schönfeld
Zweitreferent:	Prof. Dr. K. Schürger

Tag der mündlichen Prüfung: 25. Januar 1996

Markus Zenner

Learning to Become Rational

The Case of Self-Referential Autoregressive and Non-Stationary Models

Springer

Author

Dr. Markus Zenner
University of Bonn
Institute for Econometrics and Operations Research
Adenauerallee 24–42
D-53113 Bonn, Germany

Library of Congress Cataloging-in-Publication Data

Zenner, Markus, 1963-
Learning to become rational : the case of self-referential autoregressive and non-stationary models / Markus Zenner.
p. cm. -- (Lecture notes in economics and mathematical systems ; 439)
Includes bibliographical references.
ISBN 978-3-540-61279-7 ISBN 978-3-642-51876-8 (eBook)
DOI 10.1007/978-3-642-51876-8
1. Rational expectations (Economic theory)--Mathematical models.
2. Autoregression (Statistics) 3. Economics, Mathematical.
I. Title. II. Series.
HB135.Z46 1996
330'.01'51--dc20 96-19578
CIP

Typesetting: Camera ready by author
SPIN: 10516281 42/3142-543210 - Printed on acid-free paper

Contents

Chapter 1

Introduction

1.1 Rational Expectations and Learning to Become Rational

A characteristic feature of dynamic economic models is that, if future states of the economy are uncertain, the expectations of agents matter. Producers have to decide today which amount of a good they will produce not knowing what demand will be tomorrow. Consumers have to decide what they spend for consumption today not knowing what prices will prevail tomorrow. Adopting the neo-classical point of view that economic agents are 'rational' in the sense that they behave in their own best interest given their expectations about future states of the ecomomy it is usually assumed that agents are Bayesian decision makers. But, as LUCAS points out, there remains an element of indeterminacy:

> Unfortunately, the general hypothesis that economic agents are Bayesian decision makers has, in many applications, little empirical content: without some way of infering what an agent's subjective view of the future is, this hypothesis is of no help in understanding his behavior. Even psychotic behavior can be (and today, is) understood as "rational", given a sufficiently abnormal view of relevant probabilities. To practice economics, we need *some* way (short of psychoanalysis, one hopes) of understanding *which* decision problem agents are solving. (LUCAS (1977, p. 15))

1.1.1 The Rational Expectations Hypothesis

Before MUTH (1961) introduced the *rational expectations hypothesis* (REH) agents' expectations were described by different ad hoc expectations formation schemes, for instance by the *myopic* scheme $p_t^e = p_{t-1}$ (leading to the common cobweb theorem), by an extrapolative scheme, or by the adaptive scheme

$$(1.1) \qquad p_t^e - p_{t-1}^e = \eta(p_{t-1} - p_{t-1}^e), \qquad 0 < \eta < 1,$$

employed, for example, by CAGAN (1956) and NERLOVE (1958). (Here p_t denotes the price of some good in period t and p_t^e the expectation of p_t held by agents in the previous period.) Although each one of these schemes is in some sense plausible and is able to explain certain empirical phenomena[1] they all are ad hoc and lack some amount of rationality since they do not take into account the specific structure of the underlying model.

In his famous article MUTH (1961) proposes a different modelling of agents' expectations. He suggests that "expectations, since they are informed predictions of future events, are essentially the same as the predictions of the relevant theory" (p. 316). More precisely, "expectations of firms (or, more generally, the *subjective* probability distributions of outcomes) tend to be distributed, for the same information set, about the predictions of the theory (or the *objective* probability distributions of outcomes)" (p. 316).

The fundamental advantage of the concept of rational expectations is that it is not ad hoc but relies on well-defined mathematical criteria[2].

---

[1]For example, NERLOVE (1958) suggests the use of the adaptive expectations formation scheme because it is able to explain why cobweb cycles are quite rare in agricultural markets although these markets are predetermined for these phenomena to occur since production is generally more elastic than demand.

[2]From the mathematical point of view the definition of rational expectations given by MUTH is in some sense ambiguous. On the one hand he speaks of expectations as probability distributions, on the other hand he states that these distributions coincide with the predictions of the relevant theory. But predictions are usually regarded as random variables or mathematical conditional expectations.

This ambiguity goes right through the RE literature. While MUTH, in his mathematical analysis, treats rational expectations as (mathematical) conditional expectations, LUCAS (1972) regards rational expectations as conditional probability distributions. Hence, there exist two versions of the REH; a strong version as suggested by LUCAS, and a weak version as employed by MUTH and the majority of studies on RE models, including this study.

In most microeconomic and macroeconomic models agents are assumed to be

Following the REH agents do not adhere rigidly to some exogenously given expectations formation scheme but take into account the structure of the model they are part of. The expectations formation scheme they follow is thus endogenously determined. Of course, this does not exclude the case that in certain models it coincides with one of the ad hoc schemes mentioned above[3].

In the seventies the interest in RE models began to rise as a consequence of several studies in which it is shown that macroeconomic RE models can exhibit qualitative properties differing drastically from models based on different expectation formation schemes (see, e.g., SARGENT/WALLACE (1975)). In particular, if agents have rational expectations, then monetary policy has no effect on the distribution of real variables, at least in the long run.

This finding attracted much attention and started an intensive and fruitful debate between the opponents and the advocats of the REH leading to a huge literature on RE models nowadays. This literature contains not only contributions to solution theory, estimation theory, and studies on the empirical evidence of the REH, but also studies on the methodological problems related to the REH. In particular, many attempts were undertaken to develop a microeconomic foundation of the REH although MUTH regarded the REH as purely descriptional and emphasized that "it *does not* assert that the scratch work of entrepreneurs resembles the system of equations in any way; nor does it states that predictions of entrepreneurs are perfect or that their expectations are all the same" (p. 317).

---

risk-neutral so that the mean value of agents' subjective distribution of outcomes is the only relevant criterion for their decisions. Then the weak version of the REH is adequate. In other models, however, additional characteristics of the probability distribution may be relevant decision criteria. For instance, in financial market models the variance of the distribution may play an important role for agents' decisions. In such models the strong version of the REH is appropriate.

[3]Under a suitable probabilistic specification rational expectations are optimal in the sense of yielding minimum mean squared prediction errors. This optimality property, however, should not be confused with other optimality concepts. For example, rational expectations do not necessarily lead to utility maximization. See, e.g., BENASSY (1992) for a recent study in which the RE scheme is not the utility maximizing expectations formation scheme.

1.1.2 Methodological Problems of the REH

B. M. FRIEDMAN (1979) was probably the first to recognize the extreme informational assumption underlying the REH. He distinguishes between the *information exploitation assumption* and the *information availability assumption.* The former "in its broadest construction simply states, as a condition for optimizing behavior, that people exploit information until the point at which its marginal product equals its (perhaps zero) marginal cost" (p. 25) while the latter claims "that the information which is available to economic agents is sufficient to permit them to form expectations characterized by conditional subjective distibutions of outcomes that are equivalent to the conditional objective distributions of outcomes indicated by the 'relevant' economic theory" (p. 26).

While the information exploitation assumption is similar in spirit to assumptions on agents' abilities usually made in economic theory[4] the information availability assumption is more problematic to accept since it implies that agents not only know the values of past and current economic variables and parameters "but also have whatever additional knowledge is required to transform this information into *objectively* unbiased conditional expectations of the time series to be predicted" (FRIEDMAN (1979, p. 27)).

In order to understand how demanding the information availability assumption is it is useful to look at the mathematical side of the problem. Consider the following linear economic model given by its reduced form equation

$$(1.2) \qquad y_{t+1} = \phi' z_t + a y^e_{t+1} + w_{t+1}, \qquad t \geq 0,$$

with y_{t+1} the (univariate) endogenous variable, z_t a vector of explanatory variables, y^e_{t+1} the prediction of y_{t+1} made by agents at time t, w_{t+1} a disturbance term, and ϕ and a some parameters. The REH (in its weak version) states that

$$(1.3) \qquad y^e_{t+1} = \mathrm{E}[\, y_{t+1} \,|\, I_t] \qquad \text{a.s.}$$

with I_t the information set containing all variables required to calculate the objective distributions of outcomes. Substituting (1.2) in (1.3)

[4] If agents are very competent mathematical programmers, why should they not be also very competent statisticians?

leads to

$$(1.4) \qquad y_{t+1}^e = \frac{1}{1-a}\phi' \mathrm{E}[\, z_t \mid I_t \,] + \frac{1}{1-a}\mathrm{E}[\, w_{t+1} \mid I_t \,] \qquad \text{a.s.},$$

provided that $a \neq 1$. Under the additional assumption that the information set I_t contains the complete history of the model (i.e., $\{y_t, \ldots, y_0, z_t, \ldots, z_0\} \subseteq I_t$) and that the disturbance terms are independent of that history (i.e., $\mathrm{E}[w_{t+1}|I_t] = 0$ a.s.) equation (1.4) simplifies to

$$(1.5) \qquad y_{t+1}^e = \frac{1}{1-a}\phi' z_t \qquad \text{a.s.}$$

In view of (1.5) it is tempting to conclude that in order to form rational expectations agents have to know 'only' the reduced form parameters ϕ and a and the realization of z_t. But since (1.5) is the result of some mathematical transformations agents have to know how to arrive at this equation. Hence agents have to know also the reduced form structure of the model.

But even the knowledge of the reduced form structure of the model does not necessarily ensure that agents can form rational expectations. To appreciate this point it is helpful to look at the informational problem from the point of view of an individual agent. While forming his expectations he faces two different kinds of uncertainty. Firstly, there is a *parameter uncertainty* or, more generally, the uncertainty about objective or exogenously given characteristics of the model.

Secondly, there is also a *behavioural uncertainty*. A single agent generally does not know what the other agents expect; but since the market or aggregate expectation matters in the model, and the agent is aware of this fact, he cannot neglect what other agents expect. Probably, the most concise formulation was given by KEYNES who likened this kind of problem

> ... to those newspaper competitions in which the competitors have to pick out the six prettiest faces from a hundred photographs, the prize being awarded to the competitor whose choice most nearly corresponds to the average preferences of the competitors as a whole; so that each competitor has to pick, not those faces which he himself finds prettiest, but those which he thinks likeliest to catch the fancy of the competitors, all of whom are looking at the problem from the same point of view. It is not just a case

> of choosing those which, to the best of one's judgement, are really the prettiest, nor even those which average opinion genuinely thinks the prettiest. We have reached the third degree where we devote our intelligences to anticipating what average opinion expects the average opinion to be. And there are some, I believe, who practice the fourth, fifth and higher degrees. (KEYNES (1936, p. 156))

This problem is usually called the *infinite regress of expectations* and agents have to solve it somehow in order to form rational expectations.

1.1.3 Stability of Rational Expectations or Learning to Become Rational

As the above reasoning shows the concept of rational expectations is an equilibrium concept[5] and therefore inherits the fundamental problems related to equilibrium concepts in general. Beside the problems of existence and uniqueness (which are, more or less, mathematical problems) the fundamental problem is that of stability. How is an equilibrium actually attained? Is there some tâtonnement process by which agents come to form rational expectations?

Since a REE is an informational equilibrium it is usually argued that "in absence of rational expectations agents must be systematically making mistakes and should therefore modify their behavior until they have obtained rational expectations" (BLUME ET AL. (1982, p. 313)). Hence rational expectations "may be regarded as the outcome of some unspecified process of learning and adapting on the part of economic agents" (TOWNSEND (1978, p. 481)). Although this idea is intuitively appealing many authors felt the need to make such a learning process explicit since "without well-developed process models, the concept of rational expectations is essentially a black box" (CYERT/DEGROOT (1974, p. 522)). Usually, such process models incorporate, as approximation to real life learning, Bayesian learning or learning by classical statistical techniques[6].

[5]In fact, as noticed by several authors (see, e.g., TOWNSEND (1978)), in some models the REE may be regarded as some kind of Nash equilibrium. But this does not necessarily hold true in every model. For a counterexample see, e.g., BENASSY (1992).

[6]As PESARAN (1987, p. 32) points out "there is no doubt that individuals do

Unfortunately, it has turned out that the problem of learning to become rational is more complicated than it seems at first sight. The main difficulty stems from the self-referential structure of these models which implies that there exists *forecast feedback.* In self-referential models agents are learning about the relationships between the economic variables, but these relationships themselves are affected by the expectations of agents. This implies that the relationships agents observe change permanently as long as agents are learning and changing their behaviour in the light of what they have learned. Moreover, during the learning phase the relationships agents observe coincide neither with the equilibrium relationships nor with their expectations. In other words, in order to form rational expectations agents have to learn relationships between economic variables which prevail only when learning has been completed. The situation is thus different from the situation usually considered in Bayesian theory and statistics.

The presence of forecast feedback, however, does not necessarily imply that learning is impossible to occur. But in order to show that learning is eventually successful it is not possible to apply the convergence results of Bayesian theory and classical statistics, at least not directly. From the mathematical point of view the main problem is that learning introduces non-stationarity into the model. Even if all time series entering the model are assumed to be stationary the time series generated by the model are non-stationary, except in a REE, and they exhibit a complicated dependence structure. Hence the assumptions of the classical convergence results are usually not satisfied. In order to show that learning is eventually successful it is therefore necessary to develop mathematical results dealing with a much more complicated problem than the standard theories.

1.1.4 Rational and Boundedly Rational Learning

There have been numerous approaches to the problem of learning to become rational but most of the literature is characterized by two different frameworks, the *rational learning approach* and the *boundedly*

learn from their own experience as well as from the experience of others. Generally speaking, learning takes place through two separate but closely connected mechanisms, namely *repetition* and *understanding*". Bayesian learning as well as learning by statistical procedures incorporate both mechanisms assuming that agents have some prior information about the structure of the model and repeatedly update their estimates whenever additional information becomes available.

rational learning approach. In the rational learning approach it is assumed that agents know the correct specification of the model but are uncertain about some of its characteristics, for example some parameter values. These agents learn the values of the unknown characteristics through repeated application of Bayes theorem. In order to do so it is assumed that they understand what is happening well enough to form rational expectations of the characteristics they are uncertain about based on their prior distributions. Thus learning takes place in a sequence of, informationally less demanding, rational expectations equilibria.

In the boundedly rational learning approach it is not assumed that agents know the correct specification of the model. Instead, they adopt some misspecified auxiliary model which in most cases includes a correct specification of the REE but usually does not incorporate the feature of forecast feedback. Based on this auxiliary model agents learn the values of some (hypothetical) parameters applying repeatedly Bayes theorem or using a statistical estimation procedure, usually the ordinary least squares (OLS) procedure[7].

The two approaches differ mainly in the amount of rationality and a priori knowledge attributed to agents. In the rational learning approach agents are extraordinarily well informed about the structure of the model and their learning procedure is fully rational. In particular, agents are aware of the fact that their own and other agents' expectations matter; they thus recognize the problem of infinite regress of expectations and are able to solve it somehow. In order to ensure the latter it is mostly assumed that some parameter values are a priori known and that it is common knowledge that they are known[8].

The boundedly rational learning approach is informationally less demanding since it treats all parameter values as unknown by agents; but it incorporates some element of irrationality which is not justified any further. This irrationality consists in the assumption that agents neglect the problem of forecast feedback and believe in some auxiliary model which is, essentially, ad hoc. Given this auxiliary model, how-

[7]Under the stochastic specification of normally distributed random variables the Bayesian procedure and the OLS procedure are closely related, i.e., the OLS estimates may be regarded as Bayesian estimates based on a diffuse prior.

[8]For example, if agents know the structure of the model (1.2) and, in addition, know the value of the parameter a, then the problem of forming rational expectations reduces to the problem of forming conditional expectations (in the Bayesian sense) of $\phi' z_t$.

ever, their learning procedure is usually rational in the sense that it satisfies the information exploitation assumption.

Although there are some plausible behavioural reasons why agents may neglect the forecast feedback[9] the fundamental reason for this assumption is that it reduces the mathematical complexity to some degree. More precisely, the neglect of the forecast feedback in the auxiliary model avoids estimability problems. For example, in model (1.2) agents cannot consistently estimate both parameters a and ϕ since, provided that the current market expectation is not observable, there are more parameters to be estimated than data available in each period[10]. But, as (1.5) shows, it is not at all necessary to know both parameters a and ϕ to form rational expectations. Only the term $(1 - a)^{-1}\phi$ has to be known, and boundedly rational agents eventually learn this term. In other words "nothing need be revealed with asymptotic certainty except the equilibrium itself" (JORDAN (1992, p. 110)).

Both approaches have thus advantages and shortcomings on their own reflecting different points of view from which the problem of learning to become rational can be seen. (For a more detailed discussion see, e.g., FRYDMAN/PHELPS (1983) and PESARAN (1988).) From the game theoretic point of view the rational learning approach is favourable and from the econometric point of view the boundedly rational is. In this work we adopt the econometric point of view.

Beside these two main approaches there are some more, two of them being of interest in connection with this study. The first one

[9]The use of an auxiliary model which does not take into account the forecast feedback is usually defended by argueing that agents believe to act in a competitive world in which a single agents' expectation does not matter, or that agents believe the market expectation already to be rational, or that it is impossible or too costly to gather information about other agents' expectations.

But one can also adopt a more naive point of view. Suppose that agents have carried out an explorative data analysis which has revealed that certain time series influence the time series to be predicted, or that agents know, at least roughly, about the relationships between the economic variables of interest. Then they simply carry out a linear regression, i.e., they estimate some unknown, possibly only hypothetical parameters using the OLS procedure. To assume that agents use this procedure is reasonable since the OLS procedure is, probably, the only estimation procedure known also by non-statisticians.

[10]FRYDMAN (1982) shows that this estimability problem cannot be solved by introducing an intuition in the market which collects individual expectations and reports the aggregate expectation since agents would alter their predictions after receiving this additional information.

could be called the *super-rational learning approach.* As in the rational learning approach it is assumed that agents know the correct specification of the model but are uncertain about the parameter values. The super-rational agents, however, are sophisticated enough to recognize that they can use their predictions as control input variables in order to track the process of the endogenous variables as close as possible to some reference trajectory. Hence agents do not try to learn some equilibrium law of motion but form their predictions such that future realizations of the endogenous variable become close to their predictions. The problem of learning to become rational is thus transformed into a problem of adaptive control under parameter uncertainty[11].

The second approach studies the stability of rational expectations in terms of properties of some expectational operator. This operator maps the *perceived law of motion* into the *true law of motion.* Obviously, a REE law of motion is a fixed point of this operator; and it is called 'stable' if it is the limit point of successive iterations of the expectational operator applied to a 'reasonable' initial value[12].

This approach is sometimes regarded as describing a stylized learning procedure. But this interpretation is problematic since in order to give this learning procedure an operational meaning it is necessary that *within* each period agents learn the exact values of some parameters which vary from period to period. Hence learning takes place in virtual time[13]. The main advantage of this approach is that it is mathematically less demanding so that more general results can be achieved. These stability results are closely related to but do not always coincide with the stability results based on real time learning[14].

[11]See, e.g., BAŞAR (1989) and KOTTMANN (1990, Part II).

[12]See, e.g., DECANIO (1979) and EVANS (1983).

[13]BRAY (1982, Proposition 4)) gives a real time formulation of this kind of learning. She assumes that agents do not change their predictions during the learning period. This implies that the parameters agents are learning about do not change and agents eventually learn these parameters in infinitly many periods following the OLS procedure. After they have learned the exact parameter values agents simultaneously change their predictions and learn about the altered parameter values in another infinity of periods, and so on.

[14]See, e.g., EVANS (1989) and MARCET/SARGENT (1988).

1.2 The Mathematics of Learning to Become Rational

In this section we have a closer look at the mathematical side of the problem to become rational and present briefly some mathematical approaches previously employed in a boundedly rational learning setup[15]. As starting point we consider the linear model (1.2) and we suppose that agents carry out a linear regression based on the auxiliary model[16]

$$y_{t+1} = \boldsymbol{\theta}'\boldsymbol{z}_t + e_{t+1}, \qquad t \geq 0. \tag{1.6}$$

Thus agents, at time $t \geq t_0$, calculate the OLS estimator of the (hypothetical) parameter $\boldsymbol{\theta}$,

$$\boldsymbol{\theta}_t = \left(\sum_{s=0}^{t-1} \boldsymbol{z}_s \boldsymbol{z}_s'\right)^{-1} \sum_{s=0}^{t-1} \boldsymbol{z}_s y_{s+1}, \tag{1.7}$$

and predict y_{t+1} by

$$y^e_{t+1} = \boldsymbol{\theta}_t{}'\boldsymbol{z}_t. \tag{1.8}$$

The resulting true model is then

$$y_{t+1} = (\boldsymbol{\phi} + a\boldsymbol{\theta}_t)'\boldsymbol{z}_t + w_{t+1}, \qquad t \geq t_0. \tag{1.9}$$

Notice that the above construction exploits some assumptions concerning the underlying information structure. Firstly, we assume that agents know which time series determine the endogenous variable. The auxiliary model (1.6) includes the same explanatory variables as the model (1.2)[17].

[15] For the sake of expositional simplicity we do not present these approaches in their full scope.

[16] We like to emphasize that at first hand the auxiliary model is purely fictitious and does not describe any real economic activity. It describes only what we assume agents believe in and serves us as a justification for what we assume agents actually do. If agents believe in the model (1.6) and, in addition, assume the (fictitious) disturbance term e_{t+1} to be independent of the explanatory variables $\boldsymbol{z}_s$, $s \leq t$, then it is rational for them to carry out a linear regression in order to form best predictions according to the mean squared prediction error criterion.

[17] Notice that we do not assume the parameter $\boldsymbol{\phi}$ to be non-zero in each component. The vector $\boldsymbol{z}_t$ may thus contain some variables which affect the endogenous variable only via agents' predictions. These variables are usually called *sun-spot variables* since in a REE they do not affect the endogenous variable.

Secondly, we assume that the realization of z_t is observable at time t and that agents, in fact, observe z_t. The information set agents' predictions at time t are based upon is thus

$$I_t = \{y_t, \ldots, y_1, z_t, \ldots, z_0\}. \tag{1.10}$$

In addition, we explicitly assume that $a \neq 1$ and $\mathrm{E}[w_{t+1}|I_t] = 0$ a.s. As already shown, under these assumptions rational expectations exist and are uniquely determined by

$$y^*_{t+1} = \frac{1}{1-a}\phi' z_t \qquad \text{a.s.} \tag{1.11}$$

Let $\bar{\theta} = (1-a)^{-1}\phi$. In view of (1.8) and (1.11) it is obvious that agents form rational expectations if, and only if, $\theta_t = \bar{\theta}$ a.s. Generically, this equality does not hold true but one could say that *agents learn to form rational expectations* if θ_t converges in some sense towards $\bar{\theta}$. Usually, convergence is understood in the strong sense, thus as a.s. convergence.

Up to now we have made no assumptions concerning the explanatory variables z_t. We want to introduce the following distinction. If z_t contains only exogenous variables, then we speak of the *static* case. If z_t contains also lagged endogenous variables, we speak of the *dynamic* case, and if z_t contains only lagged endogenous variables, we speak of the *purely dynamic* case. In addition, we distinguish the *stable* or *stationary* case, in which all exogenous times series as well as the REE are covariance stationary, and the *non-stationary* case, in which this condition is not satisfied, for instance, because there is a polynomial trend among the exogenous variables. If it is possible to reduce the non-stationary case to the stationary case applying *one* suitable transformation to *all* explanatory variables without altering the learning procedure, we speak of the *pseudo non-stationary* case.

Now we want to have a closer look at the mathematical problems arising when trying to show $\theta_t \to \bar{\theta}$. Substituting (1.9) into (1.7) leads to

$$\theta_{t+1} = (1-a)\bar{\theta} + aZ_t^{-1}\sum_{s=0}^{t} z_s z_s' \theta_s + Z_t^{-1}\sum_{s=0}^{t} z_s w_{s+1} \tag{1.12}$$

with $Z_t = \sum_0^t z_s z_s'$.

If no forecast feedback is present, thus if $a = 0$, the mid-hand term on the right-hand side (r.h.s.) of (1.12) equals zero and $\theta_t \to \bar{\theta}$ a.s.

if, and only if, the right-hand term on the r.h.s. of (1.12) vanishes a.s. as $t \to \infty$. Verifying the latter is the usual way to prove strong consistency of the OLS estimator in linear regression models; and there exist various results (i.e., strong laws of large numbers) providing the desired result.

If forecast feedback is present, thus if $a \neq 0$, the problem is more difficult since, in addition, one has to show that the mid-hand term on the r.h.s. of (1.12) converges towards $a\bar{\boldsymbol{\theta}}$. But this is in no way obvious since the mid-hand term depends on the complete history of the estimation process $\{\boldsymbol{\theta}_t\}$. In the dynamic case the problem is even more complicated since then the time series $\{\boldsymbol{z}_t\}$ and $\{\boldsymbol{\theta}_t\}$ are correlated. This implies that we cannot use the standard techniques to show that the right-hand term on the r.h.s. of (1.12) vanishes asymptotically.

Probably, the immediate idea to show $\boldsymbol{\theta}_t \to \bar{\boldsymbol{\theta}}$ is to substitute (1.7) into (1.12). But this leads to quite complicated terms which are hardly tractable. Instead, it is more suitable to consider the recursive representation of the estimates

$$
\begin{aligned}
\boldsymbol{\theta}_{t+1} &= \boldsymbol{Z}_t^{-1}\left[\sum_{s=0}^{t-1} \boldsymbol{z}_s y_{s+1} + \boldsymbol{z}_t y_{t+1}\right] \\
&= \boldsymbol{Z}_t^{-1}\left[\boldsymbol{Z}_{t-1}\boldsymbol{\theta}_t + \boldsymbol{z}_t\boldsymbol{z}_t'(\boldsymbol{\phi} + a\boldsymbol{\theta}_t) + \boldsymbol{z}_t w_{t+1}\right] \\
&= \boldsymbol{Z}_t^{-1}\left[(\boldsymbol{Z}_t - \boldsymbol{z}_t\boldsymbol{z}_t')\boldsymbol{\theta}_t + \boldsymbol{z}_t\boldsymbol{z}_t'(\boldsymbol{\phi} + a\boldsymbol{\theta}_t) + \boldsymbol{z}_t w_{t+1}\right] \qquad (1.13) \\
&= \boldsymbol{\theta}_t + \boldsymbol{Z}_t^{-1}\boldsymbol{z}_t\boldsymbol{z}_t'(\boldsymbol{\phi} + a\boldsymbol{\theta}_t - \boldsymbol{\theta}_t) + \boldsymbol{Z}_t^{-1}\boldsymbol{z}_t w_{t+1}. \\
&= \boldsymbol{\theta}_t - (1-a)\boldsymbol{Z}_t^{-1}\boldsymbol{z}_t\boldsymbol{z}_t'(\boldsymbol{\theta}_t - \bar{\boldsymbol{\theta}}) + \boldsymbol{Z}_t^{-1}\boldsymbol{z}_t w_{t+1}.
\end{aligned}
$$

Mostly it is more convenient to consider the deviations from equilibrium $\boldsymbol{\theta}_t - \bar{\boldsymbol{\theta}}$ for which we have the recursive representation

$$(1.14) \quad \boldsymbol{\theta}_{t+1} - \bar{\boldsymbol{\theta}} = \left[\boldsymbol{I} - (1-a)\boldsymbol{Z}_t^{-1}\boldsymbol{z}_t\boldsymbol{z}_t'\right](\boldsymbol{\theta}_t - \bar{\boldsymbol{\theta}}) + \boldsymbol{Z}_t^{-1}\boldsymbol{z}_t w_{t+1}.$$

The representations (1.13) and (1.14) are interesting for several reasons. Firstly, it becomes clear that the OLS learning procedure can be regarded as an adaptive learning procedure with time-varying parameters. (Notice, however, that the estimates, and not the expectations, exhibit an adaptive structure.) Moreover, since (1.13) can be written as

$$(1.15) \qquad \boldsymbol{\theta}_{t+1} = \boldsymbol{\theta}_t + \boldsymbol{Z}_t^{-1}\boldsymbol{z}_t(y_{t+1} - y_{t+1}^e)$$

the OLS procedure can be regarded as an prediction error based learning procedure. Agents adjust their parameter estimates in the light of the previously observed prediction error. This interpretation motivates to consider also other adaptive learning procedures, for example the procedure given by

$$\theta_{t+1} = \theta_t + \frac{1}{r_t} z_t (y_{t+1} - y^e_{t+1}) \tag{1.16}$$

with $r_t = \sum_{s=0}^{t} z_s' z_s$. In the literature on recursive identification and control this procedure is known as the *stochastic gradient (SG) algorithm.* In Chapter 3 and Chapter 5 we shall consider this learning procedure.

Secondly, (1.14) shows that the process $\{\theta_t - \bar{\theta}\}$ is governed by a stochastic difference equation. But this difference equation is of a complex nature since its coeffients are random variables. Moreover, in the dynamic case these coefficients are endogenously determined and the asymptotic behaviour of a solution is by no means obvious.

Finally, (1.13) and (1.14) show that the estimate θ_{t+1} depends, apart from the disturbance term w_{t+1}, only on time t random variables. Hence the estimation process $\{\theta_t\}$ may be regarded as a Markov-process and possesses some kind of martingale structure.

1.2.1 The Martingale Approach

This approach is based on the martingale structure of the estimation process and, consequently, applies martingale convergence results in order to show consistency of the estimates. It is due to BRAY/SAVIN (1986) and applies to the static case under the following assumptions:

(i) z_t i.i.d. such that $Z^* = \mathrm{E}[z_t z_t']$ is positive definite and $\mathrm{E}[z_t^4] < \infty$,

(ii) w_t i.i.d. with $\mathrm{E}[w_t] = 0$, $\mathrm{E}[w_t^2] = \sigma^2 > 0$, and

(iii) $\{w_t\}$ and $\{z_t\}$ are stochastically independent.

For notational convenience let $\xi_t = \theta_t - \bar{\theta}$ and $\tilde{Z}_t = t^{-1} Z_t$. Then (1.14) can be rewritten as

$$\xi_{t+1} = \left(I - \frac{1-a}{t} \tilde{Z}_t^{-1} z_t z_t' \right) \xi_t + \frac{1}{t} \tilde{Z}_t^{-1} z_t w_{t+1}. \tag{1.17}$$

Define a filtration $\{\mathcal{F}_t\}$ according to $\mathcal{F}_t = \sigma(z_0, \dots, z_{t-1}, w_1, \dots, w_t)$. Then, using the assumptions (i)–(iii), squaring and taking conditional expectations leads to

$$(1.18)\quad \mathrm{E}\left[\|\boldsymbol{\xi}_{t+1}\|^2 \middle| \mathcal{F}_t\right] = \frac{\sigma^2}{t^2}\mathrm{E}\left[\boldsymbol{z}_t'\widetilde{\boldsymbol{Z}}_t^{-2}\boldsymbol{z}_t \middle| \mathcal{F}_t\right] + \boldsymbol{\xi}_t'\mathrm{E}\left[\left(I - \frac{1-a}{t}\widetilde{\boldsymbol{Z}}_t^{-1}\boldsymbol{z}_t\boldsymbol{z}_t'\right)'\left(I - \frac{1-a}{t}\widetilde{\boldsymbol{Z}}_t^{-1}\boldsymbol{z}_t\boldsymbol{z}_t'\right)\middle| \mathcal{F}_t\right]\boldsymbol{\xi}_t \quad \text{a.s.}$$

Since $\boldsymbol{z}_t$ is independent of $\mathcal{F}_t$ and $\widetilde{\boldsymbol{Z}}_t$ can be approximated by $\boldsymbol{Z}^*$ for large t the conditional expectations in (1.18) can be approximated by unconditional expectations. Then it is not difficult to show that if $a < 1$ there exist positive constants λ and μ such that

$$(1.19)\qquad \mathrm{E}\left[\|\boldsymbol{\xi}_{t+1}\|^2 \middle| \mathcal{F}_t\right] \leq \left(1 - \frac{\lambda}{t}\right)\|\boldsymbol{\xi}_t\|^2 + \frac{\mu}{t^2} \qquad \text{a.s.}$$

for t sufficiently large. Hence the process $\{\|\boldsymbol{\xi}_t\|^2\}$ possesses some kind of martingale structure. More precisely, it is an almost-supermartingale and a convergence result of ROBBINS/SIEGMUND (1971) gives $\|\boldsymbol{\xi}_t\|^2 \to 0$ a.s., hence $\boldsymbol{\theta}_t \to \bar{\boldsymbol{\theta}}$ a.s.[18]

The martingale approach provides an elegant answer to the question which conditions ensure $\boldsymbol{\theta}_t \to \bar{\boldsymbol{\theta}}$ a.s. In the above formulation, however, it relies crucially on the conditions (i)–(iii) which are satisfied only in the static case. (Notice that in the dynamic case condition (iii) is violated since $\boldsymbol{z}_t$ and w_t are dependent. In addition, the property (i) is endogenous in the dynamic case.)

Using a different formulation the martingale approach can be applied also in the dynamic case. In fact, the complete convergence analysis in this work is based upon it. For example, consider the (purely dynamic) model (1.2) with $\boldsymbol{z}_t = y_t$. Define the filtration $\{\mathcal{F}_t\}$ by $\mathcal{F}_t = \sigma(y_0, \ldots, y_t)$ and suppose that $\mathrm{E}[w_{t+1}|\mathcal{F}_t] = 0$ a.s. Then we obtain

$$\begin{aligned} \mathrm{E}\left[|\theta_{t+1} - \bar{\theta}|^2 \middle| \mathcal{F}_t\right] &= \left(1 - (1-a)\frac{y_t^2}{\sum_{s=0}^t y_s^2}\right)^2 |\theta_t - \bar{\theta}|^2 \\ (1.20)\qquad &\quad + \frac{y_t^2}{\left(\sum_{s=0}^t y_s^2\right)^2}\mathrm{E}\left[w_{t+1}^2 \middle| \mathcal{F}_t\right] \qquad \text{a.s.} \end{aligned}$$

If $\sup_t \mathrm{E}[w_{t+1}^2|\mathcal{F}_t] < \infty$ a.s. the same convergence result as above gives $\theta_t \to \bar{\theta}$ a.s. if $|a| < 1$ (see Chapter 2 for details).

[18] Obviously, the result of ROBBINS/SIEGMUND (1971) was not known to BRAY/-SAVIN (1986) since using this result simplifies the original proof considerably.

1.2.2 The Stochastic Approximation Approach

The stochastic approximation approach relies on the fact that the OLS procedure can be regarded as a stochastic approximation procedure. These procedures (the Robbins–Monro procedure is a prominent example) are studied since the fifties and various convergence results exist, the probably most elaborate ones being given by WALK/ZSIDÓ (1989). As shown in the studies of KOTTMANN (1990) and MOHR (1990) these results can be applied in a very fruitful way to the problem of learning to become rational in the stationary static case. The following result is due to WALK (1985) (but see also WALK (1992)). We apply it to the model (1.2) in the static case where the estimates are given by the OLS procedure based on the auxiliary model (1.6)[19].

Let X_t, b_t, $t \geq 1$, and b be elements in a Banach space $\mathcal{B}$ and let A_t, $t \geq 1$, and A be bounded linear operators on $\mathcal{B}$ into itself. Suppose that the recursion

$$X_{t+1} = X_t - \frac{1}{t}(A_t X_t - b_t) \tag{1.21}$$

is satisfied. If

(i) $\|\frac{1}{t}(A_1 + \cdots + A_t) - A\| \to 0$,

(ii) $\frac{1}{t}\sum_{s=1}^{t} \|A_s\| = O(1)$,

(iii) $\|\frac{1}{t}\sum_{s=1}^{t} b_s - b\| \to 0$, and

(iv) $\Re(\lambda) > 0 \ \forall \lambda \in spec(A)$,

then $X_t \to A^{-1}b$.

To apply this result set $X_t = \boldsymbol{\theta}_t - \bar{\boldsymbol{\theta}}$, $A_t = (1-a)\widetilde{\boldsymbol{Z}}_t^{-1}\boldsymbol{z}_t\boldsymbol{z}_t'$, $A = (1-a)\boldsymbol{I}$, $b_t = \widetilde{\boldsymbol{Z}}_t^{-1}\boldsymbol{z}_t w_{t+1}$, and $b = 0$. In view of (1.14) the recursion (1.21) is obviously satisfied and condition (iv) requires $a < 1$. It remains to find conditions on the time series $\{\boldsymbol{z}_t\}$ and $\{w_t\}$ which induce the conditions (i)–(iii). As shown by KOTTMANN and MOHR the assumption that $\{\boldsymbol{z}_t, w_{t+1}\}$ is stationary and ergodic is sufficient

[19] Notice that the stochastic approximation approach applies to considerably more complex models than model (1.2), in particular to (multivariate) models incorporating several prediction terms based on several different auxiliary models. For details see KOTTMANN (1990) and MOHR (1990).

for (i)–(iii) to hold on an a.s. event. Hence we can apply the above theorem pathwise and obtain $\boldsymbol{\theta}_t \to \bar{\boldsymbol{\theta}}$ a.s.

Notice that the stochastic approximation approach is, essentially, free from any stochastic assumptions. It relies only on algebraic properties of the respective times series. In the static case one can assume these properties to hold a priori. In the dynamic case, however, these properties are endogenous and have to be verified first before the convergence result can be applied. As already noticed by KOTTMANN, this is a serious problem which, practically, restricts the application of the stochastic approximation approach to the static case.

1.2.3 The ODE Approach

The ODE approach, developed by LJUNG (1977) and applied first to the problem of learning to become rational by MARCET/SARGENT (1989a,b), is based on the idea that the trajectories of an adaptive estimation procedure can be approximated by the trajectories of an associated ordinary differential equation (ODE). In order to make this idea explicit suppose that the true model is given by

$$y_{t+1} = f(\boldsymbol{\theta}_t)'\boldsymbol{z}_t + w_{t+1} \tag{1.22}$$

with some function $f : \mathbb{R}^n \to \mathbb{R}^n$, where n is the dimension of $\boldsymbol{z}_t$. The function f which maps the *perceived law of motion*, $\boldsymbol{\theta}_t$, into the *actual* or *true law of motion*, $f(\boldsymbol{\theta}_t)$, is sometimes called *feedback function.* (For the model (1.2) we have $f(\boldsymbol{\theta}) = \boldsymbol{\phi} + a\boldsymbol{\theta}$.) Obviously, the fixed points of this function are REE parameters. For simplicity we assume that only one fixed point $\bar{\boldsymbol{\theta}}$ exists.

The vector $\boldsymbol{z}_t$ of explanatory variables may contain lagged endogenous variables as well as exogenous variables. But the exogenous variables, as well as the disturbance terms, have to be covariance stationary. Then we can rewrite (1.22) in a state space representation

$$\boldsymbol{z}_{t+1} = A(\boldsymbol{\theta}_t)\boldsymbol{z}_t + B(\boldsymbol{\theta}_t)\boldsymbol{u}_{t+1} \tag{1.23}$$

with $A(\cdot), B(\cdot)$ appropriate matrix valued functions and $\{\boldsymbol{u}_t\}$ a (possibly multivariate) covariance stationary process. The process $\{\boldsymbol{z}_t\}$ can thus be regarded as a Markov-chain controlled by the parameter $\boldsymbol{\theta}_t$.

The approximation suggested by the ODE approach is based on the assumption that the Markov-chain $\{\boldsymbol{z}_t\}$ behaves sufficiently 'regular' if the estimates θ_t do not vary by much. More formally, let $D_S \subset \mathbb{R}^n$ be the set such that $\{z_t\}$ given by (1.23) under the fixed parameter assumption $\theta_t \equiv \theta$, $\theta \in D_S$, is covariance stationary and $M_z(\theta) = \mathrm{E}[z_t z_t']$ is regular. Under fairly weak regularity assumptions for the function $B(\cdot)$ the *stability region* D_S depends solely on the function $A(\cdot)$, i.e.

$$D_S = \left\{\theta \in \mathbb{R}^n \,|\, |\lambda| < 1 \;\forall \lambda \in spec\,(A(\theta))\right\}. \tag{1.24}$$

Suppose that D_S is non-empty and that the fixed point $\bar{\theta}$ lies in the interior of D_S. (Notice that this implies that the REE is a covariance stationary process.) Suppose furthermore that the parameter estimates are given by the OLS procedure based on the auxiliary model (1.6)[20]. Hence

$$\begin{aligned} \theta_{t+1} &= \theta_t + \frac{1}{t}\widetilde{Z}_t^{-1} z_t z_t' [f(\theta_t) - \theta_t] + \frac{1}{t}\widetilde{Z}_t^{-1} z_t w_{t+1} \\ \widetilde{Z}_{t+1} &= \widetilde{Z}_t + \frac{1}{t+1}\left(z_{t+1} z_{t+1}' - \widetilde{Z}_t\right). \end{aligned} \tag{1.25}$$

The ODE approach claims that under suitable regularity conditions the trajectories of this estimation scheme mimic the behaviour of the trajectories of the associated ODE

$$\frac{d}{dt}\begin{pmatrix} \theta(t) \\ \widetilde{Z}(t) \end{pmatrix} = \begin{pmatrix} \widetilde{Z}(t)^{-1} M_z(\theta(t))[f(\theta(t)) - \theta(t)] \\ M_z(\theta(t)) - \widetilde{Z}(t) \end{pmatrix} \tag{1.26}$$

given some appropriate initial value[21]. In particular, if $(\bar{\theta}, M_z(\bar{\theta}))$ is a stable equilibrium point of the ODE (1.26), then θ_t converges towards $\bar{\theta}$. Moreover, the asymptotic behaviour of $\{\theta_t\}$ in a neighbourhood of the equilibrium is already determined by the simpler ODE

$$\dot{\theta} = f(\theta) - \theta. \tag{1.27}$$

The (local) consistency of the OLS procedure can thus be studied in terms of (local) stability of the ODE (1.27)[22].

---

[20]The ODE approach does not require that that the auxiliary model includes all relevant time series. Furthermore it applies also to the case of multivariate endogenous variables as long as the state space representation (1.23) holds true.

[21]Notice that the trajectories of the estimation process are denoted by θ_t and the trajectories of the ODE by $\theta(t)$. Notice furthermore that the time index is used differently in (1.25) and (1.26).

[22]The concept of expectational stability developed by EVANS (1989) and applied

The above approximation is based on the idea that, for large t, the estimates θ_t do not vary by much. Hence, under suitable regularity conditions for the feedback function f, the true law of motion $f(\theta_t)$ does not vary by much and the data process $\{z_t\}$ behaves as if it were generated by (1.23) under a fixed parameter. According to some averaging principle (some kind of law of large numbers) the term $z_t z_t'$ in (1.25) may be replaced by $M_z(\theta_t)$ and substituting the difference quotients by the respective differential quotients leads to the ODE (1.26). Although this idea is simple a rigorous mathematical justification is quite involved and complicated (see, e.g., BENVENISTE ET AL. (1991)).

The main difficulty associated with the ODE approach is to legitimate the above approximation. This is somewhat problematic. Firstly, the approximation works only if the estimates θ_t have already stabilized. Before that the ODE approach cannot explain anything. Secondly, it is necessary to ensure that the estimates θ_t leave neither the stability region D_S nor the domain of attraction D_A of the ODE (1.26). LJUNG (1977) tries to overcome this problem by introducing a so-called *projection facility.* This projection facility is a mechanism which projects the estimates back into some set D_2 containing the equilibrium $(\bar{\theta}, M_z(\bar{\theta}))$ whenever the estimates $(\theta_t, \widetilde{Z}_t)$ leave some set D_1 with $D_2 \subset D_1$. For the projection facility to work it is necessary that the sets D_1 and D_2 are chosen in a very special way[23]. Usually, a proper choice of these sets exists if the equilibrium point is stable, but even for moderately complex models it can be very difficult to determine these sets exactly[24].

Finally, the convergence analysis of LJUNG raises another problem since it requires that the process $\{z_t\}$ is infinitely often bounded a.s. Although computer simulations suggest that this is usually the case

in a series of subsequent studies (see, e.g., EVANS/HONKAPOHJA (1994a) for references) is based on the study of the 'smaller' ODE (1.27) but incorporates no explicit real time learning procedure.

[23]The set D_1 has to be open and D_2 has to be closed. Furthermore D_1 has to be a subset of the domain of attraction D_A of the ODE (1.26) and, in its first n components, also a subset of the stability region D_S. Moreover, the vector field of the ODE (1.26) has to point inside D_1 everywhere on the boundary of D_1.

The problem of a proper choice of the set D_1 and D_2 is overlooked in many studies applying the ODE approach. See, e.g., MOORE (1993) and EVANS/HONKAPOHJA (1994c).

[24]See, for example, the application of the ODE approach to specific economic models in the studies of MARCET/SARGENT (1989a) and CHANG ET AL. (1991a).

it is extremely difficult to verify this property mathematically in the dynamic case. To our knowledge, no fairly general and satisfactory results exist[25].

To us the use of the projection facility is the main shortcoming of the ODE approach since the projection facility is introduced *on the level of agents' behaviour.* Agents have to choose the proper sets D_1 and D_2, not the model builder. Since the determination of these sets can be quite difficult even if the feedback function is known it is highly unrealistic to assume that agents have this ability without knowing the feedback function. But without a proper determination of these sets the ODE approach gives only local results. Another shortcoming of the ODE approach is that it applies only to the stationary case[26].

Thus, summarizing the preceding discussion, it may be said that the ODE approach essentially gives only local convergence results. If, however, only local results are requested it provides an elegant way to achieve them since in most applications the stability of the ODE (1.27) is not difficult to determine. In addition, the notion of the feedback function generally allows for a intuitively appealing economic interpretation of the stability results.

1.3 Literature Review

In this section we give a brief review of some literature on learning to become rational in a boundedly rational framework. Since it has become popular to consider learning procedures in almost every field of economics[27] and the concept of boundedly rational learning is not

[25]Some special cases are treated by MARCET/SARGENT (1989a) and CHANG ET AL. (1991b).

[26]In engineering applications, for which the ODE approach was originally developed, this means no restriction since unstable processes do not play a prominent role in this field. In economic applications, however, unstable processes, like unit root processes or polynomial trends, are quite common.

[27]In some studies considering overlapping generations models and general equilibrium models the term 'learning' is used in a somewhat euphemistic manner (see, e.g., HOMMES (1991), GRANDMONT (1992), and BALASKO/ROYER (1994)). In these studies agents' predictions are given by a fixed adaptive expectations formation scheme, for example, a moving average of lagged endogenous variables. If the predictions generated by these schemes converge towards a steady state equilibrium,

sharply defined this literature has become huge and a complete review is beyond our scope. We therefore restrict ourselves to those studies which in formulation and in spirit are similar to our work. More precisely, we review only those studies in which agents learn about the law of motion of the endogenous variable by use of some reasonable statistical procedure based on a misspecified auxiliary model and applied to previously observed data[28]. In particular, agents learn about the reduced form parameters of the REE.

1.3.1 The Static Case

As already mentioned the static case (the case that the vector of explanatory variables contains no lagged endogenous variables) is easier to analyze than the dynamic one. For that reason several studies give exact convergence results. Common to these studies is that the learning procedure, usually the OLS procedure, converges with probability

---

then it is said that agents have learned this equilibrium value. But since agents do not adjust their expectations formation scheme over time this modelling lacks an important characteristic of learning.

The recently grown interest in this kind of adaptive models is somewhat surprising since, basically, it means a step back into pre-REH times. We believe that the reason for this interest can be found in the fact that, on the one hand, these models are easy to analyze mathematically since the endogenous variable is governed by a time-invariant law of motion and, on the other hand, they are able to explain not only convergence towards a steady state equilibrium but also business cycles and other kinds of interesting dynamical behaviour (e.g., chaotic movements) without leaving the neo-classical framework.

In some studies, however, different concepts are confused. BALASKO/ROYER (1994), for example, argue that the OLS procedure can be regarded as a special case of such adaptive schemes overlooking the fact that the *estimates* generated by the OLS procedure exhibit an adaptive structure, but not the *predictions* based on these estimates. Moreover, they compare their adaptive schemes for a first order autoregressive model to the OLS estimates generated by a regression on a constant as the only explanatory variable.

[28]Some interesting studies not satisfying these conditions are given by KIRMAN (1975, 1983), BRAY (1982), and WOODFORD (1990). In these studies agents learn about the relationships between endogenous variables (KIRMAN), between exogenous variables and a sun-spot variable (WOODFORD), or about the law of motion of an exogenous variable by a regression on the endogenous variable (BRAY).

The results obtained by these studies are mixed. While BRAY shows a.s. convergence of the OLS procedure towards rational expectations under suitable parameter conditions KIRMAN and WOODFORD show that agents can learn to believe in a sun-spot or *misinformed expectational equilibrium* where "they are ignorant, incompetent but happy" (KIRMAN (1975, p. 152)).

one under suitable parameter conditions. (For that reason we shall omit the additional term 'almost sure' in this subsection and briefly speak of convergence.) The resulting limit points are parameters of either a *full information REE* or a *limited information REE* depending on whether agents' learning procedure is based upon all relevant time series, only a subset of them, or just upon a set of instrumental variables which may or may not be correlated with the relevant time series. In the first case we say that agents use the *proper* auxiliary model.

The first rigorous convergence results are given by BRAY (1983) and FRYDMAN (1983). Both authors consider a multivariate version of the linear model (1.2) where agents are learning by means of the OLS procedure. BRAY studies the case of a constant as the only exogenous variable and assumes that agents adopt the proper auxiliary model. She shows convergence under a parameter condition analogous to $a < 1$ for the model (1.2).

FRYDMAN (1983) considers the case that the exogenous variables follow a stable multivariate ARMA process and assumes that agents adopt the same auxiliary model as in BRAY's study, thus an improper model in his setup. Under a condition analogous to $|a| < 1$ for the model (1.2) he shows convergence towards a limited information REE which he calls an *unconditional expectational equilibrium.* Due to the specification of the auxiliary model the analysis of the OLS procedure is relatively simple in both studies since the OLS estimates are simply arithmetic means of past variables.

More general convergence results for the OLS procedure are given by FOURGEAUD ET AL. (1986) and BRAY/SAVIN (1986). Both studies consider the model (1.2) with z_t a vector of exogenous variables. Using different mathematical techniques they arrive at slightly different convergence results. BRAY/SAVIN study the case that agents adopt the proper auxiliary model. Applying the martingale approach they show convergence towards a full information REE if $a < 1$.

FOURGEAUD ET AL. (1986) consider the case that agents adopt an improper auxiliary model. Under the assumption that the relationship between the exogenous variables and the instruments employed is stationary they show convergence towards a limited information REE under the condition $a < 1$ in the case of univariate instruments. In the case of multivariate instruments they show convergence under the more restrictive condition $a < 1/2$. The convergence analysis of

FOURGEAUD ET AL. is mainly algebraic and the assumptions on the time series are given in terms of algebraic properties. These assumptions are less demanding than the i.i.d. assumption of BRAY/SAVIN and are satisfied also in the pseudo non-stationary case[29].

A comprehensive study of the static case based on the stochastic approximation approach is given by KOTTMANN (1990) and MOHR (1990). They extend the results previously obtained in several directions allowing for multivariate linear models with several expectation terms. This allows one to consider the case that agents form expectations of several future values of the endogenous variable as well as the case that different types of agents use different auxiliary models for their predictions. These auxiliary models may be improper ones. KOTTMANN and MOHR give convergence results under suitable parameter conditions for a whole class of learning procedures containing the OLS procedure as a special case. Although the results achieved are considerably more general than the ones previously obtained they are restricted to the stationary static case.

1.3.2 The Dynamic Case

The dynamic case (the case that the vector of explanatory variables contains lagged endogenous variables) is much more difficult to analyze since it cannot be assumed that all the time series used as regressors in the OLS procedure exhibit the properties required by the convergence theorems. For this reason many studies concerned with the dynamic case are based on computer simulations and exact mathematical results are scarce. The dynamic case differs qualitatively from the static one in that convergence does not necessarily occur with probability one but may be a path-dependent property.

In a pioneering study CYERT/DEGROOT (1974) consider the linear partial equilibrium model already employed by MUTH (1961) but

[29]The most restrictive assumption in the study of FOURGEAUD ET AL. (1986) requires that the maximum and minimum eigenvalues of the matrix of moments diverge at the same rate. This holds true if, e.g., the involved time series are (covariance) stationary and ergodic. It is also satisfied if all variables explode at the same rate. But it fails to hold if the variables grow at different rates, for example, if some variables are stationary and some follow a polynomial trend. In Chapter 4 we shall show that we can relax the assumption on the eigenvalues and still obtain convergence if $a < 1/2$.

assume that agents are learning by the OLS procedure based on an improper auxiliary model. Although the original model is static CYERT/DEGROOT adopt a dynamic auxiliary model such that the resulting true model becomes dynamic, except in the REE. (Since agents' learning procedure is not fully rational they call the resulting model an 'inconsistent model'.) In a Monte–Carlo study they show that if the influence of the forecast feedback is sufficiently strong, then convergence is a path-dependent property. More precisely, they show that whether convergence or divergence occurs sometimes depends crucially on the respective trajectory of the disturbance terms[30].

The most general results for the dynamic case are given by MARCET/SARGENT (1989a,b) and KUAN/WHITE (1994). These studies both rely on the ODE approach but use different techniques to legitimate the approximation of the estimation process by an associated ODE.

The ODE approach is introduced first in the literature on boundedly rational learning in a formulation of MARCET/SARGENT (1989a). As mentioned by the authors, it allows a unified treatment of the static and the dynamic case, at least if convergence is studied only in the local sense[31] and the REE is stationary. They give convergence results for a weighted least squares procedure based on the proper auxiliary model in the static as well as in the dynamic case and apply these results to several previously studied models, including the ones of BRAY (1983) and BRAY/SAVIN (1986). However, some of the static examples are not analyzed in an appropriate manner[32] and MARCET/SARGENT failed in verifying the boundedness condition for the endogenous variables in the dynamic case.

In a subsequent study MARCET/SARGENT (1989b) extend their formulation by allowing for hidden state variables and private information among different types of agents. However, they do not provide formal proofs[33].

---

[30]Clearly, such a result is discouraging for an economist. Possibly for that reason CYERT/DEGROOT (1974) came to the conclusion "that the construction of inconsistent models is not the most fruitful way to progress in this field" (p. 524).

[31]The global stability of least squares learning is analyzed properly by CHANG ET AL. (1991a).

[32]CHANG ET AL. (1991b) point out that the formulation by MARCET/SARGENT does not allow for an intercept term among the exogenous variables and provide a reformulation which overcomes this shortcoming.

[33]Again, CHANG ET AL. (1991b) provide a proper reformulation and give formal

In spite of its shortcomings the results of MARCET/SARGENT are applied in a series of subsequent studies to several microeconomic and macroeconomic models[34]. Other studies rely directly on the results of LJUNG (1977) and LJUNG/SÖDERSTRÖM (1983) which are applicable to a large class of recursive learning procedures[35]. Since these studies do not provide new theoretical results we do not review them in detail.

Further progress is achieved by KUAN/WHITE (1994). They extend the framework of LJUNG (1977) in two directions. Firstly, they allow the law of motion of the endogenous variable to be nonlinear also in the explanatory variables and, secondly, they allow the disturbance terms to exhibit moderate dependence. They give a convergence result for a general class of adaptive learning procedures, containing the OLS procedure as a special case. The convergence analysis relies on stochastic approxiamtion results by KUSHNER/CLARK (1978) and parallels the theory of LJUNG in that the asymptotic behaviour of the estimates is determined by an ODE. To legitimate this correspondence KUAN/WHITE employ a projection facility similar to the one appearing in the theory of LJUNG and assume the exogenous variables to be uniformly bounded. (This assumption considerably facilitates the verification of the boundedness condition.)

Although the results by KUAN/WHITE are more general than the ones previously obtained they do not cover the dynamic case in its full scope. Firstly, since the approximation technique is similar in spirit to the one of LJUNG the convergence results are restricted to the stationary case. Secondly, due to the application of the projection facility it is problematic to accept them as global global convergence results. Finally, the assumption that the exogenous variables are uniformly bounded is quite restrictive in an economic context.

The performance of the OLS procedure in the univariate purely dynamic case is analyzed in a series of studies using different techniques. MARCET/SARGENT (1989c) consider a simple deterministic macroeconomic model with a non-stationary (explosive) REE. They state a convergence result but provide only a heuristical justification based on the recursive representation of the estimates.

KOTTMANN/KULIBERDA (1990) consider the univariate purely dy-

proofs of the propositions claimed by MARCET/SARGENT (1989b).

[34]See, e.g., SARGENT (1991), MOORE (1993), and EVANS/HONKAPOHJA (1994a).

[35]See, e.g., BULLARD (1992), HONKAPOHJA (1993), and EVANS/HONKAPOHJA (1994b,c).

namic case in a deterministic as well as in a stochastic setting. They present results of a Monte–Carlo study but also give theoretical results for the stochastic case. These results employ the modified martingale approach. Unfortunately, the proofs given are not fully correct[36].

A more detailed study, as well in a deterministic as in a stochastic setting, is given by ZENNER (1992a,b). Based on computer simulation it is shown that if agents form multi-period ahead predictions, various kinds of qualitative long-term behaviour of the estimation process may occur; and it is investigated which parameter configurations lead to the respective long-term behaviour. In particular, it is shown that the OLS procedure is able to induce stable limit cycles and chaotic movements of the estimation process, even in the stochastic case. These limit cycles, however, are usually not rational and occur only if the process of the endogenous variables explodes[37].

In a study similar in the techniques employed BULLARD (1994) shows for a deterministic overlapping generations model that the OLS procedure can generate cycles and chaos. In particular, he proves the existence of a Hopf bifurcation under parameter conditions which are economically interpretable.

Finally, we quote the study of EVANS/HONKAPOHJA (1994c) in which convergence of a modified OLS procedure towards an explosive REE is shown. This result is achieved reducing the non-stationary case to the stationary case such that the results of LJUNG (1977) can be applied. But this reduction is problematic to accept since it is performed on the level of agents' behaviour and requires that agents initially know approximately the rate at which the system explodes.

1.3.3 Summary

It may be said that the problem whether agents can learn to become rational following a reasonable learning procedure based on a misspecified auxiliary model is not yet completely solved, neither in the static

[36] In Section 2.6 we shall restate, as a special case, the convergence result of KOTTMANN/KULIBERDA (1990). This result applies as well to the stationary as to the non-stationary case.

[37] The existence of endogenously generated cycles is shown in many recent studies, most of them based on the pioneering work of GRANDMONT (1985). These cycles are usually rational in the sense that they occur in spite of perfect foresight (the deterministic analogon to rational expectations) while the cycles observed by ZENNER (1992a,b) should be regarded as a pathological outcome.

nor in the dynamic case. For the static case satisfactory results exist only for the stationary case, and some results are available for the pseudo non-stationary case. But even the simple situation that agents use as instruments a stationary (exogenous) variable and a polynomial trend is not covered by any one of the studies mentioned above.

For the dynamic case the results are rather poor. Apart from special cases no global convergence results exist which do not rely on the projection facility. If one is willing to accept the projection facility, which is introduced on the level of agents' behaviour, then at least the stationary case is, more or less, solved. For the non-stationary case, however, virtually nothing is known.

In the remainder of this work we give some results which provide a first answer to the questions left open. In Chapter 2 we consider the univariate purely dynamic case and give some convergence results for a class of adaptive learning procedures including the OLS procedure as a special case. Depending on the shape of the feedback function these results are either global convergence results or local ones. But, in contrast to all previous studies, we give a rigorous proof of the fact that convergence can occur with positive but not unit probability. This kind of result is completely new in the literature on boundedly rational learning and formalizes the previously observed phenomenon that convergence can be a path-dependent property.

In Chapter 3 we give global convergence results for the SG procedure in univariate ARX(p) models with $p \geq 1$. In particular, we show that agents following this learning procedure cannot destabilize the system and that they can eventually learn the REE parameters with probability one under suitable parameter conditions. Since the convergence analysis does not make use of a projection facility the convergence result is a proper global result. To our knowledge, it is the first global convergence result for the dynamic case.

In Chapter 4 we consider the performance of the OLS procedure in non-stationary static models. We show that agents can learn the parameters of the REE with probability one even if some time series entering the model are non-stationary, e.g., are polynomial trends or unit root processes. To our knowledge, also this result has no counterpart in literature.

Finally, in Chapter 5 and Chapter 6 we generalize the results of the two preceding chapters to the multivariate case, the case of multivariate endogenous variables.

Chapter 2

Univariate AR(1) Models

2.1 Introduction

This chapter is devoted to the mathematical analysis of learning to become rational in the simplest purely dynamic case. More precisely, we consider a model in which the univariate endogenous variable depends only on its one period lagged value, the predictions of agents, and a disturbance term. Since this model exhibits a very simple structure (the estimates of agents as well as the endogenous variables are real valued) it is a suitable platform for introducing our mathematical approach. Due to this simple structure the mathematical techniques employed in this chapter are easy to understand and do not obscure the fundamental properties and problems.

Although some of the results are covered by more general results in subsequent chapters the content of this chapter is not completely redundant. On the one hand the simple structure of the model allows us to consider a more general class of learning procedures and enables us to obtain broader convergence results than in the general case; on the other hand many auxiliary results and considerations of this chapter will also be employed later on.

The content of this chapter can be outlined as follows. In Section 2 we introduce the basic assumptions and derive some preliminary results. As a first theoretical result we show in Section 3 that the learning procedures under consideration can converge only towards rational expectations. In Section 4 we develop a static concept of stability of rational expectations with respect to a learning procedure and give a characterization of stable and unstable rational expectations. Section 5 contains the basic convergence analysis which is applied in Section 6 to obtain global convergence results and in Section 7 to obtain local convergence results (convergence with positive but not unit probability). In Section 8 we determine the rate of convergence for some learning procedures and in Section 9 we give an economic example.

2.2 Basic Assumptions

We consider the following univariate autoregressive model given by its reduced form equation

(2.1) $$y_t = F(y_{t-1}, y_t^e, y_{t+1}^e, \ldots, y_{t+K}^e) + w_t, \qquad t \geq 1,$$

where

- the endogenous variables y_t are real valued random variables with some, possibly random, initial value y_0,
- y_{t+k}^e, $k = 0, \ldots, N$, are the predictions of y_{t+k} made by agents at time $t-1$ based on the information set $I_{t-1} = \{y_{t-1}, \ldots, y_0\}$,
- w_t are disturbance terms,
- F is a real valued function, and $K \in \mathbb{N}_0$.

We call such a model a *generalized first order autoregressive model with forecast feedback.*

With the following three basic assumptions we specify the formation of the predictions, the function F, and the probabilistic structure of the model. All probabilistic statements are to be understood with respect to a basic probability space $(\Omega, \mathcal{F}, \mathrm{P})$ with elementary events $\omega \in \Omega$.

Assumption (A.1) (Behavioural Assumption)
Agents form their predictions y_t^e according to

(2.2) $$y_t^e = \theta_{t-1} y_{t-1}, \qquad t \geq 1,$$

where θ_t is recursively given by

$$\theta_t = \theta_{t-1} + \gamma_{t-1} \frac{y_t - y_t^e}{y_{t-1}}, \qquad t \geq 1, \tag{2.3}$$

with some, possibly random, initial value θ_0 and $\{\gamma_t\}$ a sequence of real valued random variables adapted to the filtration $\{\mathcal{G}_t\} = \{\sigma(I_t)\}$. The *sequence of gains*[1] $\{\gamma_t\}$ satisfies

(i) $\gamma_t \in [0,1]$ for all $t \geq 0$,

(ii) $[y_t = 0] \subset [\gamma_t = 0]$ for all $t \geq 0$,

(iii) $\sum_{t=0}^{\infty} \gamma_t = \infty$ a.s., and

(iv) $\sum_{t=0}^{\infty} \frac{\gamma_t^2}{y_t^2} < \infty$ a.s.

where we follow the convention $0/0 := 0$. Such a sequence of gains is called *admissible*. The multi-period ahead predictions are given by

$$y_{t+k}^e = \theta_{t-1}^{k+1} y_{t-1} \tag{2.4}$$

for all $1 \leq k \leq K$ and $t \geq 1$.

Assumption (A.2)
There exists a continuous function $f : \mathbb{R} \to \mathbb{R}$ such that

$$F(y, \theta y, \theta^2 y, \ldots, \theta^{K+1} y) = f(\theta) y \qquad \forall\, y \in \mathbb{R}, \quad \forall\, \theta \in \mathbb{R}, \tag{2.5}$$

and f possesses at least one fixed point $\bar{\theta} = f(\bar{\theta})$. We assume furthermore that the set of fixed points consists of isolated points only.

---

[1]In the sequel we regard the stochastic process $\{\theta_t\}$ as the outcome of an adaptive on-line estimation algorithm, a concept which is well-known in engineering and control sciences (see, e.g., LJUNG/SÖDERSTRÖM (1983) and BENVENISTE ET AL. (1990)) and for which the weighting coefficients γ_t are called 'gains'.

Assumption (A.3) (Probabilistic Assumption)
The disturbance terms $\{w_t\}$ form a martingale difference sequence (MDS) with respect to the filtration $\{\mathcal{F}_t\}$ defined as $\mathcal{F}_0 = \sigma(y_0, \theta_0)$ and $\mathcal{F}_t = \sigma(w_t, w_{t-1}, \ldots, w_1, y_0, \theta_0)$, $t \geq 1$, such that

$$(2.6) \qquad \sup_{t\geq 1} \mathrm{E}\left[|w_t|^{2+\delta}\middle| \mathcal{F}_{t-1}\right] < \infty \qquad \text{a.s.}$$

with some fixed constant $\delta > 0$, and

$$(2.7) \qquad \liminf_{T\to\infty} \frac{1}{T}\sum_{t=1}^{T} \mathrm{E}\left[w_t^2\middle| \mathcal{F}_{t-1}\right] > 0 \qquad \text{a.s.}$$

We probably should discuss these three assumptions in some detail. The Behavioural Assumption (A.1) seems to be somewhat ad hoc at first sight but can be rationalized as follows. We suppose that agents are aware of an autoregressive relationship between the endogenous variables and try to learn about this relationship. Since we consider a dynamic model this relationship can also be understood as *law of motion* which governs the *data process* $\{y_t\}$. The learning procedure agents follow is made explicit in Assumption (A.1).

At time $t = 0$ agents start with an initial guess θ_0 of the law of motion and form their prediction of y_1 according to $y_1^e = \theta_0 y_0$. (We suppose that at any time t the value of y_t is observed by agents and known before they form their predictions y_{t+k+1}^e.) This initial guess is modified, or adjusted, successively in the light of the observed predition error (PE). Since economic agents, on the average, prefer to think in terms of relative change the *relative prediction error* (RPE) seems to be the proper adjustment criterion. The RPE at time t is defined as

$$(2.8) \quad RPE_t = \frac{1}{y_{t-1}}(y_t - y_t^e) = \frac{1}{y_{t-1}}(y_t - \theta_{t-1}y_{t-1}) = \frac{y_t}{y_{t-1}} - \theta_{t-1}.$$

Then equation (2.3) becomes evident. At time t the previous estimate of the law of motion, θ_{t-1}, is adjusted by some amount into the direction suggested by the RPE_t. The weighting coefficients γ_t reflect the sensitivity of the learning procedure w.r.t. the RPE. This sensitivity is allowed to vary over time as well as to depend on the history of the model.

Understanding the learning procedure given by Assumption (A.1) in this way as a recursive PE algorithm[2] the conditions (i)–(iv) become clear. Since $\gamma_t = 0$ and $\gamma_t = 1$ represent the boundary cases of learning procedures which are completely insensitive or totally sensitive w.r.t. the RPE a reasonable learning procedure should be based on a sequence of gains with $0 \leq \gamma_t \leq 1$.

Since the updating equation (2.3) includes a quotient we have to ensure that this quotient is always well-defined. This is achieved by condition (ii) jointly with the convention $0/0 = 0$.

Condition (iii) requires the sequence of gains not to decrease too rapidly towards zero. A decreasing sequence of gains represents the behaviour of agents which believe in the success of their learning procedure and therefore adjust their estimates by smaller and smaller amounts over time. The gains should, however, not decrease too rapidly since otherwise the learning procedure becomes too insensitive towards the RPE and the *estimation process* $\{\theta_t\}$ converges only because agents are convinced of their success in learning. In such a case the resulting limit point usually will be arbitrary. A sequence of gains which satisfies condition (iii) is, e.g., given by $\gamma_t = 1/t$. This sequence is the standard choice in the theory of stochastic approximation but it has also some empirical evidence[3].

Condition (iv) is more difficult to understand. As will become clear later on it is a necessary condition for our convergence results but it has also a behavioural interpretation. As already mentioned above, the learning procedures specified by (A.1) are based on the RPE as adjustment criterion. In the unstable case, thus if the data process explodes, this adjustment criterion is obviously the proper one. In the stable case, however, the use of the RPE as adjustment criterion is sometimes problematic since the RPE is very large if the realizations of the data process are very small. In such a case the (absolute) PE would be the proper adjustment criterion. Of course, real economic agents are able to choose the proper adjustment criterion given the situation they face but it is difficult to model this 'switching ability' mathematically. With condition (iv) which, loosely speaking, requires that if y_t is very small, then γ_t is even smaller, we can overcome this problem, however only at the cost that the gains depend on the history of the model.

[2]We use the terms 'learning procedure' and 'algorithm' synonymously.

[3]See, ROTTER (1954) for an early experimental study on the formation of expectations and the empirical evidence of the choice $\gamma_t = 1/t$.

(Notice that if we could ensure $\liminf_{t\to\infty} y_t^2 > 0$ a.s., then condition (iv) could be replaced by the more familiar one[4] $\sum_{t=0}^{\infty} \gamma_t^2 < \infty$ a.s.)

The two other assumptions are more easy to understand. Assumption (A.2) specifies the structure of the model. The functions F and f are given by the underlying economic model and the qualifications introduced in (A.2) are quite plausible. Under Assumption (A.1) and (A.2) equation (2.1) can be rewritten as

$$y_t = f(\theta_{t-1})y_{t-1} + w_t. \tag{2.9}$$

The time t endogenous variable thus depends linearly on its one period lagged value but it may depend in a non-linear way on the estimate θ_{t-1}. (Such processes $\{y_t\}$ are sometimes called *processes with conditionally linear dynamics.*) At first sight this construction seems to be somewhat artificial but non-linearities of this kind arise naturally whenever agents form multi-period ahead predictions (cf. (2.4)).

The function f, which we call *feedback function*, was introduced first into the analysis of self-referential models by MARCET/SARGENT (1989a). It maps the *perceived law of motion*, θ_t, into the actual or *true law of motion*, $f(\theta_t)$, and allows us to characterize some properties of the model in a simple and intuitively appealing manner. We therefore adopt this construction.

Assumption (A.3) specifies the probabilistic structure of the model. The disturbance terms are assumed to form a MDS w.r.t. the filtration $\{\mathcal{F}_t\}$, hence $\mathrm{E}[w_t|\mathcal{F}_{t-1}] = 0$ a.s. Since $\mathcal{G}_t \subset \mathcal{F}_t$ by construction we have also $\mathrm{E}[w_t|\mathcal{G}_{t-1}] = 0$ a.s. Thus there is no effect of the disturbance terms which is foreseeable by agents[5].

The conditions (2.6) and (2.7) specify the amount of stochastic fluctuation the disturbance terms introduce into the model. Condition (2.6) ensures that there is not too much fluctuation and (2.7) ensures that the fluctuation does not die out.

Most results only require that condition (2.6) is fulfilled with $\delta = 0$; but occasionally we need the stronger assumption with $\delta > 0$. In

[4]The conditions $\gamma_t \in [0,1]$, $\sum_0^\infty \gamma_t = \infty$, and $\sum_0^\infty \gamma_t^2 < \infty$ are the so-called *Dvoretzky–Conditions* which are a kind of natural conditions for sequences of gains of stochastic approximation procedures (see, e.g., DVORETZKY (1956)).

[5]Notice that all information about the history of the model available at time t is contained in the σ–algebra $\mathcal{F}_t$. Notice furthermore that, by construction, y_t is always $\mathcal{F}_t$-measurable.

order to keep the assumptions as consistent as possible we disregard the slight generalization and refer always to the stronger assumption. Nevertheless, as a careful examination of the respective proofs shows, Assumption (A.3) can be replaced without any loss by the common assumption that $\{w_t\}$ is an i.i.d. sequence with $\mathrm{E}w_t = 0$ and $\mathrm{E}w_t^2 > 0$.

In the remainder of this section we derive some preliminary results. The first one concerns the data process. In view of (2.9) we can regard $\{y_t\}$ as a first order autoregression with time-varying parameters. In Appendix A we have collected some fundamental properties of such processes which are of an interest on their own. The following lemma formalizes the intuitively appealing idea that the persistent stochastic fluctuation introduced by the disturbance terms implies persistent fluctuation of $\{y_t\}$. It is proved in Appendix A, Theorem A.7.

Lemma 2.2.1
Suppose that (A.1)–(A.3) are satisfied. Then

$$\liminf_{T\to\infty} \frac{1}{T}\sum_{t=1}^{T} y_t^2 > 0 \qquad a.s. \tag{2.10}$$

Now we want to come back to Assumption (A.1). Since condition (iv) concerns an endogenous property it is not yet clear whether learning procedures exist satisfying (A.1). We show that there exists at least one, namely the OLS learning procedure. Recall that this learning procedure is based on the idea that the agents are aware of an autoregressive relationship between the endogenous variables and simply carry out a linear regression based on the hypothetical auxiliary model

$$y_t = \theta y_{t-1} + e_t \tag{2.11}$$

with some (hypothetical) disturbance term e_t which agents assume to be independent of past values of the endogenous variable and to have zero mean. The (hypothetical) parameter θ would then reasonably be approximated by the time t OLS estimate

$$\theta_t = \left(\sum_{\tau=0}^{t-1} y_\tau^2\right)^{-1} \sum_{\tau=0}^{t-1} y_\tau y_{\tau+1}. \tag{2.12}$$

In order to show that the OLS estimates possess a recursive representation which satisfies Assumption (A.1) we need the following simple but useful lemma which is known as Theorem of ABEL/DINI and Theorem of PRINGSHEIM and can be found in KNOPP (1964).

Lemma 2.2.2
Let (d_t) be a sequence of non-negative real numbers with $d_0 > 0$ such that $D_t = \sum_{\tau=0}^{t} d_\tau \to \infty$ as $t \to \infty$. Let $\alpha, \rho \geq 0$ be constants. Then

(a) $\displaystyle\sum_{t=0}^{\infty} \frac{d_t}{D_t^\alpha} < \infty \quad \Longleftrightarrow \quad \alpha > 1$, *and*

(b) $\displaystyle\sum_{t=1}^{\infty} \frac{d_t}{D_t D_{t-1}^\rho} < \infty \quad \Longleftrightarrow \quad \rho > 0.$

Lemma 2.2.3
Suppose that (A.2) and (A.3) are satisfied. Let θ_0 be a real valued random variable and θ_t, $t \geq 1$, be given by (2.12). Then $\{\theta_t\}$ satisfies Assumption (A.1) with the sequence of gains $\{\gamma_t\}$ given by

$$\gamma_t = \frac{y_t^2}{\sum_{\tau=0}^{t} y_\tau^2}. \tag{2.13}$$

The OLS sequence of gains is thus admissible.

Proof
We have

$$\begin{aligned}
\theta_t &= \left(\sum_{\tau=0}^{t-1} y_\tau^2\right)^{-1} \sum_{\tau=0}^{t-1} y_\tau y_{\tau+1} \\
&= \left(\sum_{\tau=0}^{t-1} y_\tau^2\right)^{-1} \left(\sum_{\tau=0}^{t-2} y_\tau y_{\tau+1} + y_{t-1} y_t\right) \\
&= \left(\sum_{\tau=0}^{t-1} y_\tau^2\right)^{-1} \left(\left(\sum_{\tau=0}^{t-2} y_\tau^2\right) \theta_{t-1} + y_{t-1} y_t\right) \qquad (2.14) \\
&= \left(\sum_{\tau=0}^{t-1} y_\tau^2\right)^{-1} \left(\left(\sum_{\tau=0}^{t-1} y_\tau^2\right) \theta_{t-1} - y_{t-1}^2 \theta_{t-1} + y_{t-1} y_t\right) \\
&= \theta_{t-1} + \left(\sum_{\tau=0}^{t-1} y_\tau^2\right)^{-1} y_{t-1}^2 \left(\frac{y_t}{y_{t-1}} - \theta_{t-1}\right).
\end{aligned}$$

Hence $\{\theta_t\}$ possesses the recursive representation (2.3). To show that $\{\gamma_t\}$ is admissible we have to verify the conditions (i)–(iv). The first two conditions are evidently satisfied and the third and fourth are implied by Lemma 2.1 and Lemma 2.2. ■

Example 2.2.4
In the sequel we refer sometimes to the following special case which covers most economic examples. We call it *linear model with additive forecasts.* Its reduced form equation is

$$y_t = \phi y_{t-1} + a y^e_{t+k} + w_t, \qquad t \geq 0, \tag{2.15}$$

with some $k \geq 0$ and $a, \phi \in I\!R$. Under (A.1) we have $f(\theta) = \phi + a\theta^{k+1}$ and (A.2) is satisfied under suitable parameter conditions[6].

Finally, we define what we regard as rational expectations in this model. If (A.1)–(A.3) are satisfied, then it is obvious that agents form rational expectations, i.e., $\mathrm{E}[y_{t+k}|\mathcal{F}_{t-1}] = y^e_{t+k}$ a.s., whenever

$$\theta_{t-1} y_{t-1} = f(\theta_{t-1}) y_{t-1} \qquad \text{a.s.} \tag{2.16}$$

In such a case the process $\{y_t\}$ will be called a *rational expectations equilibrium* (REE). Hence agents form rational expectations if their parameter estimates θ_t are fixed points of the feedback function, more precisely, if $\theta_t = f(\theta_t)$ a.s.

Notice that this definition of rational expectations is very general since in the case of multiple fixed points of the feedback function it allows for path-dependent rational expectations ($\theta_t(\omega) \neq \vartheta_t(\omega')$) as well as for time-varying rational expectations ($\theta_t(\omega) \neq \theta_{t+1}(\omega)$). In view of the convergence analysis this generality is not problematic since we employ a kind of deterministic reduction such that convergence of the estimation process can be studied pathwise. In addition, the design of the learning procedures specified by (A.1) implies that possible limit points are generally time-invariant. But from the point of view of economics path-dependent as well as time-varying rational expectations are problematic. In the case of path-dependent rational expectations

[6] If $k = 0$ then $a \neq 1$ ensures the existence of a unique fixed point. If $k \geq 1$ more complicated conditions on a and ϕ are necessary (see, e.g., ZENNER (1992a,b)).

certain long run properties of the model (which, first of all, economics is interested in) may become path-dependent properties and the model may become meaningless or, at least, looses its explorative and normative power. In addition, if rational expectations are time-varying these long run properties may be very difficult to determine. For these reasons we restrict our convergence analysis to time-invariant and path-independent RE. In other words, whenever we speak of a fixed point of the function f this fixed point should be understood as a constant.

2.3 Rationality of Limit Expectations

In this section we determine the possible limit points of the estimation process $\{\theta_t\}$. These limit points, understood in a pathwise manner in this section, will be called *limit expectations*.

Theorem 2.3.1
Suppose that (A.1)-(A.3) are satisfied and $P[\theta_t \to \bar{\theta}] > 0$ with some a.s. finite random variable $\bar{\theta}$. Then $f(\bar{\theta}) = \bar{\theta}$ a.s. on the event $[\theta_t \to \bar{\theta}]$.

For the proof we need the following result on weighted sums of martingale difference sequences. This result, which relies on the local martingale convergence theorem of CHOW (1965), is a keystone in our convergence analysis since it provides a kind a deterministic reduction and allows us to state local convergence results.

Lemma 2.3.2 (LAI/WEI (1982a))
Suppose that $\{w_t\}$ is a MDS with respect to a filtration $\{\mathcal{F}_t\}$ such that $\sup_t \mathrm{E}[w_t^2|\mathcal{F}_{t-1}] < \infty$ a.s. Let $\{\xi_t\}$ be a sequence of $\mathcal{F}_t$-adapted random variables. Then

(i) $\sum_{t=0}^{T} \xi_t w_{t+1}$ *converges a.s. on the event* $\left[\sum_{t=0}^{\infty} \xi_t^2 < \infty\right]$, *and*

(ii) $\sum_{t=0}^{T} \xi_t w_{t+1} = o\left(\sum_{t=0}^{T} \xi_t^2\right)$ *a.s. on the event* $\left[\sum_{t=0}^{\infty} \xi_t^2 = \infty\right]$.

Proof of Theorem 3.1

Suppose that $\mathrm{P}[\theta_t \to \bar{\theta}, f(\bar{\theta}) \neq \bar{\theta}] > 0$. In view of (2.3) and (2.9) we have

$$\theta_t = \theta_{t-1} + \gamma_{t-1}\left(f(\theta_{t-1}) - \theta_{t-1}\right) + \frac{\gamma_{t-1}}{y_{t-1}} w_t \tag{2.17}$$

with some initial value θ_0. Iteration of (2.17) leads to

$$\theta_T - \theta_0 = \sum_{t=0}^{T-1} \gamma_t(f(\theta_t) - \theta_t) + \sum_{t=0}^{T-1} \frac{\gamma_t}{y_t} w_{t+1}. \tag{2.18}$$

Lemma 3.2 (i) and condition (iv) of Assumption (A.1) imply that the second term on the r.h.s. converges a.s. The left-hand term converges by assumption on the event $[\theta_t \to \bar{\theta}]$. Hence the first term on the r.h.s. has to converge too a.s. on this event. But this term diverges a.s. because of $f(\bar{\theta}) \neq \bar{\theta}$, the continuity of the function f, and condition (iii) of (A.1). Hence we obtain a contradiction. ■

The interpretation of Theorem 3.1 is the following. If agents follow a learning procedure satisfying (A.1)–(A.3) they cannot learn to form non-rational limit expectations. These learning procedures are thus consistent with the aim of learning to become rational. Notice, however, that we have not yet shown that these learning procedures always lead to rational limit expectations. But whenever there is pathwise convergence the limit points are rational.

2.4 Stability of Rational Expectations

From Theorem 3.1 we know that the possible limit points of the learning procedures are fixed points of the feedback function f, thus REE parameters. The converse, however, is not necessarily true. Not every REE parameter is a possible limit point of the learning procedure. In the following we show that whether a REE parameter is a possible limit point or not depends not only on the parameter value itself but also on the respective learning procedure.

At this point we face for the first time the problem of the forecast feedback. As (2.9) shows the evolution of the data process $\{y_t\}$ depends on the evolution of the estimation process $\{\theta_t\}$; and in view of (2.3) the evolution of the estimation process $\{\theta_t\}$ depends on the sequence of gains $\{\gamma_t\}$. Since we allow $\{\gamma_t\}$ to depend on the history of the model the evolution of $\{\gamma_t\}$ may depend on the evolution of the data process $\{y_t\}$. Hence we have to consider the evolution of the three processes $\{y_t\}$, $\{\theta_t\}$, and $\{\gamma_t\}$ simultaneously.

In a first step we deal with the feedback problem as follows. We assume that the estimation process $\{\theta_t\}$ converges (pathwise) towards a fixed point $\bar{\theta}$ of the feedback function f. This assumption implies certain long run properties for the data process $\{y_t\}$ and, in case of history-dependent gains, also certain long run properties for the sequence of gains $\{\gamma_t\}$. If the long run properties of these three processes are compatible in the sense that they do not imply a contradiction, we will call the respective fixed point $\bar{\theta}$ *stable w.r.t. the learning procedure given by* $\{\gamma_t\}$. Otherwise $\bar{\theta}$ will be called *unstable* and convergence $\theta_t \to \bar{\theta}$ is obviously impossible.

We start with the recursive representation (2.17). It is useful to decompose the r.h.s. into a *structural adjustment term*,

$$S_t = \gamma_t(f(\theta_t) - \theta_t), \tag{2.19}$$

which depends only on the *augmented estimation process* $\{(\theta_t, \gamma_t)\}$ and the feedback function, and an *accidental adjustment term*

$$A_t = \frac{\gamma_t}{y_t} w_{t+1}. \tag{2.20}$$

Obviously, there are two necessary conditions for convergence of $\{\theta_t\}$ towards $\bar{\theta}$. On the one hand the accidental adjustment terms have to converge towards zero as t increases, on the other hand the structural adjustment terms have to shift the estimates θ_t closer to $\bar{\theta}$, at least in some neighbourhood of $\bar{\theta}$. In this section we are concerned with the second condition. Since the contraction property of the structural adjustment terms is an algebraic property all considerations in this section apply pathwise.

Definition 2.4.1
Let $\bar{\theta}$ be a fixed point of the function f. The *attracting region* $D(\bar{\theta})$ of $\bar{\theta}$ is defined as the largest connected set $D(\bar{\theta}) \subset \mathbb{R} \times [0,1]$ which is open in $\mathbb{R} \times [0,1]$ and satisfies

$$D(\bar{\theta}) \subset \left\{(\theta,\gamma) \;\middle|\; \left((1-\gamma)\theta + \gamma f(\theta) - \bar{\theta}\right)^2 \leq (\theta - \bar{\theta})^2\right\} \tag{2.21}$$

such that $(\bar{\theta},\gamma) \in D(\bar{\theta})$ for all $\gamma \in [0,1]$.

The Figures 2.1 and 2.2 give an example how the feedback function and the attracting region are related. Figure 2.1 shows a quadratic

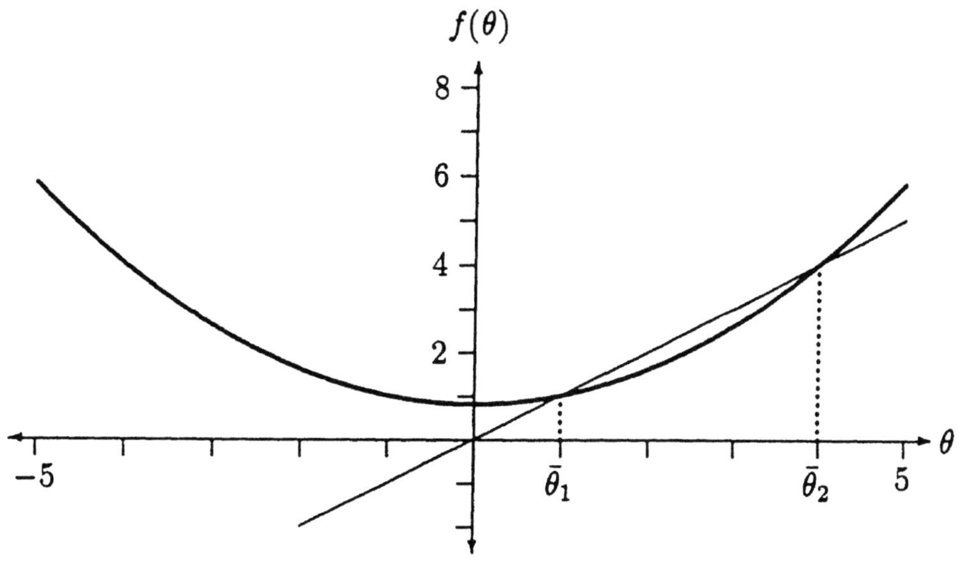

Figure 2.1: The function $f(\theta) = 0.8 + 0.2\,\theta^2$

feedback function f which possesses two distinct fixed points, $\bar{\theta}_1$ and $\bar{\theta}_2$, and Figure 2.2 shows the attracting region $D(\bar{\theta}_1)$. The attracting region $D(\bar{\theta}_2)$ is the empty set because the set on the r.h.s. of (2.21) is $\{\bar{\theta}_2\} \times [0,1]$ which possesses as open subset only the empty set.

Now we can introduce our concept of stability of rational expectations w.r.t. a learning procedure. The underlying idea is quite simple. A fixed point $\bar{\theta}$ is called stable if the attracting region $D(\bar{\theta})$ is *non-trivial* in the sense that $\theta_t \to \bar{\theta}$ implies $(\theta_t, \gamma_t) \in D(\bar{\theta})$ for all t

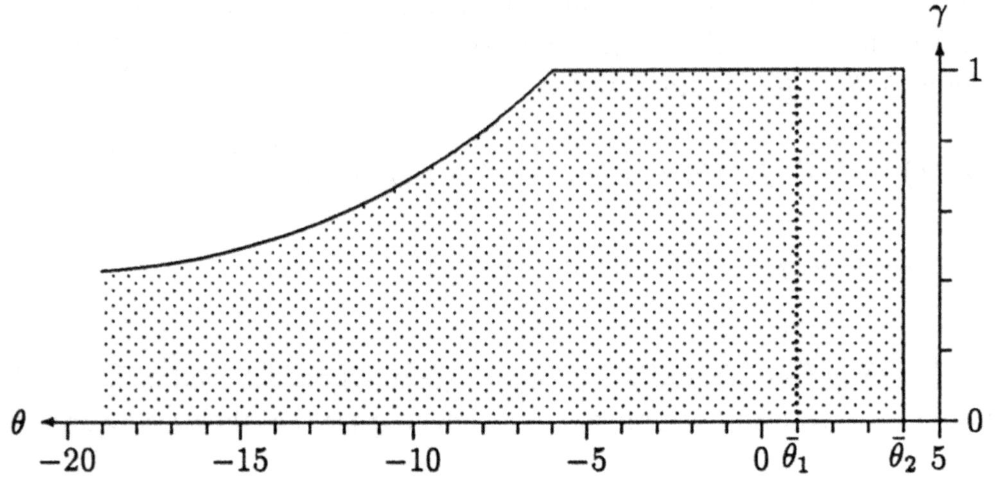

Figure 2.2: The attracting region $D(\bar{\theta}_1)$

sufficiently large. Hence stability depends also on the evolution of the sequence of gains. For convenience we assume that the evolution of $\{\gamma_t\}$ is linked to the evolution of $\{\theta_t\}$ in the following way[7].

Definition 2.4.2
Let $\bar{\theta}$ be a fixed point of the function f and let $\{\gamma_t\}$ be an admissible sequence of gains. If

(2.22) $\qquad \gamma_t \longrightarrow \bar{\gamma} \qquad \text{a.s. on the event} \qquad [\theta_t \rightarrow \bar{\theta}]$

with $\bar{\gamma} = \bar{\gamma}(\bar{\theta}) \in [0, 1]$, then $\{\gamma_t\}$ is called *convergence preserving.*

In the sequel we consider only convergence preserving sequences of gains since this class contains nearly all interesting cases. The following result shows that the gains of the OLS procedure are 'almost convergence preserving' in the sense that (2.22) holds true except for $|\bar{\theta}| = 1$.[8] The proof is given in Appendix A, Theorem A.13.

[7]It is possible to admit also sequences of gains with an evolution not linked to the evolution of the estimation process. This case of 'fluctuating gains' is covered by the analysis in ZENNER (1994). We decided to disregard this generalization here since it gives only little additional gain but requires additional notational effort.

[8]The reason why we exclude the case $|\bar{\theta}| = 1$ is that we did not succeed in verifying (2.22) in that case without imposing additional assumptions. We are, however, convinced that (2.22) generally holds true with $\bar{\gamma} = 0$ if $|\bar{\theta}| = 1$.

Proposition 2.4.3
Suppose that (A.2) and (A.3) are satisfied. Let $\bar{\theta}$ be a fixed point of the function f and let $\{\gamma_t\}$ be given by the OLS learning procedure. Then

$$(2.23)\quad \gamma_t \longrightarrow \bar{\gamma}(\bar{\theta}) = \begin{cases} 0 & \text{if } |\bar{\theta}| < 1 \\ \dfrac{\bar{\theta}^2 - 1}{\bar{\theta}^2} & \text{if } |\bar{\theta}| > 1 \end{cases} \qquad a.s. \text{ on } \quad [\theta_t \rightarrow \bar{\theta}].$$

Definition 2.4.4
Let $\{\gamma_t\}$ be a convergence preserving sequence of gains. A fixed point $\bar{\theta}$ of the function f is called *stable w.r.t. the learning procedure given by the sequence of gains* $\{\gamma_t\}$ if the attracting region $D(\bar{\theta})$ is non-trivial in the sense that there exist some $\epsilon > 0$, $\delta > 0$ such that

$$(2.24)\qquad (\bar{\theta} - \epsilon, \bar{\theta} + \epsilon) \times (\bar{\gamma} - \delta, \bar{\gamma} + \delta) \subset D(\bar{\theta})$$

if $\bar{\gamma} > 0$, and

$$(2.25)\qquad (\bar{\theta} - \epsilon, \bar{\theta} + \epsilon) \times (0, \delta) \subset D(\bar{\theta})$$

if $\bar{\gamma} = 0$. Otherwise $\bar{\theta}$ is called *unstable.*

If the following additional assumption is satisfied, then it is possible to characterize the stable fixed points in simple terms of the feedback function.

Assumption (A.4)
The function f is differentiable and f' is continuous at the fixed points $\bar{\theta}$ of f.

Theorem 2.4.5
Suppose that (A.1)-(A.4) are satisfied. A fixed point $\bar{\theta}$ of f is stable w.r.t. the learning procedure given by a convergence preserving sequence of gains $\{\gamma_t\}$ with limit point $\bar{\gamma} = \bar{\gamma}(\bar{\theta})$ if, and only if, one of the following conditions holds:

(i) $1 - \dfrac{2}{\bar{\gamma}} < f'(\bar{\theta}) < 1 \quad$ *and* $\quad \bar{\gamma} > 0,$

(ii) $f'(\bar{\theta}) < 1$ *and* $\bar{\gamma} = 0$,

(iii) $f'(\bar{\theta}) = 1$ *and* $f'(\cdot)$ *has a local maximum at* $\bar{\theta}$,

(iv) $f'(\bar{\theta}) = 1 - \frac{2}{\bar{\gamma}}$, $\bar{\gamma} \neq 0$, *and* $f'(\cdot)$ *has a local minimum at* $\bar{\theta}$.

Proof

The proof is simple and elementary. Firstly, notice that for every $\gamma > 0, \theta \in \mathbb{R}$

$$\begin{aligned} (\theta,\gamma) \in D(\bar{\theta}) &\iff ((1-\gamma)\theta + \gamma f(\theta) - \bar{\theta})^2 \leq (\theta - \bar{\theta})^2 \\ &\iff |1-\gamma(1-f'(\xi))| \leq 1 \\ &\iff 1 - \frac{2}{\gamma} \leq f'(\xi) \leq 1 \end{aligned} \tag{2.26}$$

where $\xi = \xi(\theta)$ is given by the mean value theorem of differential calculus. Since $f'(\cdot)$ is continuous at $\bar{\theta}$, it is easy to see that (i)–(iv) are sufficient conditions for stability.

To see that (i)–(iv) are necessary conditions notice that $f'(\bar{\theta}) > 1$ always implies $D(\bar{\theta}) = \emptyset$ since $D(\bar{\theta})$ is defined as open and $(\theta, \cdot) \notin D(\bar{\theta})$ for all $\theta > \bar{\theta}$ in some small neighbourhood of $\bar{\theta}$. The same kind of reasoning applies if $f'(\bar{\theta}) = 1$ and $f'(\theta) > 1$ for all $\theta \in (\bar{\theta}, \bar{\theta} + \epsilon)$ or $\theta \in (\bar{\theta} - \epsilon, \bar{\theta})$ for some $\epsilon > 0$. Hence in the case of $f'(\bar{\theta}) = 1$ the fixed point $\bar{\theta}$ is stable only if $f'(\cdot)$ possesses a local maximum at $\bar{\theta}$.

Analogously, if $f'(\bar{\theta}) = 1 - 2/\bar{\gamma}$ with $\bar{\gamma} > 0$, then the fixed point $\bar{\theta}$ is stable only if $f'(\cdot)$ has a local minimum at $\bar{\theta}$. ■

Notice that the concept of stability of rational expectations w.r.t. a learning procedure is, up to now, only an 'static' concept[9]. If a fixed point $\bar{\theta}$ is stable w.r.t. $\{\gamma_t\}$, this does not necessarily imply that the estimation process converges towards $\bar{\theta}$. Of course, it *might* but it *need not.* Notice furthermore that stability in our sense is only a *local*

[9] Our concept of stability of rational expectations is closely related to the one of EVANS (1989). But since his concept does not incorporate a real time learning procedure the two concepts do not fully coincide. The stability results obtained by EVANS coincide with our stability results for learning procedures given by a sequence of gains with limit point one.

property. If a fixed point $\bar{\theta}$ is stable there exists a (possibly very small) neighbourhood of $(\bar{\theta}, \bar{\gamma})$ such that for (θ_t, γ_t) in this neighbourhood the structural adjustment terms shift the estimates $\{\theta_t\}$ closer to $\bar{\theta}$. Hence if the accidental adjustment terms do not force (θ_t, γ_t) to leave this neighbourhood, we can expect convergence to occur.

Understanding f as the function which maps the perceived law of motion into the true law of motion Theorem 4.5 can be interpreted in the following way. If the feedback function is very sensible w.r.t. changes of belief at a REE parameter $\bar{\theta}$, i.e. if $|f'(\bar{\theta})|$ is large, it is impossible for the agents to learn this parameter by a simple trial-and-error mechanism. In particular, in case of $f'(\bar{\theta}) > 1$ the forecast feedback destabilizes the whole system. Notice, however, that if the feedback is negative, thus $f'(\bar{\theta}) < 0$, and the sequence of gains converges to zero, then the fixed point $\bar{\theta}$ is stable even if $f'(\bar{\theta}) < -1$.

2.5 Basic Convergence Analysis

As mentioned above one can expect $\{\theta_t\}$ to converge towards a fixed point $\bar{\theta}$ of f whenever the *augmented estimation process* $\{(\theta_t, \gamma_t)\}$ stays in the attracting region $D(\bar{\theta})$ after some finite time. We show that this is, in fact, true with a few qualifications. Hence the attracting region possesses the (stochastic version of the) property attributed to attracting regions in the theory of differential equations. Our convergence analysis is based on the following convergence result for almost-supermartingales.

Proposition 2.5.1 (ROBBINS/SIEGMUND (1971))
Suppose that $\{z_t\}, \{\alpha_t\}, \{\beta_t\}$, and $\{\eta_t\}$ are sequences of non-negative $\mathcal{F}_t$-measurable random variables such that for $t \geq 0$

$$\text{(2.27)} \qquad \mathrm{E}[z_{t+1}|\mathcal{F}_t] \leq (1+\alpha_t)z_t + \beta_t - \eta_t \qquad a.s.$$

Then on the event $\left[\sum_{t=0}^{\infty} \alpha_t < \infty, \sum_{t=0}^{\infty} \beta_t < \infty\right]$, $\lim_{t\to\infty} z_t$ *exists and is finite a.s. and* $\sum_{t=0}^{\infty} \eta_t < \infty$ *a.s.*

Theorem 2.5.2
Suppose that (A.1)–(A.3) are satisfied. Let $\bar{\theta}$ be fixed point of the function f. Then $\{|\theta_t - \bar{\theta}|\}$ converges a.s. towards an a.s. finite random variable on the event

$$\mathcal{A} = \left[(\theta_t, \gamma_t) \in D(\bar{\theta}) \text{ for all but finitely many } t \geq 0\right]. \tag{2.28}$$

Proof
For the process $\{\theta_t - \bar{\theta}\}$ we have the recursion

$$\theta_{t+1} - \bar{\theta} = (1-\gamma_t)(\theta_t - \bar{\theta}) + \gamma_t(f(\theta_t) - \bar{\theta}) + \frac{\gamma_t}{y_t} w_{t+1}. \tag{2.29}$$

Squaring and taking conditional expectations leads to

$$\begin{aligned} \mathrm{E}\left[(\theta_{t+1} - \bar{\theta})^2 \middle| \mathcal{F}_t\right] &= [(1-\gamma_t)\theta_t + \gamma_t f(\theta_t) - \bar{\theta}]^2 \\ &\quad + \frac{\gamma_t^2}{y_t^2} \mathrm{E}[w_{t+1}^2 | \mathcal{F}_t]. \end{aligned} \tag{2.30}$$

Let

$$\begin{aligned} z_t &= (\theta_t - \bar{\theta})^2, \\ \beta_t &= \frac{\gamma_t^2}{y_t^2} \mathrm{E}\left[w_{t+1}^2 | \mathcal{F}_t\right], \text{ and} \\ \alpha_t &= \begin{cases} 0 & \text{if } (\theta_t, \gamma_t) \in D(\bar{\theta}), \\ \dfrac{[(1-\gamma_t)\theta_t + \gamma_t f(\theta_t) - \bar{\theta}]^2}{(\theta_t - \bar{\theta})^2} - 1 & \text{if } (\theta_t, \gamma_t) \notin D(\bar{\theta}). \end{cases} \end{aligned} \tag{2.31}$$

Then (2.30) implies

$$\mathrm{E}[z_{t+1} | \mathcal{F}_t] \leq (1 + \alpha_t) z_t + \beta_t. \tag{2.32}$$

Assumption (A.1) and (A.3) obviously imply $\sum_{t=0}^{\infty} \beta_t < \infty$ a.s.[10] Since $\mathcal{A} \subset [\sum_{t=0}^{\infty} \alpha_t < \infty]$ Proposition 5.1 finally gives the desired result. ■

[10] Notice that the conditional Lyapunov inequality jointly with condition (2.6) implies $\sup_t \mathrm{E}[w_{t+1}^2 | \mathcal{F}_t] < \infty$ a.s.

It is tempting to conclude that given the assumptions of Theorem 5.2, $\{\theta_t\}$ by itself converges a.s.[11] and to infer from the rationality of limit expectations (Theorem 3.1) that the limit point is rational. But convergence of $|\theta_t - \bar{\theta}|$ does not necessarily imply convergence of $\{\theta_t\}$. The following result shows that given some additional assumptions we can exclude the possibility that $\{\theta_t\}$ possesses two distinct (possibly path-dependent) accumulation points.

Theorem 2.5.3
Suppose that (A.1)–(A.4) are satisfied. If

(i) $\gamma_t \to 0$ *a.s. on* $\mathcal{A}$, *or*

(ii) $\limsup_{t\to\infty} \gamma_t \le \gamma^*$ *a.s. on* $\mathcal{A}$ *with some fixed value* $\gamma^* \in [0,1]$ *s.t.*

$$f'(\theta) > 1 - \frac{2}{\gamma^*} + \epsilon \qquad \text{with some } \epsilon > 0 \tag{2.33}$$

for all $\theta \in \mathbb{R}$ *such that* $(\theta, \gamma) \in D(\bar{\theta})$ *for some* $\gamma > 0$,

then $\{\theta_t\}$ *converges a.s. on the event* $\mathcal{A}$.

Proof
Consider

$$\theta_{t+1} - \theta_t = \gamma_t(f(\theta_t) - \theta_t) + \frac{\gamma_t}{y_t} w_{t+1}. \tag{2.34}$$

Assumption (A.1) and Lemma 3.2 imply $\gamma_t w_{t+1}/y_t \to 0$ a.s., and from Theorem 5.2 we know that $\{\theta_t\}$ is pathwise bounded a.s. on $\mathcal{A}$. If $\gamma_t \to 0$ a.s. on $\mathcal{A}$, then we obtain $|\theta_{t+1} - \theta_t| \to 0$ a.s. on $\mathcal{A}$ since f is continuous. Hence $\{\theta_t\}$ cannot possess two distinct accumulation points. In view of Theorem 5.2 we can conclude that $\{\theta_t\}$ converges a.s. on $\mathcal{A}$ if condition (i) holds true.

To show that condition (ii) implies the same result suppose that the sequence $(\theta_{t+1} - \bar{\theta})/(\theta_t - \bar{\theta})$ possesses also the accumulation point $\theta^* = -1$. In the subsequence converging to this point we have for sufficiently large t (dropping the subsequence index)

$$\begin{aligned} -(\theta_t - \bar{\theta}) &\approx \theta_{t+1} - \bar{\theta} \\ &\approx (1 - \gamma_t + \gamma_t f'(\xi_t))\,(\theta_t - \bar{\theta}) \end{aligned} \tag{2.35}$$

[11] KOTTMANN/KULIBERDA (1990) made this mistake in the proof of their Theorem 2.4.

with some mean value ξ_t between θ_t and $\bar{\theta}$. Hence

$$\begin{array}{rrcl} & -1 & \approx & 1-\gamma_t+\gamma_t f'(\xi_t) \\ \Longleftrightarrow & -2+\gamma_t & \approx & \gamma_t f'(\xi_t) \\ \Longleftrightarrow & 1-\frac{2}{\gamma_t} & \approx & f'(\xi_t) \end{array} \tag{2.36}$$

Clearly, this is a contradiction to condition (ii). ∎

Under the assumptions of Theorem 5.3 we thus can exclude the case that $\{\theta_t\}$ possesses two distinct accumulation points. This, however, does not yet mean that we have convergence $\theta_t \to \bar{\theta}$. There can be some other fixed point $\theta^* \neq \bar{\theta}$ such that $\theta_t \to \theta^*$. Although attracting regions of distinct fixed points are disjunct (see Lemma 4.3 in ZENNER (1994)) the boundary of the attracting region of one fixed point may contain another fixed point. Hence $\theta_t \to \theta^*$ with a fixed point $\theta^* \neq \bar{\theta}$ is possible even on the event $\mathcal{A}$. To exclude this case we consider the following subsets $D^\epsilon(\bar{\theta})$ of $D(\bar{\theta})$ which are defined, for small $\epsilon > 0$, as the largest connected subsets of $D(\bar{\theta})$ such that

$$D^\epsilon(\bar{\theta}) \subset \left\{(\theta,\gamma)\middle|\left((1-\gamma)\theta+\gamma f(\theta)-\bar{\theta}\right)^2 \leq (1-\epsilon\gamma)^2(\theta-\bar{\theta})^2\right\}. \tag{2.37}$$

It is easy to see that the closure of $D^\epsilon(\bar{\theta})$ contains no other fixed point than $\bar{\theta}$.

We shall show that if the augmented estimation process stays in this *ϵ–attracting region* $D^\epsilon(\bar{\theta})$, then $\{\theta_t\}$ actually converges towards $\bar{\theta}$.

Theorem 2.5.4
Suppose that (A.1)–(A.3) are satisfied and $\bar{\theta}$ is a fixed point of f. Then $\theta_t \to \bar{\theta}$ a.s. on $\mathcal{A}^\epsilon := [(\theta_t,\gamma_t) \in D^\epsilon(\bar{\theta})$ for all but finitely many $t \geq 0]$.

Proof
Since $(1-\epsilon\gamma)^2 \leq 1-\epsilon\gamma$ for small $\epsilon > 0$ we obtain, analogously to (2.30),

$$\begin{aligned} \mathrm{E}\left[|\theta_{t+1}-\bar{\theta}|^2\middle|\mathcal{F}_t\right] \leq\ & (1-\epsilon\gamma_t)(\theta_t-\bar{\theta})^2 \\ & +\frac{\gamma_t^2}{y_t^2}\mathrm{E}\left[w_{t+1}^2\middle|\mathcal{F}_t\right] \quad \text{a.s.} \end{aligned} \tag{2.38}$$

Define z_t and β_t as in (2.31) and let

$$\eta_t = \epsilon \gamma_t(\theta_t - \bar{\theta})^2. \tag{2.39}$$

Then Proposition 5.1, with $\alpha_t \equiv 0$, implies

$$\sum_{t=1}^{\infty} \gamma_t(\theta_t - \bar{\theta})^2 < \infty \qquad \text{a.s. on } \mathcal{A}^\epsilon. \tag{2.40}$$

Also, since $\mathcal{A}^\epsilon \subset \mathcal{A}$, $(\theta_t - \bar{\theta})^2$ converges a.s. on $\mathcal{A}^\epsilon$ by Theorem 5.2. Since $\sum_0^\infty \gamma_t = \infty$ a.s. by Assumption (A.1) we finally obtain $\theta_t \to \bar{\theta}$ a.s. on $\mathcal{A}^\epsilon$. ■

We like to remark that the convergence results in this section remain valid if $\bar{\theta}$ is understood as a random variable and, consequently, the attracting region $D(\bar{\theta})$ is understood as a random set, provided that $\bar{\theta}$ is $\mathcal{F}_0$-measurable.

2.6 Global Convergence Results

Now we apply the results of the preceding section in order to derive some convergence results. In this section we consider only results which give convergence with probability one. We shall call these results *global convergence results.* These results generally rely on a global stability condition for the feedback function which ensures $D(\bar{\theta}) = \mathbb{R} \times [0, 1]$.

Theorem 2.6.1
Suppose that (A.1)-(A.3) are satisfied. Suppose furthermore that f possesses only one fixed point $\bar{\theta}$ and satisfies

$$\left(f(\theta) - \bar{\theta}\right)^2 \leq (\theta - \bar{\theta})^2 \qquad \forall\, \theta \in \mathbb{R}. \tag{2.41}$$

Let $\{\gamma_t\}$ be an admissible sequence of gains such that $\limsup_{t\to\infty} \gamma_t < 1$ *a.s. Then $\theta_t \to \bar{\theta}$ a.s.*

In particular, $\theta_t \to \bar{\theta}$ a.s. if $\{\theta_t\}$ is given by the OLS procedure.

Proof
It is easy to see that the global contraction condition (2.41) implies $D(\bar{\theta}) = I\!R \times [0,1]$. From Theorem 5.2 we obtain that $\{|\theta_t - \bar{\theta}|\}$ converges a.s. In view of Theorem 3.1, since $\bar{\theta}$ is the unique fixed point of f, we only have to exclude the case that $\{\theta_t\}$ possesses two distinct accumulation points. This can be done as in the proof of Theorem 5.3 (ii) replacing the differential quotients in (2.35) and (2.36) by the respective difference quotients. (Notice that Theorem 6.1 does not require that Assumption (A.4) is satisfied.) The global contraction condition (2.41) implies that $|(f(\theta_t) - \bar{\theta})/(\theta_t - \bar{\theta})| \leq 1$ while, by assumption, we have $\limsup_{t\to\infty} \gamma_t < 1$. Hence, analogously to (2.36), we obtain a contradiction. Since these considerations apply pathwise we do not need that $\limsup_{t\to\infty} \gamma_t$ is uniformly bounded away from 1.

For the OLS learning procedure we know that the evolution of the sequence of gains depends on the evolution of the process $\{y_t\}$ which in turn depends on the evolution of the estimates $\{\theta_t\}$. As it is shown in Appendix A, Theorem A.12, $\limsup_{t\to\infty} \gamma_t = 1$, understood as a pathwise property, requires that $f(\theta_t)$ grows beyond every boundary. But from Theorem 5.2 we know that $\{\theta_t\}$ is pathwise bounded a.s. Hence, since f is continuous, $\limsup_{t\to\infty} \gamma_t < 1$ a.s. and thus $\theta_t \to \bar{\theta}$ a.s. ■

For learning procedures given by a sequence of gains which converges a.s. towards zero we obtain a stronger result.

Theorem 2.6.2
Suppose that (A.1)–(A.4) are satisfied. Let $\{\gamma_t\}$ be an admissible sequence of gains such that $\gamma_t \to 0$ a.s. and let $\bar{\theta}$ be a fixed point of f which is stable w.r.t. $\{\gamma_t\}$. If

$$-C \leq f'(\theta) \leq 1 \qquad \forall\, \theta \in I\!R \tag{2.42}$$

with some positive constant C, then $\theta_t \to \bar{\theta}$ a.s.

Proof
In view of property (2.26) condition (2.42) implies that $(\theta_t, \gamma_t) \in D(\bar{\theta})$ for t sufficiently large. Again, this holds pathwise a.s. Then Theorem 5.3 implies that $\{\theta_t\}$ converges a.s. Since (2.42) jointly with

$f'(\bar{\theta}) < 1$, which follows from Theorem 4.5 (ii), ensures that f possesses only one fixed point we can conclude that $\theta_t \to \bar{\theta}$ a.s. ■

For the OLS procedure we obtain

Corollary 2.6.3
Suppose that (A.2)-(A.4) are satisfied and let $\{\theta_t\}$ be given by the OLS procedure. Let $\bar{\theta}$ be a fixed point of f such that $f'(\bar{\theta}) < 1$. If, in addition,

$$(2.43) \qquad |f(\theta)| \leq 1 \quad \text{and} \quad -C \leq f'(\theta) \leq 1 \qquad \forall\, \theta \in \mathbb{R}$$

with some positive constant C, then $\theta_t \to \bar{\theta}$ a.s.

Proof
As shown in Appendix A, Theorem 9, the condition $|f(\theta)| \leq 1$ for all $\theta \in \mathbb{R}$ implies $\gamma_t \to 0$ a.s. Hence we can apply Theorem 6.2. ■

The following result applies for any learning procedure given by an admissible sequence of gains.

Theorem 2.6.4
Suppose that (A.1)-(A.4) are satisfied. Let $\{\gamma_t\}$ be an admissible sequence of gains and $\bar{\theta}$ a fixed point of f. If

$$(2.44) \qquad |f'(\theta)| \leq 1 - \epsilon \qquad \forall\, \theta \in \mathbb{R}$$

with some $\epsilon > 0$, then $\theta_t \to \bar{\theta}$ a.s.

Proof
Since (2.44) implies $D^{\epsilon}(\bar{\theta}) = \mathbb{R} \times [0, 1]$, Theorem 5.4 gives the desired result. ■

Example 2.6.5
Consider the linear model with additive forecasts one period ahead

$$y_{t+1} = \phi y_t + a y^e_{t+1} + w_{t+1} \tag{2.45}$$

with $a \neq 1$. The feedback function is $f(\theta) = \phi + a\theta$ which has an unique fixed point $\bar{\theta} = (1-a)^{-1}\phi$. Then we have

(i) If $|a| < 1$, then $\theta_t \to \bar{\theta}$ a.s. for any admissible learning procedure[12].

(ii) If $\gamma_t \to 0$ a.s. then $\theta_t \to \bar{\theta}$ a.s. if $a < 1$.

2.7 Local Convergence Results

The global convergence results in the preceding section all rely on the fact that, given the respective assumptions, the sets $D(\bar{\theta})$ or $D^\epsilon(\bar{\theta})$ are unbounded in the θ-coordinate. Now we consider the case that these global stability conditions do not hold.

Suppose that $\bar{\theta}$ is a stable fixed point of the function f. Then Theorem 5.4 states that $\{\theta_t\}$ converges towards $\bar{\theta}$ whenever the augmented estimation process $\{(\theta_t, \gamma_t)\}$ stays in the attracting region $D(\bar{\theta})$ after some finite time. But does the augmented estimation process actually stay in this region? Or, what is the probability of this event? In this section we give a first answer. For the proofs we need the following auxiliary result.

Lemma 2.7.1 (Wei (1987))
Let $\{w_t\}$ be a MDS w.r.t. a filtration $\{\mathcal{F}_t\}$ such that

$$\sup_{t\geq 1} \mathrm{E}\left[\,|w_t|^\alpha\,|\,\mathcal{F}_{t-1}\right] \leq C \qquad a.s. \tag{2.46}$$

with some $\alpha \geq 2$ and some positive constant C. Let $\{\xi_t\}$ be a sequence of $\mathcal{F}_t$-adapted random variables. Then

$$\mathrm{E}\left[\sup_{0\leq t\leq T}\left|\sum_{\tau=0}^{t} \xi_t w_{t+1}\right|\right]^\alpha \leq K\mathrm{E}\left[\sum_{t=0}^{T}\xi_t^2\right]^{\alpha/2}, \tag{2.47}$$

where K depends only on α and C.

---

[12]This result was already stated by Kottmann/Kuliberda (1990) for the special case of the OLS procedure but, as already mentioned, their proof was not correct.

The following sets play a central role in the proof of the next result. Let $\bar{\theta}$ be a fixed point of f such that $|f'(\bar{\theta})| < 1$. Let $B \subset I\!R$ be defined as bounded connected set with non-empty interior such that

$$\bar{\theta} \in B, \quad f(B) \subset B \quad \text{and} \quad B \times [0,1] \subset D(\bar{\theta}). \tag{2.48}$$

Let $\epsilon > 0$ and define $B^\epsilon \subset B$ as the largest connected subset of B such that (2.48) holds with B replaced by B^ϵ and

$$\inf\Big\{|\theta - \theta'| \Bigm| \theta \in B^\epsilon, \theta' \in B^c\Big\} \geq \epsilon \tag{2.49}$$

where B^c denotes the complement of B in $I\!R$. It is easy to see that if $|f'(\bar{\theta})| < 1$ such sets B and B^ϵ exist and are non-empty if ϵ is sufficiently small.

Theorem 2.7.2
Suppose that (A.1)–(A.3) are satisfied. Suppose furthermore that $\{w_t\}$ also satisfies

$$\mathrm{P}\left[|w_t| \leq \epsilon\right] > 0 \qquad \forall \epsilon > 0, \quad \forall t \geq 1, \tag{2.50}$$

and

$$\sup_{t \geq 1} \mathrm{E}\left[w_t^2 \Big| \mathcal{F}_{t-1}\right] \leq C \qquad a.s. \tag{2.51}$$

with some finite constant C. Let $\bar{\theta}$ be a fixed point of f such that $|f'(\bar{\theta})| < 1$ and let $\{\gamma_t\}$ be an admissible sequence of gains such that

$$\mathrm{E}\left[\sum_{t=0}^{\infty} \frac{\gamma_t^2}{y_t^2}\right] < \infty. \tag{2.52}$$

If $\mathrm{P}[\theta_0 \in B^\epsilon] > 0$ for some $\epsilon > 0$, then

$$\mathrm{P}\left[(\theta_t, \gamma_t) \in D(\bar{\theta}) \text{ for all but finitely many } t \geq 1\right] > 0. \tag{2.53}$$

Proof
The proof is somewhat involved although the main idea is quite simple. Since inside the attracting region the structural adjustment terms shift the estimates θ_t closer to the fixed point $\bar{\theta}$ the estimates θ_t tend to stay inside this region unless accidental adjustment terms force θ_t to leave it. We show that this only happens with a probability less than one.

Let $B \subset I\!R$ be defined as above. Define the sets $B_0 \subset B_1 \subset B$ by $B_0 = B^{\epsilon}$ and $B_1 = B^{\epsilon/2}$ with $\epsilon > 0$ given by the assumption. We shall show the assertions

$$\mathrm{P}[\theta_T \in B_1 | \theta_0 \in B_0] > 0, \tag{2.54}$$

and

$$\mathrm{P}\left[(\theta_t, \gamma_t) \in D(\bar{\theta}) \text{ for all but finitely many } t > T \,|\theta_T \in B_1\right] > 0 \tag{2.55}$$

with some fixed T. Together with the assumption $\mathrm{P}[\theta_0 \in B_0] > 0$ these assertions evidently imply (2.53).

To show (2.54) notice that $\theta_t \in B_0$ implies $(1-\gamma_t)\theta_t + \gamma_t f(\theta_t) \in B_0$. Hence

$$\begin{aligned} \mathrm{P}[\theta_{t+1} \in B_1 | \theta_t \in B_0] &= \frac{\mathrm{P}[\theta_{t+1} \in B_1, \theta_t \in B_0]}{\mathrm{P}[\theta_t \in B_0]} \\ &\geq \frac{\mathrm{P}[|\gamma_t w_{t+1}/y_t| \leq \epsilon/2]}{\mathrm{P}[\theta_t \in B_0]} \\ &\geq \frac{\mathrm{P}[|w_{t+1}| \leq \epsilon/2]}{\mathrm{P}[\theta_t \in B_0]} \\ &> 0, \end{aligned} \tag{2.56}$$

provided that the probability in the denominator is positive. Then (2.54) can be shown by iteratively applying (2.56) with the initial condition $\mathrm{P}[\theta_0 \in B_0] > 0$. To do so it is necessary to define a sequence of sets B_{01}^i such that $B_0 = B_{01}^0 \subset B_{01}^1 \subset \cdots \subset B_{01}^T = B_1$ where the inclusions are strict and each set B_{01}^i possesses the properties of B_0 or B_1. Since $|f'(\bar{\theta})| < 1$ such a sequence of sets exists.

To show (2.55) notice that since

$$\begin{aligned} &\mathrm{P}\left[\theta_{T+t} \in B \text{ for all but finitely many } t \geq 1 \,|\, \theta_T \in B_1\right] \\ &\geq \mathrm{P}\left[\theta_{T+t} \in B \;\forall\, t \geq 1 \,|\, \theta_T \in B_1\right] \\ &= 1 - \mathrm{P}\left[\theta_{T+t} \notin B \text{ for some } t \geq 1 \,|\, \theta_T \in B_1\right] \end{aligned} \tag{2.57}$$

$$= 1 - \mathrm{P}\left[\bigcup_{N \geq 1} [\theta_{T+k} \notin B \text{ for some } 1 \leq k \leq N] \,\middle|\, \theta_T \in B_1\right]$$
$$= 1 - \lim_{N\to\infty} \mathrm{P}\left[\theta_{T+k} \notin B \text{ for some } 1 \leq k \leq N \mid \theta_T \in B_1\right]$$

it is sufficient to show that

$$\mathrm{P}\left[\theta_{T+k} \notin B \text{ for some } 1 \leq k \leq N \mid \theta_T \in B_1\right] < \delta \tag{2.58}$$

uniformly in N with some $\delta \in (0,1)$.

Now fix some $\delta \in (0,1)$. Let $A_t = \gamma_t w_{t+1}/y_t$ be the time t accidental adjustment term. We have

$$\left[\theta_{T+k} \notin B \text{ for some } 1 \leq k \leq N \,\middle|\, \theta_T \in B_1\right]$$
$$\subset \left[\sup_{1\leq k\leq N}\left|\sum_{t=T}^{T+k-1} A_t\right| > \frac{\epsilon}{2}\right]. \tag{2.59}$$

Define $Q_n^T = \sum_{t=T}^{T+n-1} A_{t+1}$. Then the Chebyshev inequality and Lemma 7.1 imply

$$\mathrm{P}\left[\sup_{1\leq k\leq N}\left|Q_k^T\right| > \frac{\epsilon}{2}\right] \leq \frac{4}{\epsilon^2}\mathrm{E}\left[\sup_{1\leq k\leq N}\left|Q_k^T\right|\right]^2$$
$$\leq \frac{4K}{\epsilon^2}\mathrm{E}\left[\sum_{t=T}^{T+N-1}\frac{\gamma_t^2}{y_t^2}\right]. \tag{2.60}$$

By assumption we know that the expectation is finite, moreover

$$\lim_{T\to\infty} \mathrm{E}\left[\sum_{t=T}^{\infty}\frac{\gamma_t^2}{y_t^2}\right] = 0. \tag{2.61}$$

Hence for $\delta > 0$ there exists a number $T = T(\delta)$ such that

$$\mathrm{E}\left[\sum_{t=T}^{\infty}\frac{\gamma_t^2}{y_t^2}\right] < \frac{\epsilon^2}{4K}\delta. \tag{2.62}$$

This implies

$$\mathrm{P}\left[\sup_{1\leq k\leq N}|Q_k^{T^*}| > \epsilon/2\right] < \delta. \tag{2.63}$$

Hence (2.55) holds and the proof is complete. ■

Because the proof of Theorem 7.2 applies in exactly the same way if we replace $D(\bar{\theta})$ by $D^\varepsilon(\bar{\theta})$ with $\varepsilon > 0$ sufficiently small (to ensure the existence of the sets B and B_0 defined by (2.48) with $D(\bar{\theta})$ replaced by $D^\varepsilon(\bar{\theta})$) Theorem 5.4 implies

Corollary 2.7.3
Suppose that the assumptions of Theorem 7.2 are satisfied and suppose that $\mathrm{P}[\theta_0 \in B^\epsilon] > 0$ *for some* $\epsilon > 0$. *Then* $\mathrm{P}[\theta_t \to \bar{\theta}] > 0$.

We probably should discuss the assumptions of Theorem 7.2 a little further. Since the attracting region can be really small, for instance if $f'(\bar{\theta})$ is close to one, we have to exclude such 'pathological' disturbance processes like

$$(2.64) \qquad w_t \text{ i.i.d. such that } \mathrm{P}\left[w_t = 10^9\right] = \mathrm{P}\left[w_t = -10^9\right] = \frac{1}{2}$$

from our considerations. Of course, the asymptotic part of the proof of Theorem 7.2 holds also for such extreme disturbance terms but it is much more difficult to show that $\mathrm{P}[\theta_T \in B_1 | \theta_0 \in B_0] > 0$ for some fixed $T \in I\!N$.

The assumption (2.52) is generally difficult to verify a priori since the variables y_t are endogenous. This is the same kind of problem as verifying condition (iv) in Assumption (A.1). In view of this condition it is not too restrictive to assume that also (2.52) holds. If we consider the OLS procedure, it is easily shown that

$$(2.65) \qquad \sum_{t=0}^{\infty} \frac{\gamma_t^2}{y_t^2} = \sum_{t=0}^{\infty} \frac{y^2}{(\sum_{\tau=0}^{t} y_\tau^2)^2} \le \frac{2}{y_0^2}.$$

Hence the assumption (2.52) is satisfied whenever $\mathrm{E}[y_0^{-2}] < \infty$, for example, whenever we assume y_0 to be deterministic and non-zero.

The above results are weaker than the global convergence results in Section 6 but apply also to situations where the attracting region is bounded in the θ–coordinate, i.e. when the fixed point $\bar{\theta}$ is not globally stable. It is therefore reasonable to ask whether also in such a situation we can obtain a.s. convergence if the initial value θ_0 is sufficiently close to $\bar{\theta}$. The answer is negative in general. We show that there are situations in which convergence occurs with positive but not with unit probability. To do so we need the following result which is a generalization of Theorem 7.2.

Theorem 2.7.4
Suppose that $\{\gamma_t\}$ and $\{w_t\}$ satisfy the assumptions of Theorem 7.2. Suppose furthermore that there exists a connected bounded set with non-empty interior $D \subset \mathbb{R}$ such that $f(D) \subset D$. Then

$$\mathrm{P}[\theta_t \in D \textit{ for all but finitely many } t \geq 1] > 0, \tag{2.66}$$

provided that $\mathrm{P}[\theta_0 \in D^\epsilon] > 0$, where D^ϵ is defined as in (2.48).

Proof
Since

$$(1-\gamma)\theta + \gamma f(\theta) \in D \qquad \forall\, \theta \in D,\ \forall\, \gamma \in [0,1] \tag{2.67}$$

the structural adjustment terms force $\{\theta_t\}$ to stay in D whenever $\{\theta_t\}$ has reached D. A careful examination of the proof of Theorem 7.2 shows that we can imitate the proof in order to obtain the desired result. ■

Notice that if we allow the disturbance terms to be unbounded, e.g., if we assume $\{w_t\}$ to be a sequence of independent Gaussian random variables, we can dispense with any assumption on the initial value θ_0 since with positive probability there exist sufficiently large realizations of the disturbance terms to ensure that the estimation process reaches or leaves any bounded set.

Theorem 2.7.5
Suppose that (A.1)-(A.3) are satisfied. Suppose furthermore that w_t possesses a positive density function and that (2.51) holds true. Let $\{\gamma_t\}$ be an admissible sequence of gains such that (2.52) holds and let $\bar{\theta}$ be a fixed point of f such that $|f'(\bar{\theta})| < 1$. If there exists some connected set $D \subset \mathbb{R}$ with non-empty interior such that

$$f(D) \subset D \qquad \textit{and} \qquad D \cap D(\bar{\theta}) = \emptyset \tag{2.68}$$

then $\mathrm{P}[\theta_t \to \bar{\theta}] > 0$ and $\mathrm{P}[\theta_t \not\to \bar{\theta}] > 0$.

Proof

Notice that the assumptions of Theorem 7.2 are met. Since the disturbance terms are not bounded and possess a continuous distribution we have

$$\text{(2.69)} \qquad \mathrm{P}[\theta_1 \in D^\epsilon] > 0 \qquad \text{and} \qquad \mathrm{P}[\theta_1 \in B^\epsilon] > 0$$

for some $\epsilon > 0$ where B^ϵ is defined as in Corollary 7.3 and D^ϵ, B^ϵ are chosen with non-empty interior. Then Corollary 7.3, with θ_1 playing the role of θ_0, implies $\mathrm{P}[\theta_t \to \bar{\theta}] > 0$ while Theorem 7.4 gives $\mathrm{P}[\theta_t \not\to \bar{\theta}] > 0$. ∎

Since the pioneering Monte–Carlo study of CYERT/DEGROOT in 1974 it is well-known that in the dynamic case convergence does not always occurs with probability one[13]. This finding was confirmed in the Monte–Carlo study of KOTTMANN/KULIBERDA (1990) but the interpretation given therein is not correct[14]. We like to emphasize that, under certain assumptions on the feedback function and the disturbance terms, *convergence is a path-dependent property*, i.e., whether convergence or divergence of the estimation process occurs depends on the respective trajectory of the disturbance terms. Theorem 7.5 formalizes this assertion.

[13] CYERT/DEGROOT (1974) considered the linear model with additive forecasts one period ahead jointly with the OLS procedure and observed that, for the same deterministic initial values θ_0 and y_0, some simulation runs showed convergence of the estimation process while other runs ended in divergence. They observed this phenomenon in the case of $f'(\bar{\theta}) = a < -1$, for a stable as well as for an unstable REE. This finding indicates that if a fixed point is stable w.r.t. a learning procedure, then the respective learning procedure does not necessarily converges a.s. towards the fixed point if the evolution of the gains depends on the evolution of the endogenous variable.

[14] KOTTMANN/KULIBERDA (1990) remarked that for linear models with additive forecasts more than one period ahead "almost everything can happen". They considered the OLS procedure with a slightly different formation scheme for multi-period ahead predictions which results in a slightly different feedback function.

Although KOTTMANN/KULIBERDA observed the same qualitative features of the model as we did they conjectured "that for models with $k > 0$ there is a bounded domain of attraction depending on ϕ and a [...] containing all starting configurations [...] which give almost sure convergence"(p. 11). In fact, this conjecture is false in the stochastic case as shown in our own Monte–Carlo study of their model (see ZENNER (1992b)).

Example 2.7.6
Consider the linear model with additive forecasts two periods ahead

$$(2.70) \qquad y_{t+1} = \phi y_t + a y^e_{t+2} + w_{t+1}, \qquad t \geq 0.$$

The feedback function is thus $f(\theta) = \phi + a\theta^2$ which obviously does not satisfy any of the global stability conditions of Section 6.

If $4a\phi < 1$, $a \neq 0$, then f possesses two distinct fixed points

$$(2.71) \quad \bar{\theta}_1 = \frac{1}{2a}\left(1 - \sqrt{1 - 4a\phi}\right) \quad \text{and} \quad \bar{\theta}_2 = \frac{1}{2a}\left(1 + \sqrt{1 - 4a\phi}\right).$$

Since

$$(2.72) \quad f'(\bar{\theta}_1) = 1 - \sqrt{1 - 4a\phi} \quad \text{and} \quad f'(\bar{\theta}_2) = 1 + \sqrt{1 - 4a\phi}$$

the fixed point $\bar{\theta}_2$ is unstable.

In order to ensure that $\bar{\theta}_1$ is stable we assume, in addition to $4a\phi < 1$, that $a > 0$ and $4a\phi \in (-3, 1)$. Then $\bar{\theta}_1$ is stable with respect to any admissible learning procedure since $|f'(\bar{\theta}_1)| < 1$. Since $f(\theta) > \theta$ for all $\theta > \bar{\theta}_2$ the attracting region $D(\bar{\theta}_1)$ is bounded above in the θ-coordinate and there exists some value $\theta^* < \bar{\theta}_2$ such that

$$(2.73) \quad f([\theta^*, \bar{\theta}_2]) \subset [\theta^*, \bar{\theta}_2] \quad \text{and} \quad [\theta^*, \bar{\theta}_2] \times [0,1] \subset D(\bar{\theta}_1).$$

In view of (2.68) we define $D = (\bar{\theta}_2, \infty)$. Now suppose that the disturbance terms satisfy the assumptions of Theorem 7.5, the initial value y_0 is deterministic and non-zero, and the estimates θ_t are given by the OLS procedure. Then we have $\mathrm{P}[\theta_t \to \bar{\theta}] \in (0, 1)$.

As the above example indicates the situation arises quite naturally that rational expectations are stable but not globally stable w.r.t. a learning procedure, even in simple models. In particular, if the feedback function is a polynomial of degree higher than one, for example in the case of multi-period ahead expectations in the linear model with additive forecasts, then rational expectations are at most locally stable. Hence a *risk of explosion*[15] exists and convergence occurs with

[15] By explosion we mean divergence of the estimation process and the data process caused by the feedback mechanism. For example, if the function f is shaped such that overestimation of the rational expectations parameter, $\theta_t > \bar{\theta}$, leads to underestimation of the actual law of motion, $\theta_t < f(\theta_t)$, such a feedback to cause explosion is likely to occur.

probability less than one. This feature is exclusive to the dynamic case. In the static case multi-period ahead expectations do not cause any (additional) problems (see, e.g., KOTTMANN (1990)).

Although explosions occur also in real economic life (as the hyperinflation in the twenties shows) most studies on learning to become rational in the dynamic case try to avoid the risk of explosion by introducing a mechanism which ensures that the estimates do not leave a certain neighbourhood of the REE parameter (see, e.g., MARCET/SARGENT (1989a,b)). In our setup such a mechanism could ensure that the augmented estimation process never leaves the attracting region. This would considerably facilitate the convergence analysis but, as already mentioned in the preceding chapter, the use of such mechanisms is problematic since they have to be introduced at the level of agents' behaviour. Hence agents have to understand the model well enough to determine the attracting region. To us, such an assumption is highly implausible and unrealistic.

Based on our Monte–Carlo study we give some final remarks on the long-term behaviour of the estimation process $\{\theta_t\}$. Firstly, if there are two or more stable fixed points it is possible that the estimation process moves from one attracting region into another one with positive probability. We conjecture that this can happen only finitely often.

Secondly, the probability that the estimation process stays in a particular region depends on the shape of the feedback function f, which determines the size of the attracting regions, but also on the long-term behaviour of the data process $\{y_t\}$. If the data process is explosive, then the influence of the accidental adjustment terms decreases rapidly. Various Monte–Carlo runs, reported in ZENNER (1992b), have shown that in such cases the transient phase in which the estimation process eventually leaves the attracting region after starting there is relatively short — say about 10 periods — and if the estimation process stays in the attracting region, then convergence takes place quite rapidly.

On the other hand, if the data process is stable, i.e., if the estimation process stays in a region which implies $|f(\theta_t)| \leq 1$, the transient phase can be relatively long. We faced situations in which the the estimation process seemed to stabilize but exploded suddenly after more than 300 periods, due only to some 'unpleasant' disturbances.

Finally, the behaviour of the estimation process depends also on the initial value θ_0. An initial value far-away from the attracting region reduces the probability of convergence but, as already mentioned and unlike to the theory of differential equations, in general there *does not* exist a region D for the initial values θ_0 such that $\theta_0 \in D$ implies a.s. convergence of $\{\theta_t\}$.

All these findings are of a qualitative nature and, to us, it seems to be impossible to calculate exact probability values even in particular cases.

2.8 The Rate of Convergence

In this section we determine the rate of convergence of the estimation processes. The rate of convergence is not only of interest as a purely theoretical result but also in view of the plausibility of the learning produres. If convergence is fast then it is plausible to assume that agents stick to their learning procedure. Otherwise they will likely look for another learning procedure.

It turns out that the rate of convergence depends as well on the respective learning procedure as on the long-term behaviour of the data process $\{y_t\}$. If this process explodes the rate of convergence is much higher than in the case of a stable data process. This phenomenon is very similar to the superefficiency of the least squares estimator in the case of an exploding autoregression.

The following theorem is the central tool in this section.

Theorem 2.8.1
Suppose that (A.1)-(A.3) are satisfied. Let $\bar{\theta}$ be a fixed point of the function f and $\{\pi_t\}$ be a sequence of positive predetermined random variables (i.e., π_t is $\mathcal{F}_{t-1}$-measurable) such that for all $t \geq 0$,

$$(2.74) \quad \frac{\pi_{t+1}^2}{\pi_t^2}\left[(1-\gamma_t)(\theta_t-\bar{\theta})+\gamma_t(f(\theta_t)-\bar{\theta})\right]^2 \leq (1+\alpha_t)(\theta_t-\bar{\theta})^2$$

with $\{\alpha_t\}$ a sequence of non-negative $\mathcal{F}_t$-measurable random variables. If on the event $[\theta_t \to \bar{\theta}]$

(i) $\sum_{t=0}^{\infty} \alpha_t < \infty$ *a.s., and*

(ii) $\sum_{t=0}^{\infty} \frac{\gamma_t^2}{y_t^2}\pi_{t+1}^2 < \infty \qquad a.s.,$

then $|\theta_t - \bar{\theta}| = O(\pi_t^{-1})$ *a.s. on* $[\theta_t \to \bar{\theta}]$.

Proof
In view of (2.30) and (2.74) we have

$$\begin{aligned} \mathrm{E}\left[\pi_{t+1}^2(\theta_{t+1}-\bar{\theta})^2\middle|\mathcal{F}_t\right] &\leq (1+\alpha_t)\pi_t^2(\theta_t-\bar{\theta})^2 \\ &+\frac{\gamma_t^2}{y_t^2}\pi_{t+1}^2\mathrm{E}\left[w_{t+1}^2\middle|\mathcal{F}_t\right]. \end{aligned} \tag{2.75}$$

Then Proposition 5.1 implies that $\{\pi_t^2(\theta_t - \bar{\theta})^2\}$ converges a.s. towards some finite limit on the event $[\theta_t \to \bar{\theta}]$. Hence $|\theta_t - \bar{\theta}| = O(\pi_t^{-1})$. ■

Now it is obvious how to proceed. Given a fixed point $\bar{\theta}$ and a sequence of gains $\{\gamma_t\}$ we have to find a sequence $\{\pi_t\}$ such that the conditions (i) and (ii) of Theorem 8.1 are satisfied and, if possible, $\{\pi_t\}$ grows at a maximum rate.

Since the sequence $\{\pi_t\}$ usually depends as well on the respective sequence of gains as on the evolution of $\{y_t^2\}$ which is, at least qualitatively, determined by the respective fixed point $\bar{\theta}$ one cannot expect to obtain a result which is, on the one hand, fairly general and applies for a large class of sequences of gains and, on the other hand, determines the rate of convergence quite sharply. We therefore distinguish several cases.

First we consider the *explosive case* $|\bar{\theta}| > 1$. In this case the process $\{y_t\}$ explodes a.s. at approximately a geometrical rate on $[\theta_t \to \bar{\theta}]$. This property considerably facilitates the verification of condition (ii) of Theorem 8.1. We shall give results for (convergence preserving) sequences of gains with positive limit points and limit point zero.

Then we consider the *stable case* $|\bar{\theta}| < 1$. In this case the situation is more complicated since the process $\{y_t\}$ does not possess a minimum rate of divergence so that the verification of condition (ii) of Theorem 8.1 is difficult in general. We will therefore give a result only for a special case, the OLS procedure.

2.8.1 The Explosive Case

The first result applies to sequences of gains with a positive limit point.

Theorem 2.8.2
Suppose that (A.1)–(A.4) are satisfied. Let $\bar{\theta}$ be a fixed point of f with $|\bar{\theta}| > 1$ and let $\{\gamma_t\}$ be a convergence preserving sequence of gains with limit point $\bar{\gamma} = \bar{\gamma}(\bar{\theta}) > 0$. Suppose that $1 - 2/\bar{\gamma} < f'(\bar{\theta}) < 1$, thus $\bar{\theta}$ is stable w.r.t. $\{\gamma_t\}$. Then on the event $[\theta_t \to \bar{\theta}]$

$$|\theta_t - \bar{\theta}| = O\left(\rho^{-t}\right) \qquad a.s. \tag{2.76}$$

for every $\rho > 1$ such that

$$\rho < \min\left\{|\bar{\theta}|, \frac{1}{|1 - \bar{\gamma}(1 - f'(\bar{\theta}))|}\right\}. \tag{2.77}$$

Proof
Since $1 - 2/\bar{\gamma} < f'(\bar{\theta}) < 1$ is equivalent to $|1 - \bar{\gamma}(1 - f'(\bar{\theta}))| < 1$ there exist constants ρ which satisfy (2.77). In order to apply Theorem 8.1 we set $\pi_t^2 = \rho^{2t}$ with ρ satisfying (2.77). Then

$$\begin{aligned} &\frac{\pi_{t+1}^2}{\pi_t^2}\left[(1-\gamma_t)(\theta_t - \bar{\theta}) + \gamma_t(f(\theta_t) - \bar{\theta})\right]^2 \\ &\qquad = \rho^2\left[1 - \gamma_t(1 - f'(\xi_t))\right]^2 (\theta_t - \bar{\theta})^2 \end{aligned} \tag{2.78}$$

with some mean value ξ_t between θ_t and $\bar{\theta}$. Define the random variables α_t by

$$\alpha_t = \left(\rho^2\left[1 - \gamma_t(1 - f'(\xi_t))\right]^2 - 1\right)^+. \tag{2.79}$$

Then the representation (2.74) holds. Let N be a (path-dependent) number such that $\alpha_t = 0$ for all $t \geq N$. Since $f'(\cdot)$ is continuous at $\bar{\theta}$, $\gamma_t \to \bar{\gamma}$, and (2.77) is satisfied this number is finite a.s. on the event $[\theta_t \to \bar{\theta}]$. Hence $\sum_0^\infty \alpha_t < \infty$ a.s. on $[\theta_t \to \bar{\theta}]$ and condition (i) of Theorem 8.1 is verified.

To verify condition (ii) we choose some $\tilde{\rho}$ such that $\rho < \tilde{\rho} < |\bar{\theta}|$. Because $\gamma_t \leq 1$ we obtain on the event $[\theta_t \to \bar{\theta}]$

$$\sum_{t=0}^{T} \frac{\gamma_t^2}{y_t^2}\pi_{t+1}^2 \leq \sum_{t=0}^{T} \frac{\tilde{\rho}^{2(t+1)}}{y_t^2}\left(\frac{\rho}{\tilde{\rho}}\right)^{2(t+1)} < \infty \quad \text{a.s.} \tag{2.80}$$

where the finiteness of the sum follows from $\rho < \tilde{\rho}$ and since $\tilde{\rho}^{2t} = O(y_t^2)$ a.s. on $[\theta_t \to \bar{\theta}]$ as shown in Theorem A.11 in Appendix A. Hence condition (ii) of Theorem 8.1 is verified and (2.76) follows. ■

Now we consider the case $\gamma_t \to 0$ a.s. on $[\theta_t \to \bar{\theta}]$. Because the term $1 - \gamma_t(1 - f'(\xi_t))$ approaches 1 on $[\theta_t \to \bar{\theta}]$ the choice of $\{\pi_t\}$ as above does not satisfy condition (i) of Theorem 8.1. We thus have to find another sequence $\{\pi_t\}$ which increases with lower speed.

Theorem 2.8.3
Suppose that (A.1)–(A.4) are satisfied. Let $\bar{\theta}$ be a fixed point of f with $|\bar{\theta}| > 1$ and let $\{\gamma_t\}$ be an admissible sequence of gains such that $\gamma_t \to 0$ a.s. on $[\theta_t \to \bar{\theta}]$. Suppose that $f'(\bar{\theta}) < 1$, thus $\bar{\theta}$ is stable with respect to $\{\gamma_t\}$. Then on the event $[\theta_t \to \bar{\theta}]$

$$(2.81) \qquad |\theta_t - \bar{\theta}| = O\left(\exp\left(-c\sum_{s=0}^{t}\gamma_s\right)\right) \qquad a.s.$$

for every $c \in (0, 1 - f'(\bar{\theta}))$.

Proof
Fix some $0 < c < 1 - f'(\bar{\theta})$. Define $\{\pi_t^2\}$ recursively by $\pi_0^2 = 1$ and

$$(2.82) \qquad \pi_{t+1}^2 = \begin{cases} \pi_t^2 & \text{if} \quad 1 - c\gamma_t = 0, \\ \dfrac{\pi_t^2}{(1 - c\gamma_t)^2} & \text{otherwise.} \end{cases}$$

Hence π_{t+1}^2 is positive and $\mathcal{F}_t$-measurable. Furthermore define random variables α_t by

$$(2.83) \quad \alpha_t = \begin{cases} \left([1 - \gamma_t(1 - f'(\xi_t))]^2 - 1\right)^+ & \text{if} \quad 1 - c\gamma_t = 0, \\ \left(\dfrac{[1 - \gamma_t(1 - f'(\xi_t))]^2}{[1 - c\gamma_t]^2} - 1\right)^+ & \text{otherwise,} \end{cases}$$

with some mean value ξ_t. Hence α_t is non-negative and $\mathcal{F}_t$-measurable. It is easy to see that with π_t^2 and α_t as in (2.82) and (2.83) the representation (2.74) holds.

In order to verify condition (i) of Theorem 8.1 notice firstly that $\gamma_t \to 0$ a.s. on $[\theta_t \to \bar{\theta}]$ implies that $1 - c\gamma_t = 0$ only finitely often a.s. on $[\theta_t \to \bar{\theta}]$. Hence the first case in the split-case definitions (2.82) and (2.83) applies only finitely often a.s. on $[\theta_t \to \bar{\theta}]$.

Secondly, notice that since $\gamma_t \to 0$ a.s. on $[\theta_t \to \bar{\theta}]$, $c < 1 - f'(\bar{\theta})$, and since f is continuous at $\bar{\theta}$ we can conclude that

$$\frac{[1 - \gamma_t(1 - f'(\xi_t))]^2}{[1 - c\gamma_t]^2} \le 1 \tag{2.84}$$

for all but finitely many $t \ge 0$ a.s. on $[\theta_t \to \bar{\theta}]$. This implies that $\alpha_t = 0$ a.s. for all but finitely many t on $[\theta_t \to \bar{\theta}]$. Hence $\sum_0^\infty \alpha_t < \infty$ a.s. on $[\theta_t \to \bar{\theta}]$ and condition (i) is verified.

To verify condition (ii) we fix two constants $\rho, \tilde{\rho}$ such that $1 < \rho < \tilde{\rho} < |\bar{\theta}|$. We want to show that $\pi_t^2 = O(\rho^{2t})$ a.s. on $[\theta_t \to \bar{\theta}]$. To see this notice that the first case in definition (2.82) applies only finitely often a.s. on $[\theta_t \to \bar{\theta}]$. Notice furthermore that $\gamma_t \to 0$ a.s. on $[\theta_t \to \bar{\theta}]$ implies that $(1 - c\gamma_t)^{-2} < \rho^2$ for all but finitely many t a.s. on $[\theta_t \to \bar{\theta}]$. Hence $\pi_t^2 = O(\rho^{2t})$ a.s. on $[\theta_t \to \bar{\theta}]$. Now we can proceed as in the proof of Theorem 8.2 to show that (ii) holds.

To finish the proof let N be the (path-dependent) number such that $1 - c\gamma_t > 0$ for all $t \ge N$. Obviously, N is finite a.s. on $[\theta_t \to \bar{\theta}]$. Using the inequality $\log x \le x - 1$ we obtain

$$\begin{aligned}
\pi_{t+1}^{-1} &= O\left(\prod_{s=N}^{t}(1 - c\gamma_s)\right) \\
&= O\left(\exp\left(\log\left(\prod_{s=N}^{t}(1 - c\gamma_s)\right)\right)\right) \\
&= O\left(\exp\left(\sum_{s=N}^{t}\log(1 - c\gamma_s)\right)\right) \qquad (2.85) \\
&= O\left(\exp\left(-c\sum_{s=N}^{t}\gamma_s\right)\right) \\
&= O\left(\exp\left(-c\sum_{s=0}^{t}\gamma_s\right)\right)
\end{aligned}$$

This completes the proof. ■

As an example we quote the OLS procedure since (cf. Proposition 4.3) the OLS sequence of gains is convergence preserving with a positive limit point if $|\bar{\theta}| > 1$. Then Theorem 8.3 implies $|\theta_t - \bar{\theta}| = O(\rho^{-t})$ a.s. with ρ given as in (2.77). The OLS estimates thus converge geometrically.

2.8.2 The Stable Case

The stable case, $|\bar{\theta}| < 1$, is more difficult to analyze since the asymptotic behaviour of the data process is not as simple as in the explosive case. In particular, $\{y_t\}$ possesses no minimum rate of divergence. This complicates the verification of condition (ii) of Theorem 8.1.

First we consider a convergence preserving sequence of gains with limit point $\bar{\gamma} > 0$. Since Theorem 8.1 makes sense only if the sequence $\{\pi_t^2\}$ is increasing in the long run condition (ii) of Theorem 8.1 requires as a necessary condition

$$\sum_{t=1}^{\infty} \frac{1}{y_t^2} < \infty \qquad \text{a.s.} \tag{2.86}$$

on the event $[\theta_t \to \bar{\theta}]$. In Appendix A, Theorem A.4, it is shown that $y_t^2 = o(t)$ a.s. on $[\theta_t \to \bar{\theta}]$ if $|\bar{\theta}| < 1$. Hence (2.86) is violated and, consequently, condition (ii) cannot hold for sequence of gains with positive limit point[16].

For that reason let $\{\gamma_t\}$ be a sequence of gains with $\gamma_t \to 0$ a.s. on $[\theta_t \to \bar{\theta}]$ and $\bar{\theta}$ a fixed point of f such that $|\bar{\theta}| < 1$. In order to apply Theorem 8.1 it is not difficult to find a sequence $\{\pi_t^2\}$ such that (i) holds but it is a serious problem to show (ii) for general $\{\gamma_t\}$. We therefore present a solution only for a special case, the OLS procedure.

---

[16]Nevertheless, this does not necessarily imply that $\pi_t^2(\theta_t - \bar{\theta})^2$ does not converge. Only if we impose additional assumptions on the disturbance terms, more precisely, if we assume $\{w_t\}$ to be normed regular in the sense of Marcinkiewicz and Zygmund, then $\sum_{t=0}^{\infty} y_t^{-2} = \infty$ implies that $\pi_t^2(\theta_t - \bar{\theta})^2$ does not converge (see, e.g., STOUT (1974), pp. 80).

Notice that, e.g., every sequence $\{w_t\}$ of independently distributed random variables such that $Ew_t = 0$, $Ew_t^2 = 1$, and w_t^2 is uniformly integrable is a normed regular MDS in the sense of Marcinkiewicz and Zygmund. Other examples are MDS with $E[w_{t+1}^2|\mathcal{F}_t] = 1$ which are uniformly bounded by a constant.

Theorem 2.8.4
Suppose that (A.1)-(A.4) are satisfied. Let $\bar{\theta}$ be an OLS-stable fixed point of the function f with $|\bar{\theta}| < 1$. Then on the event $[\theta_t \to \bar{\theta}]$

$$\theta_t - \bar{\theta} = O\left(t^{-c}\right) \qquad a.s. \tag{2.87}$$

for every $c > 0$ such that

$$c < \min\left\{\frac{1}{2}, 1 - f'(\bar{\theta})\right\}. \tag{2.88}$$

For the proof we need the following auxiliary result due to CESÀRO which can be found in KNOPP (1964).

Lemma 2.8.5
Let (d_t) be a sequence of non-negative real numbers with $d_0 > 0$ and let $D_t = \sum_{\tau=0}^{t} d_\tau$. Suppose that $D_t \to \infty$ and $d_t/D_t \to 0$ as $t \to \infty$. Then

$$(\log D_T)^{-1} \sum_{t=0}^{T} \frac{d_t}{D_t} \longrightarrow 1 \qquad as \quad T \to \infty. \tag{2.89}$$

Proof of Theorem 8.4
We imitate the proof of Theorem 8.3. This is possible since $\gamma_t \to 0$ a.s. on $[\theta_t \to \bar{\theta}]$ as shown in Theorem A.13 in Appendix A. We choose π_{t+1}^2 as in the proof of Theorem 8.3 with c satisfying (2.88). (Notice that $c \in (0, 1/2)$ implies that $1 - c\gamma_t$ is always positive. Hence the split-case definitions (2.82) and (2.83) can be avoided.) Then, by the same reasoning as in the proof of Theorem 8.3, condition (i) of Theorem 8.1 can be verified. Hence it remains to verify condition (ii).

Recall that the gains of the OLS procedure are given as $\gamma_t = y_t^2 / \sum_{\tau=0}^{t} y_\tau^2$. Hence

$$\sum_{t=0}^{T} \frac{\gamma_t^2}{y_t^2} \pi_{t+1}^2 = \sum_{t=0}^{T} \frac{y_t^2}{\left(\sum_{\tau=0}^{t} y_\tau^2\right)^2} \prod_{s=0}^{t} (1 - c\gamma_s)^{-2}. \tag{2.90}$$

Using the inequality $\log x \geq 1 - 1/x$ and Lemma 8.5 we obtain

$$\begin{aligned} \pi_{t+1}^2 &= \exp\left(\log\left(\prod_{s=0}^{t}(1-c\gamma_s)^{-2}\right)\right) \\ &= \exp\left(-2\sum_{s=0}^{t}\log(1-c\gamma_s)\right) \\ &= O\left(\exp\left(2\sum_{s=0}^{t}\left(\frac{c\gamma_s}{1-c\gamma_s}\right)\right)\right) \qquad (2.91) \\ &= O\left(\exp\left(2c\sum_{s=0}^{t}\gamma_s\right)\right) \\ &= O\left(\left(\sum_{s=0}^{t}y_s^2\right)^{2c}\right). \end{aligned}$$

Hence

$$(2.92) \qquad \sum_{t=0}^{T}\frac{\gamma_t^2}{y_t^2}\pi_{t+1}^2 \quad \leq \quad C\sum_{t=0}^{\infty}\frac{y_t^2}{\left(\sum_{\tau=0}^{t}y_\tau^2\right)^{2(1-c)}} \quad < \quad \infty$$

with some constant $C > 0$ and where the finiteness follows from Lemma 2.2 since $c < 1/2$. Thus condition (ii) of Theorem 8.1 is satisfied and we obtain

$$(2.93) \qquad |\theta_t - \bar{\theta}| = O(\pi_{t+1}^{-1}) = O\left(\left(\sum_{0}^{t}y_s^2\right)^{-c}\right) = O(t^{-c}) \quad \text{a.s.}$$

where the second equality follows from (2.85) and Lemma 8.5 and the last equality follows from Lemma 2.1. ■

This result corresponds to results determining the rate of convergence for linear models with forecast feedback incorporating only exogenous variables as explanatory variables. FOURGEAUD ET AL. (1986) and KOTTMANN (1990) obtain the same rate of convergence for these models. This coincidence is not surprising since in case of $\theta_t \to \bar{\theta}$ a.s. with $|\bar{\theta}| < 1$ the data process exhibits the properties usually attributed to exogenous inputs.

For the OLS procedure it is possible to derive a slightly stronger result that Theorem 8.4. In ZENNER (1994) we have shown under the assumptions of Theorem 8.4 and, in addition, if $f'(\bar{\theta}) < 1/2$, then

$$|\theta_t - \bar{\theta}|^2 = O\left(\frac{\log t}{t}\right) \quad \text{a.s.} \tag{2.94}$$

on $[\theta_t \to \bar{\theta}]$. If Assumption (A.3) is only fulfilled with $\delta = 0$, then

$$|\theta_t - \bar{\theta}|^2 = o\left(\frac{(\log t)^{1+\delta}}{t}\right) \quad \text{a.s.} \tag{2.95}$$

These results are achieved by a related but more involved technique. We refer to Chapter 4 where we shall use this technique to derive a convergence result for the OLS procedure in the non-stationary case.

We conclude this section with the remark that the rate of convergence given in (2.94) and (2.95) corresponds exactly with the respective rates of convergence of the OLS estimates in a constant parameter autoregressive model determined by LAI/WEI (1982a). Moreover, LAI/WEI show that these results cannot be sharpend without additional assumptions on the disturbance terms. It is therefore somewhat surprising that we can introduce forecast feedback in the model up to $f'(\bar{\theta}) < 1/2$ without obtaining a slower rate of convergence of the OLS estimates.

2.9 An Example

In this section we give an example in order to illustrate the preceding theory. It is a modification of the cobweb model employed by MUTH (1961) in his famous paper and analyzed by several authors in connection with learning procedures[17]. In its text book formulation the cobweb model is not autoregressive since the endogenous variables are intertemporally linked only via the predictions of agents. We modify the model by introducing a special type of agents that generates a persistent autoregressive relationship between the endogenous variables.

[17]See, e.g., CYERT/DEGROOT (1974), BRAY/SAVIN (1986), FOURGEAUD ET AL. (1986), MARCET/SARGENT (1989a), KOTTMANN (1990) and MOHR (1990)).

2.9.1 The Model

Consider the model of an isolated market with a fixed production lag of a commodity which cannot be stored, for instance an agricultural market. The market equations are of the usual form

$$\begin{aligned} D_t &= -\beta p_t && \text{(Demand)} \\ S_t &= \alpha p_t^e + u_t && \text{(Supply)} \\ D_t &= S_t && \text{(Market Equilibrium)} \end{aligned} \tag{2.96}$$

where

- S_t represents the number of units produced in a period lasting as long as the production lag,
- D_t is the amount consumed in period t,
- p_t is the market price in period t,
- p_t^e is the market price expected to prevail during period t based on information available through the $(t-1)$'st period,
- u_t is an error term — representing, say, variations in yields due to weather, and
- $\alpha > 0$, $\beta > 0$ are the model's parameters.

Demand and supply are thus linear functions in prices and expected prices, resp. The supply equation can be understood as the result of maximizing expected profits under a quadratic cost function. Notice that both equations are formulated in terms of deviations from equilibrium values[18].

The quantity variables may be eliminated from (2.96) to give

$$p_t = -\frac{\alpha}{\beta} p_t^e - \frac{1}{\beta} u_t. \tag{2.97}$$

We assume that there exist two different types of agents (producers) in the market which differ in the way they form their predictions. The first type adopts the naive or myopic prediction rule $p_t^e = p_{t-1}$ (possibly since they believe to act in a competitive steady state economy or

[18] In the next chapter we consider the same model without this simplification.

just do not know better) while the other type follows a learning procedure as given in Assumption (A.1). With $a_1, a_2 \in [0,1]$, $a_1 + a_2 = 1$, we denote the fractions of the respective types of agents measured by their output capacity. The special cases $a_2 = 0$ and $a_1 = 0$ correspond to the common cobweb model and to the model in which all agents follow a learning procedure. (The latter case is considered, for example, in the study of CYERT/DEGROOT (1974)). Since in case of $a_2 = 0$ there are no agents following a learning procedure we assume $a_2 > 0$.

The aggregate or market prediction is then given by

$$p_t^e = a_1 p_{t-1} + a_2 \theta_{t-1} p_{t-1} = (a_1 + a_2 \theta_{t-1}) p_{t-1} \tag{2.98}$$

with $\{\theta_t\}$ given by Assumption (A.1). Hence the reduced form equation can be rewritten as

$$p_t = -\frac{\alpha}{\beta}(a_1 + a_2\theta_{t-1})p_{t-1} - \frac{1}{\beta}u_t. \tag{2.99}$$

The feedback function of the model is

$$f(\theta) = -\frac{\alpha}{\beta}(a_1 + a_2\theta) \tag{2.100}$$

which satisfies Assumption (A.2) and possesses a unique fixed point

$$\bar{\theta} = -\frac{a_1\alpha}{a_2\alpha + \beta}. \tag{2.101}$$

(Notice that the economic parameter restrictions $\alpha > 0$ and $\beta > 0$ ensure that this fixed point always exists.) Finally we assume that the disturbance terms $\{u_t\}$ satisfy Assumption (A.3). The model is thus a special case of a linear model with additive forecasts.

2.9.2 Stability of Rational Expectations

Obviously, agents form rational expectations if their predictions are given as $p_t^e = \bar{\theta} p_{t-1}$. In order to determine the stability of $\bar{\theta}$ we consider

$$f'(\bar{\theta}) = -a_2\frac{\alpha}{\beta} \tag{2.102}$$

which is always negative. Now Theorem 4.5 gives

(i) If $\alpha/\beta < 1/a_2$, then $\bar{\theta}$ is stable w.r.t. every admissible learning procedure.

(ii) If $\alpha/\beta \geq 1/a_2$, then $\bar{\theta}$ is stable w.r.t. every admissible learning procedure such that

$$\bar{\gamma} < \frac{2\beta}{a_2\alpha + \beta}. \tag{2.103}$$

(iii) $\bar{\theta}$ is stable w.r.t. every admissible learning procedure such that $\gamma_t \to 0$ a.s.

2.9.3 Convergence Results

We can apply Theorem 6.2 and Theorem 6.4 to obtain the following global convergence result.

(i) If $\alpha/\beta < 1/a_2$, then $\theta_t \to \bar{\theta}$ a.s. for every admissible learning procedure.

(ii) If $\alpha/\beta \geq 1/a_2$ and the learning procedure is given by a sequence of gains such that $\limsup_t \gamma_t \leq \bar{\gamma}$ a.s. and $\bar{\gamma}$ satisfies (2.103), then $\theta_t \to \bar{\theta}$ a.s.

(iii) If the learning procedure is given by a sequence of gains such that $\gamma_t \to 0$ a.s. then $\theta_t \to \bar{\theta}$ a.s. no matter of the values of a_2, α, and β.

For all other cases we do not have convergence results since the local convergence results in Section 7 do not apply for this model. (If $\alpha/\beta \geq 1/a_2$ the attracting region $D(\bar{\theta})$ does not contain $B \times [0,1]$ for any $B \subset \mathbb{R}$ such that $B \neq \emptyset$ and $B \neq \{\bar{\theta}\} \times [0,1]$.) However, computer simulations suggest that if $\bar{\theta}$ is stable w.r.t. some learning procedure, then $\mathrm{P}[\theta_t \to \bar{\theta}] > 0$. This probability decreases as α/β increases or as a_2 increases.

2.9.4 Results for the OLS Procedure

Now we consider the special case that the estimates θ_t are given by the OLS procedure. From Proposition 4.3 we know that the OLS sequence of gains is convergence preserving with $\bar{\gamma}(\bar{\theta}) = 0$ if $|\bar{\theta}| < 1$ and $\bar{\gamma}(\bar{\theta}) = (\bar{\theta}^2 - 1)/\bar{\theta}^2$ if $|\bar{\theta}| > 1$. For notational convenience define two constants c_1 and c_2 by

$$c_1 = \frac{\beta}{\alpha} \quad \text{and} \quad c_2 = \frac{1}{2}\left(1 - \frac{\beta}{\alpha}\right). \tag{2.104}$$

Then it is easy to see that

$$|\bar{\theta}| > 1 \iff a_2 < c_2 \tag{2.105}$$

and

$$|f'(\bar{\theta})| \leq 1 \iff a_2 \leq c_1. \tag{2.106}$$

In view of Proposition 4.3, Theorem 4.5, and Theorem 6.4 we obtain the following result where the assertions of partly convergence rely on computer simulation results.

(i) If $\alpha/\beta < 1/a_2$, then $\bar{\theta}$ is OLS-stable and $\theta_t \to \bar{\theta}$ a.s.

(ii) If $\alpha/\beta \geq 1/a_2$, then the results reported in Table 2.1 hold where (*) denotes the property that the inequaltity

$$\bar{\theta}^2 = \left(\frac{a_1\alpha}{a_2\alpha + \beta}\right)^2 > \frac{a_2\alpha + \beta}{a_2\alpha - \beta}, \tag{2.107}$$

is satisfied.

	$\beta < \alpha < 3\beta$	$\alpha \geq 3\beta$
$a_2 < c_2$	$\lvert\bar{\theta}\rvert > 1$, $\bar{\theta}$ is OLS-stable $\theta_t \to \bar{\theta}$ a.s.	
$c_2 \leq a_2 \leq c_1$	$\lvert\bar{\theta}\rvert \leq 1$, $\bar{\theta}$ is OLS-stable $\theta_t \to \bar{\theta}$ a.s.	
$c_1 < a_2$	$\lvert\bar{\theta}\rvert \leq 1$, $\bar{\theta}$ is OLS-stable $P[\theta_t \to \bar{\theta}] \in (0,1)$	
$a_2 \leq c_1$		$\lvert\bar{\theta}\rvert > 1$, $\bar{\theta}$ is OLS-stable $\theta_t \to \bar{\theta}$ a.s.
$c_1 < a_2 < c_2$		$\lvert\bar{\theta}\rvert > 1$, $\bar{\theta}$ is OLS-stable if (*) $P[\theta_t \to \bar{\theta}] \in (0,1)$ if (*)
$c_2 \leq a_2$		$\lvert\bar{\theta}\rvert \leq 1$, $\bar{\theta}$ is OLS-stable $P[\theta_t \to \bar{\theta}] \in (0,1)$

Table 2.1

Summerizing the above result we can conclude that the RE parameter $\bar{\theta}$ is OLS-stable for nearly all parameter configurations. But for an unstable market situation ($\alpha > \beta$) we have a.s. convergence of the OLS estimates only if the fraction of the learning firms is sufficiently small. Hence the success of learning is some kind of insider effect which gets lost if too many firms follow the OLS procedure. On the other hand the learning firms have a stabilizing effect in the sense that if the fraction of the learning firms is sufficiently large, then the REE is a stable autoregression.

Finally, we want to remark that whenever $\bar{\theta} \neq 1$ the naive agents do not participate in the success of learning and do not form rational expectations. Moreover, also the aggregate prediction is not rational unless $\bar{\theta} = 1$. But the other type of agents can learn to form rational expectations. This finding supports the application of boundedly rational learning procedures since agents following such a learning procedure implicitly learn about the irrational behaviour of the naive agents without facing the problem of forming expectations about other agents' expectations.

Chapter 3

Univariate ARX Models

3.1 Introduction

In this chapter we generalize the previous model in that we allow the endogenous variable to depend not only on its one period lagged value but also on more period lagged values and, in addition, on exogenous variables. This implies that the REE parameters and the learning procedure agents follow are multivariate. Unlike to the preceding chapter we consider only one specific learning procedure, the so-called *stochastic gradient (SG) algorithm.* This algorithm is well-known in the literature on recursive identification and control not at least because of its pleasant analytical properties[1]. We adopt the SG algorithm since it enables us to obtain global convergence results. Since it can be regarded as a multivariate PE algorithm it is also plausible in view of agents' behaviour.

From the mathematical point of view the generalization to the case of multivariate explanatory variables causes some problems. In Chapter 2 the estimates θ_{t+1} could be written as $(1-\gamma_t)\theta_t + \gamma_t f(\theta_t)$ plus some accidental adjustment term, hence as a convex combination of θ_t and $f(\theta_t)$ with $\gamma_t \in [0,1]$. Based on the geometrical properties of this

[1]For example, the stochastic regulator problem was first solved by GOODWIN ET AL. (1981) using the SG algorithm for the parameter estimates. Based on this result KOTTMANN (1990) showed that agents can learn to form some kind of optimal expectations in autoregressive models with forecast feedback if the estimation problem is embedded in a control problem and agents employ the SG algorithm. CHANG ET AL. (1991c) showed that agents learn to form rational expectations using a modified version of the SG algorithm.

representation we defined in an intuitively appealing way the attracting region of a REE parameter and developed our stability concept for rational expectations with respect to a learning procedure.

For the generalized model we obtain a similar representation, i.e., $\boldsymbol{\theta}_{t+1} = (\boldsymbol{I} - \boldsymbol{\Gamma}_t)\boldsymbol{\theta}_t + \boldsymbol{\Gamma}_t f(\boldsymbol{\theta}_t)$ plus some accidental adjustment term. But this representation lacks the geometrical properties a stability concept can be based upon since the coefficients $\boldsymbol{\Gamma}_t$ are matrices and, in addition, depend on the current explanatory variables. For this reason we shall not consider stability of rational expectations as a static concept.

The remainder of this chapter is structured as follows. The basic assumptions are introduced in Section 2. These assumptions are similar to the ones of Chapter 2. In Section 3 we develop the convergence analysis. It turns out that the matrix of moments plays a central role in the convergence analysis. Only if it remains stable in the sense that its condition number remains bounded over time we can show convergence. This motivates the condition analysis in Section 4 where we determine the order of the minimum and the maximum eigenvalues of that matrix. Using these results we obtain some convergence results in Section 5. In Section 6 we restate the economic example of Section 2.9 in a proper form, and in Section 7 we conclude this chapter with some interesting computer simulation results.

3.2 Basic Assumptions

We consider the following model given by its reduced form equation

(3.1) $$y_{t+1} = \boldsymbol{\phi}'\boldsymbol{z}_t + a y^e_{t+1} + w_{t+1}, \qquad t \geq 0,$$

where

- y_t is the real valued time t endogenous variable,
- $\boldsymbol{z}_t$ is a n-dimensional random vector which may contain as well lagged endogenous variables as exogenous variables, i.e., $\boldsymbol{z}'_t = (\boldsymbol{y}'_t, \boldsymbol{x}'_t)$ with

  (3.2) $$\boldsymbol{y}'_t = (y_t, y_{t-1}, \ldots, y_{t-p+1}) \quad \text{and} \quad \boldsymbol{x}'_t = (x_{t,1}, \ldots, x_{t,q})$$

  where $p \geq 0$, $q \geq 0$ and $n = p + q \geq 1$,

- the initial values $y_0, \ldots, y_{1-p}$ are real valued random variables,
- y_t^e is the aggregate or market prediction of y_t made by agents at time $t-1$,
- w_t is the time t disturbance term, and
- $\phi \in \mathbb{R}^n$ and $a \in \mathbb{R}$ are the model parameters.

We call such a model an *ARX model with additive forecasts* or an *ARX model with linear forecast feedback.*

Analogously to Chapter 2 our analysis relies on three basic assumptions.

Assumption (A.1) (Behavioural Assumption)
Agents' predictions y_{t+1}^e are given as

$$y_{t+1}^e = \boldsymbol{\theta}_t{}'\boldsymbol{z}_t, \qquad t \geq 0, \tag{3.3}$$

where the coefficients $\boldsymbol{\theta}_t \in \mathbb{R}^n$ are recursively given by

$$\boldsymbol{\theta}_{t+1} = \boldsymbol{\theta}_t + r_t^{-1}\boldsymbol{z}_t(y_{t+1} - \boldsymbol{\theta}_t{}'\boldsymbol{z}_t), \qquad t \geq 0, \tag{3.4}$$

with some initial value $\boldsymbol{\theta}_0$ which may be random and $r_t = \sum_{s=0}^{t} \boldsymbol{z}_s'\boldsymbol{z}_s$.

Assumption (A.2) (Probabilistic Assumption)
The disturbance terms $\{w_t\}_{t\geq 1}$ form a MDS w.r.t. a filtration $\{\mathcal{F}_t\}_{t\geq 0}$ such that

$$\sup_{t\geq 0} \mathrm{E}\left[\left|w_{t+1}\right|^{2+\delta}\Big|\,\mathcal{F}_t\right] < \infty \qquad \text{a.s.} \tag{3.5}$$

with some fixed $\delta > 0$ and

$$\liminf_{T\to\infty} \frac{1}{T}\sum_{t=0}^{T} \mathrm{E}\left[w_{t+1}^2\Big|\,\mathcal{F}_t\right] > 0 \qquad \text{a.s.} \tag{3.6}$$

We assume furthermore that $\boldsymbol{\theta}_0$ and $\boldsymbol{y}_0$ are $\mathcal{F}_0$-measurable and that $\boldsymbol{x}_t$ is $\mathcal{F}_{t-p-1}$-measurable for all $t \geq p+1$ and $\mathcal{F}_0$-measurable otherwise.

Assumption (A.3) (Stability of Exogenous Inputs)
The exogenous variables $\boldsymbol{x}_t = (x_{t,1}, \ldots, x_{t,q})'$ satisfy

$$tr\left(\sum_{t=0}^{T} \boldsymbol{x}_t \boldsymbol{x}_t'\right) = O(T) \qquad \text{a.s.} \tag{3.7}$$

and

$$\liminf_{T\to\infty} \frac{1}{T}\lambda_{min}\left(\sum_{t=0}^{T} \boldsymbol{x}_t \boldsymbol{x}_t'\right) > 0 \qquad \text{a.s.} \tag{3.8}$$

Exogeneity of the $\boldsymbol{x}_t$'s is taken to mean stochastic independence of the processes $\{\boldsymbol{x}_t\}$ and $\{w_t\}$.

Assumption (A.1) specifies the learning procedure agents follow. This learning procedure can be interpreted as an adaptive, or recursive, PE algorithm. Agents successively adjust their parameter estimates in the light of the previous PE. Since the estimates $\boldsymbol{\theta}_t$ are multivariate while the PE, $y_{t+1} - \boldsymbol{\theta}_t{}'\boldsymbol{z}_t$, is univariate the latter has to be split up to give the adjustments for the respective components of $\boldsymbol{\theta}_t$. As (3.4) indicates the PE is split up into amounts proportional to the respective components of $\boldsymbol{z}_t$. Thus if $|z_{t,i}|$ is large relative to the other components of $\boldsymbol{z}_t$ the estimate $\theta_{t,i}$ will be adjusted by a relatively large amount. The direction of the adjustment is determined jointly by the signs of $z_{t,i}$ and of $y_{t+1} - \boldsymbol{\theta}_t{}'\boldsymbol{z}_t$.

The learning procedure specified by Assumption (A.1) is known in the literature on recursive identification and control as the *stochastic gradient (SG) algorithm* for the reason that the time t adjustment is, up to a scaling factor, equal to the negative gradient of the squared PE, i.e.,

$$\begin{aligned} \Delta\boldsymbol{\theta}_t &= \boldsymbol{\theta}_{t+1} - \boldsymbol{\theta}_t \\ &= \frac{1}{r_t}\boldsymbol{z}_t(y_{t+1} - \boldsymbol{\theta}_t{}'\boldsymbol{z}_t) \\ &= -\frac{1}{2r_t}\nabla_{\boldsymbol{\theta}}(y_{t+1} - \boldsymbol{\theta}_t{}'\boldsymbol{z}_t)^2. \end{aligned} \tag{3.9}$$

Since its adjustments point in direction of the steepest descent of the squared PE the SG algorithm is also known as *recursive steepest descent algorithm.*

The SG algorithm is closely related to the RPE learning procedures considered in Chapter 2. But since the SG algorithm is based on the

PE, and not on the RPE, the scaling factors[2] $1/r_t$ do not correspond directly to the gains γ_t of the RPE learning procedure. Instead, $1/r_t$ corresponds to γ_t/y_t^2.

The SG algorithm is also closely related to the OLS algorithm since replacing r_t^{-1} in (3.4) by the inverse of the matrix $Z_t = \sum_0^t z_s z_s'$ leads to the recursive representation of the OLS estimates (cf. (1.13)). The SG algorithm and the OLS algorithm thus differ only in the weighting of the PE. (Notice that they coincide if $n = 1$.) Since r_t is the trace of the matrix Z_t the SG algorithm does not use all the information available at time t and contained in Z_t. Hence one can expect the SG algorithm to be less efficient than the OLS algorithm. In fact, this is true and results in a slower rate of convergence. On the other hand the computation of the SG algorithm estimates requires no matrix inversion and could be performed with a simple pocket calculator.

Notice that by (A.1) we implicitly assume that agents' predictions are based on the information set $I_t = \{y_t, \ldots, y_0, x_t, \ldots, x_0\}$. Hence agents know which time series influence the endogenous variable. Since we do not assume the parameter ϕ to be non-zero in each component some components of z_t may influence y_{t+1} only via agents' predictions. Such variables are usually called *sun-spot variables*. We thus allow agents to initially believe in sun-spots.

Assumption (A.2) specifies the stochastic structure of the model. The conditions (3.5) and (3.6) and the measurability condition for θ_0 and y_0 were already discussed in Chapter 2 and there is nothing to add. Only the measurability condition for the x_t's has to be explained. Since the filtration $\{\mathcal{F}_t\}$ is usually understood in the sense that $\mathcal{F}_t$ contains all information about the system available at time t the condition that x_t is $\mathcal{F}_{t-p-1}$-measurable seems to require that it is possible to look some periods ahead into the future. But since we assume the variables x_t to be exogenous the knowledge of the future of x_t is worth nothing in order to predict the future of y_t. Formally, we can define the filtration $\{\mathcal{F}_t\}$ by $\mathcal{F}_t = \sigma(w_t, w_{t-1}, \ldots, w_0, \theta_0, y_0, x_0, x_1, \ldots, x_{t+p+1})$ for $t \geq 1$ and by $\mathcal{F}_0 = \sigma(\theta_0, y_0, x_0, x_1, \ldots, x_{p+1})$.

[2]In the literature on recursive identification and control the SG algorithm is sometimes defined for general sequences of gains which satisfy the so-called Dvoretzky Conditions (see, e.g., GRAUPE (1984), Chapter 7). This generalization is possible also in our model but, due to the forecast feedback, only at the cost of additional difficulties we like avoid.

Assumption (A.3) requires the exogenous variables to possess certain time series properties which we shall need later on in some results. This assumption is slightly more general than the assumption usually employed in this context[3] and holds for a large class of stochastic as well as deterministic processes including all covariance stationary and ergodic processes, such as stable ARMA processes, ARCH processes, i.i.d. sequences, but also for some non-stationary processes.

Throughout this chapter we assume $a \neq 1$ for the following reason. Since under (A.1)–(A.3) equation (3.1) can be rewritten as

$$y_{t+1} = (\phi + a\theta_t)' z_t + w_{t+1} \tag{3.10}$$

it is obvious that agents form rational expectations, i.e., $\mathrm{E}[y_{t+1}|I_t] = y^e_{t+1}$ a.s., if, and only if,

$$\theta_t = \bar{\theta} := \frac{1}{1-a}\phi. \tag{3.11}$$

Hence if $a \neq 1$, rational expectations exist and are unique.

Analogously to Chapter 2 we can show that the disturbance terms satisfying (A.2) introduce persistent stochastic fluctuation into the model. The proof follows the same lines as the one of Theorem A.7 in Appendix A and is therefore omitted.

Lemma 3.2.1
Suppose that (A.1) and (A.2) are satisfied. Then

$$\liminf_{T\to\infty} \frac{1}{T}\sum_{t=1}^{T} y_t^2 > 0 \qquad a.s. \tag{3.12}$$

[3]For example, BRAY/SAVIN (1986), MARCET/SARGENT (1989a,b), and KOTTMANN (1990) assume the exogenous variables to be stationary and ergodic with a positive definite variance-covariance matrix.

3.3 Convergence Analysis

The present section is devoted to the convergence analysis. In a first step we use the almost-supermartingale property of the process $\{||\boldsymbol{\theta}_t - \bar{\boldsymbol{\theta}}||^2\}$ and the convergence result of ROBBINS/SIEGMUND (1971) to show that $\{\boldsymbol{\theta}_t\}$ remains bounded a.s. under suitable parameter conditions. This property holds regardless of any assumptions on the time series $\{\boldsymbol{z}_t\}$ except the measurability conditions of Assumption (A.2). Then we show that $\{\boldsymbol{\theta}_t\}$ converges a.s. towards $\bar{\boldsymbol{\theta}}$ if the times series $\{\boldsymbol{z}_t\}$ satisfies the so-called *persistent excitation condition* (PEC). (In the following section we shall analyze which conditions ensure the PEC to hold.) Finally, if $\{\boldsymbol{z}_t\}$ fails to satisfy the PEC, then we can still show that at least some components of $\boldsymbol{\theta}_t$ converge towards the respective components of $\bar{\boldsymbol{\theta}}$.

Theorem 3.3.1

Suppose that (A.1) and (A.2) are satisfied. If $q \geq 1$, thus if the model includes exogenous variables, suppose that

$$(3.13) \qquad \sum_{t=0}^{\infty} \boldsymbol{x}_t'\boldsymbol{x}_t = \infty \quad a.s. \quad and \quad \limsup_{t\to\infty} \frac{\boldsymbol{x}_t'\boldsymbol{x}_t}{\sum_{s=0}^{t} \boldsymbol{x}_s'\boldsymbol{x}_s} < 1 \quad a.s.$$

Define

$$(3.14) \qquad Z_t = \sum_{s=0}^{t} \boldsymbol{z}_s\boldsymbol{z}_s', \quad r_t = \sum_{s=0}^{t} \boldsymbol{z}_s'\boldsymbol{z}_s, \quad and \quad \lambda_t = \frac{\boldsymbol{z}_t'\boldsymbol{z}_t}{r_t}.$$

(i) *If $-1 \leq a < 1$, then*

$$(3.15) \qquad ||\boldsymbol{\theta}_t - \bar{\boldsymbol{\theta}}||^2 \quad converges\ a.s.,$$

$$(3.16) \qquad \sum_{t=0}^{\infty} \frac{[\boldsymbol{z}_t'(\boldsymbol{\theta}_t - \bar{\boldsymbol{\theta}})]^2}{r_t} < \infty \quad a.s.,\ and$$

$$(3.17) \qquad \boldsymbol{\theta}_t \longrightarrow \bar{\boldsymbol{\theta}} \quad a.s.\ on \quad \left[\frac{\lambda_{max}(Z_t)}{\lambda_{min}(Z_t)} = O(1)\right].$$

(ii) *If $a < -1$, then (3.15)–(3.17) hold on the event where*

$$(3.18) \qquad \limsup_{t\to\infty} \lambda_t < \frac{2}{1-a}.$$

Proof
Firstly, notice that the event (3.18) is the full ω–space if $|a| < 1$. Giving special consideration to the case $a = -1$ we can thus avoid the distinction between the cases (i) and (ii) and prove all results on the event (3.18).

The estimates $\boldsymbol{\theta}_t$ are recursively given as

$$\begin{aligned}\boldsymbol{\theta}_{t+1} &= \boldsymbol{\theta}_t + r_t^{-1}\boldsymbol{z}_t(y_{t+1} - \boldsymbol{\theta}_t{}'\boldsymbol{z}_t) \\ &= \boldsymbol{\theta}_t + r_t^{-1}\boldsymbol{z}_t\boldsymbol{z}_t'(\boldsymbol{\phi} + a\boldsymbol{\theta}_t - \boldsymbol{\theta}_t) + r_t^{-1}\boldsymbol{z}_t w_{t+1} \\ &= \boldsymbol{\theta}_t + r_t^{-1}\boldsymbol{z}_t\boldsymbol{z}_t'(\boldsymbol{\phi} - (1-a)\boldsymbol{\theta}_t) + r_t^{-1}\boldsymbol{z}_t w_{t+1}.\end{aligned} \tag{3.19}$$

Hence, since $\boldsymbol{\phi} = (1-a)\bar{\boldsymbol{\theta}}$,

$$\boldsymbol{\theta}_{t+1} - \bar{\boldsymbol{\theta}} = \boldsymbol{\theta}_t - \bar{\boldsymbol{\theta}} - (1-a)r_t^{-1}\boldsymbol{z}_t\boldsymbol{z}_t'(\boldsymbol{\theta}_t - \bar{\boldsymbol{\theta}}) + r_t^{-1}\boldsymbol{z}_t w_{t+1}. \tag{3.20}$$

Let $\boldsymbol{A}_t = \boldsymbol{I} - (1-a)r_t^{-1}\boldsymbol{z}_t\boldsymbol{z}_t'$ and let $V_t = ||\boldsymbol{\theta}_t - \bar{\boldsymbol{\theta}}||^2$. Then

$$\mathrm{E}[V_{t+1}|\mathcal{F}_t] = ||\boldsymbol{A}_t(\boldsymbol{\theta}_t - \bar{\boldsymbol{\theta}})||^2 + \frac{\boldsymbol{z}_t'\boldsymbol{z}_t}{r_t^2}\mathrm{E}\left[w_{t+1}^2\middle|\mathcal{F}_t\right] \quad \text{a.s.} \tag{3.21}$$

with

$$\begin{aligned}||\boldsymbol{A}_t(\boldsymbol{\theta}_t - \bar{\boldsymbol{\theta}})||^2 &= ||\boldsymbol{\theta}_t - \bar{\boldsymbol{\theta}}||^2 - 2(1-a)r_t^{-1}(\boldsymbol{\theta}_t - \bar{\boldsymbol{\theta}})'\boldsymbol{z}_t\boldsymbol{z}_t'(\boldsymbol{\theta}_t - \bar{\boldsymbol{\theta}}) \\ &\quad +(1-a)^2r_t^{-2}(\boldsymbol{\theta}_t - \bar{\boldsymbol{\theta}})'\boldsymbol{z}_t\boldsymbol{z}_t'\boldsymbol{z}_t\boldsymbol{z}_t'(\boldsymbol{\theta}_t - \bar{\boldsymbol{\theta}}) \\ &= ||\boldsymbol{\theta}_t - \bar{\boldsymbol{\theta}}||^2 - \left[2(1-a) - (1-a)^2\lambda_t\right]\frac{[\boldsymbol{z}_t'(\boldsymbol{\theta}_t - \bar{\boldsymbol{\theta}})]^2}{r_t}.\end{aligned} \tag{3.22}$$

Define furthermore

$$\begin{aligned}\tilde{\eta}_t &= \left[2(1-a) - (1-a)^2\lambda_t\right]\frac{[\boldsymbol{z}_t'(\boldsymbol{\theta}_t - \bar{\boldsymbol{\theta}})]^2}{r_t}, \\ \eta_t &= (\tilde{\eta}_t)^+, \quad \text{and} \\ \beta_t &= \frac{\boldsymbol{z}_t'\boldsymbol{z}_t}{r_t^2}\mathrm{E}\left[w_{t+1}^2\middle|\mathcal{F}_t\right] + (-\tilde{\eta}_t)^+.\end{aligned} \tag{3.23}$$

Then we have

$$\mathrm{E}[V_{t+1}|\mathcal{F}_t] \le V_t + \beta_t - \eta_t \quad \text{a.s.} \tag{3.24}$$

Now we want to apply the convergence result for almost-supermartingales of ROBBINS/SIEGMUND (1971) (Proposition 2.5.1). Since

$$2(1-a) - (1-a)^2\lambda_t \ge 0 \iff \lambda_t \le \frac{2}{1-a}, \tag{3.25}$$

provided that $a < 1$, it is obvious that $\tilde{\eta}_t \geq 0$ for all but finitely many $t \geq 0$ on the event (3.18). Moreover, if $a = -1$ the event implied by (3.25) is a.s. for all t since $0 \leq \lambda_t \leq 1$. Hence on these events

$$\sum_{t=0}^{\infty} \beta_t = O\left(\sum_{t=0}^{\infty} \frac{z_t' z_t}{r_t^2}\right) < \infty \qquad \text{a.s.} \tag{3.26}$$

which follows from Lemma 2.2.2. and the conditional Lyapunov inequality. Then Proposition 2.5.1 implies that $||\boldsymbol{\theta}_t - \bar{\boldsymbol{\theta}}||^2$ converges a.s. on these events. This proves (3.15) for both cases (i) and (ii).

To show (3.16) we establish first that

$$2(1-a) - (1-a)^2 \lambda_t \geq \epsilon \tag{3.27}$$

holds pathwise a.s. for some sufficiently small $\epsilon = \epsilon(\omega) > 0$. Notice that, since $a < 1$, (3.27) is equivalent to $\lambda_t \leq (2-\tilde{\epsilon})/(1-a)$ with some small $\tilde{\epsilon} > 0$.

If $|a| < 1$ we can choose some constant $\epsilon > 0$ such that (3.27) holds for all $t \geq 0$ since $0 \leq \lambda_t \leq 1$. If $a = -1$ we can use the fact that $\boldsymbol{\theta}_t$ is bounded a.s. to infer that λ_t is (pathwise) bounded away from one. This follows from (3.13) in the case $p = 0$ and from the fact that in the case $p \geq 1$ the quotient λ_t can approach one only if $\boldsymbol{\theta}_t$ grows beyond every boundary (see Appendix A for the special case that $\{y_t\}$ is a univariate first order regression). Since $\boldsymbol{\theta}_t$ is bounded a.s., as shown above, this is impossible with probability one. We thus can find some $\epsilon = \epsilon(\omega) > 0$ such that (3.27) holds for all but finitely many $t \geq 0$ for almost every $\omega \in \Omega$. Incidentally, this proves that (3.18) is an a.s. event on the full intervall $-1 \leq a < 1$.

If $a < -1$ we can infer in the same way that some $\epsilon = \epsilon(\omega) > 0$ exists such that (3.27) holds for all but finitely many $t \geq 0$ on the event (3.18).

Now Proposition 2.5.1 implies $\sum_0^\infty \eta_t < \infty$ a.s. on the event (3.18). Since $\epsilon > 0$ we can conclude

$$\sum_{t=0}^{\infty} \frac{[z_t'(\boldsymbol{\theta}_t - \bar{\boldsymbol{\theta}})]^2}{r_t} < \infty \qquad \text{a.s. on (3.18),} \tag{3.28}$$

hence (3.16) is shown for both cases (i) and (ii).

Before we show (3.17) we remark that, again, the following considerations are all of a pathwise nature and hold on the event (3.18).

From now on we omit the additional term "on (3.18)" in the formulae. With the aid of the Kronecker Lemma, which can be applied since $r_t \to \infty$ a.s., either by (3.13) or by Lemma 2.1, we can conclude that

$$\sum_{t=0}^{T}[z_t'(\theta_t - \bar{\theta})]^2 = o(r_T) \qquad \text{a.s.} \tag{3.29}$$

The Cauchy-Schwarz inequality implies

$$\begin{aligned} \left\| \frac{1}{r_T} \sum_{t=0}^{T} z_t z_t'(\theta_t - \bar{\theta}) \right\|^2 &\leq \left(\frac{1}{r_T} \sum_{t=0}^{T} \|z_t\| |z_t'(\theta_t - \bar{\theta})| \right)^2 \\ &\leq \left(\frac{1}{r_T} \sum_{t=0}^{T} z_t' z_t \right) \left(\frac{1}{r_T} \sum_{t=0}^{T} [z_t'(\theta_t - \bar{\theta})]^2 \right) \\ &= o(1). \end{aligned} \tag{3.30}$$

Now consider the process $\{Z_T(\theta_T - \bar{\theta})\}$. Since $Z_t - Z_{t-1} = z_t z_t'$ we have

$$\begin{aligned} \sum_{t=0}^{T} Z_t(\theta_{t+1} - \theta_t) &= Z_T(\theta_{T+1} - \bar{\theta}) - \sum_{t=1}^{T} z_t z_t'(\theta_t - \bar{\theta}) \\ &\quad - Z_0(\theta_0 - \bar{\theta}). \end{aligned} \tag{3.31}$$

Hence by (3.30)

$$\begin{aligned} \|Z_T(\theta_{T+1} - \bar{\theta})\| &\leq \left\| \sum_{t=0}^{T} Z_t(\theta_{t+1} - \theta_t) \right\| \\ &\quad + \left\| \sum_{t=1}^{T} z_t z_t'(\theta_t - \bar{\theta}) + Z_0(\theta_0 - \bar{\theta}) \right\| \\ &= \left\| \sum_{t=0}^{T} Z_t(\theta_{t+1} - \theta_t) \right\| + o(r_T). \end{aligned} \tag{3.32}$$

On the other hand the recursion (3.19) leads to

$$\begin{aligned} \sum_{t=0}^{T} Z_t(\theta_{t+1} - \theta_t) &= (a-1) \sum_{t=0}^{T} \frac{1}{r_t} Z_t z_t z_t'(\theta_t - \bar{\theta}) \\ &\quad + \sum_{t=0}^{T} \frac{1}{r_t} Z_t z_t w_{t+1}. \end{aligned} \tag{3.33}$$

Hence

$$\left\|\sum_{t=0}^{T} Z_t(\theta_{t+1} - \theta_t)\right\| \le |1-a| \left\|\sum_{t=0}^{T} \widetilde{Z}_t z_t z_t'(\theta_t - \bar{\theta})\right\| + \left\|\sum_{t=0}^{T} \widetilde{Z}_t z_t w_{t+1}\right\| \tag{3.34}$$

with $\widetilde{Z}_t = r_t^{-1} Z_t$. Since $\widetilde{Z_t}$ is bounded a.s. because $tr(\widetilde{Z_t}) = 1$, and since $r_t \to \infty$ a.s. we can apply Lemma 2.3.2 which gives

$$\sum_{t=0}^{T} \widetilde{Z}_t z_t w_{t+1} = o(r_T) \qquad \text{a.s.} \tag{3.35}$$

Replacing $z_t z_t'(\theta_t - \bar{\theta})$ by $\widetilde{Z}_t z_t z_t'(\theta_t - \bar{\theta})$ in (3.30) leads to

$$\sum_{t=0}^{T} \widetilde{Z}_t z_t z_t'(\theta_t - \bar{\theta}) = o(r_T) \qquad \text{a.s.} \tag{3.36}$$

Hence, in view of (3.34) and (3.35),

$$\sum_{t=0}^{T} Z_t(\theta_{t+1} - \theta_t) = o(r_T) \qquad \text{a.s.} \tag{3.37}$$

and, finally, by (3.32)

$$Z_T(\theta_{T+1} - \bar{\theta}) = o(r_T) \qquad \text{a.s.} \tag{3.38}$$

Using the inequalities

$$\|Z_T(\theta_{T+1} - \bar{\theta})\| \ge \lambda_{min}(Z_T)\|\theta_{T+1} - \bar{\theta}\| \tag{3.39}$$

and $r_T = tr(Z_T) \le n\lambda_{max}(Z_T)$ we can conclude that

$$\|\theta_t - \bar{\theta}\| \longrightarrow 0 \qquad \text{a.s. on} \qquad \left[\frac{\lambda_{max}(Z_t)}{\lambda_{min}(Z_t)} = O(1)\right]. \tag{3.40}$$

Hence Theorem 3.1 is proved. ■

Remark

Notice that the proof of Theorem 3.1 relies only on the properties

$$\sum_{t=0}^{T} \xi_t w_{t+1} = o\left(\sum_{t=0}^{T} \xi_t^2\right) + O(1) \quad \text{a.s.} \tag{3.41}$$

and

$$\sum_{t=0}^{T} |\xi_t| w_{t+1}^2 = O\left(\sum_{t=0}^{T} \xi_t^2\right) \quad \text{a.s.} \tag{3.42}$$

with $\xi_t = r_t^{-1} z_t'(\theta_t - \bar{\theta})$. This is easily seen since

$$||\theta_{t+1} - \bar{\theta}||^2 = ||\theta_t - \bar{\theta}||^2 + \tilde{\beta}_t - \eta_t + u_t w_{t+1} \tag{3.43}$$

with $\tilde{\eta}_t$ and η_t defined as in (3.23) and

$$\begin{aligned} \tilde{\beta}_t &= \frac{z_t' z_t}{r_t^2} w_{t+1}^2 + (-\tilde{\eta}_t)^+, \\ u_t &= 2[1 - (1-a)\lambda_t] r_t^{-1} z_t'(\theta_t - \bar{\theta}). \end{aligned} \tag{3.44}$$

Iterating equality (3.43) leads to

$$||\theta_{T+1} - \bar{\theta}||^2 = \sum_{t=0}^{T} \tilde{\beta}_t - \sum_{t=0}^{T} \eta_t + \sum_{t=0}^{T} u_t w_{t+1} + ||\theta_0 - \bar{\theta}||^2. \tag{3.45}$$

In view of (3.41) the sum $\sum_0^T u_t w_{t+1}$ is dominated by $\sum_0^T \eta_t / r_t$ and hence by $\sum_0^T \eta_t$. From (3.42) and Lemma 2.2.2 we obtain $\sum_0^T \tilde{\beta}_t < \infty$ a.s. Since $||\theta_{T+1} - \bar{\theta}||^2$ is non-negative (3.45) implies that the sum $\sum_0^T \eta_t$ is bounded a.s. Hence (3.16) is shown. Since the remaining reasoning in the proof of Theorem 3.1 is of a pathwise nature it carries over directly.

We thus can replace Assumption (A.2) by the more general assumption that (3.41) and (3.42) hold for every $\mathcal{F}_t$-adapted process $\{\xi_t\}$. This allows for a more general probabilistic (or deterministic) structure of the disturbance terms. Since it is more convenient to work with martingale difference sequences we disregard this generalization.

Theorem 3.1 states that if the *persistent excitation condition* (PEC)

$$\frac{\lambda_{max}(Z_t)}{\lambda_{min}(Z_t)} = O(1) \quad \text{a.s.} \tag{3.46}$$

is satisfied the SG algorithm estimates $\boldsymbol{\theta}_t$ are strongly consistent, at least if $|a| < 1$. This result is a generalization of the convergence results for the SG algorithm in models without forecast feedback (see, e.g., CHEN/GUO (1991)).

Now we consider the case that the PEC fails to hold. The following considerations are, again, of an algebraic nature, hence we can argue pathwise. There are different reasons for that the PEC can fail to hold. Firstly, it is possible that although

$$\liminf_{T\to\infty} \frac{1}{r_T} \sum_{t=0}^{T} z_{t,i}^2 > 0 \qquad \forall i = 1, \ldots, n, \tag{3.47}$$

with $z_{t,i}$ denoting the ith component of $\boldsymbol{z}_t$, we have $\lambda_{min}(\boldsymbol{Z}_t) = o(\lambda_{max}(\boldsymbol{Z}_t))$. Thus although all diagonal elements of the normed matrix of moments $\widetilde{\boldsymbol{Z}}_t = r_t^{-1}\boldsymbol{Z}_t$ remain bounded away from zero as $t \to \infty$ the minimum eigenvalue of $\widetilde{\boldsymbol{Z}}_t$ converges to zero. This is possible only if the vectors $\widetilde{z}_i(t) := r_t^{-1}(z_{t,i}, \ldots, z_{0,i})'$, $i = 1, \ldots, n$, are asymptotically linearly dependent.

Secondly, it is possible that

$$\liminf_{T\to\infty} \frac{1}{r_T} \sum_{t=0}^{T} z_{t,i}^2 = 0 \tag{3.48}$$

for some $i = 1, \ldots, n$. Thus some diagonal elements of $\widetilde{\boldsymbol{Z}}_t$ converge to zero. Since $\widetilde{\boldsymbol{Z}}_t$ is non-negative definite this implies that some rows and columns converge to zero. (Clearly, not all rows can converge to zero since $tr(\widetilde{\boldsymbol{Z}}_t) = 1$ and $r_t \to \infty$ a.s.) This is the case if some components of $\boldsymbol{z}_t$ grow faster than the others, for example, if $\boldsymbol{z}_t = (t, 1)'$. The following theorem states that in such a case at least the components of $\bar{\boldsymbol{\theta}}$ related to the fastest growing components of $\boldsymbol{z}_t$ are properly identified by the SG algorithm.

Theorem 3.3.2

Suppose that the assumptions of Theorem 3.1 are satisfied. Let I be a fixed subset of $\{1, \ldots, n\}$ and let $\mathcal{B}(I)$ be the event where

$$\liminf_{T\to\infty} \frac{1}{r_T} \sum_{t=0}^{T} z_{t,i}^2 = 0 \qquad \forall i \in I. \tag{3.49}$$

Let Z_t^* be the matrix $\tilde{Z}_t$ with the ith row and ith column removed for all $i \in I$ and let $C(I)$ be the event where

$$\liminf_{t\to\infty} \lambda_{min}(Z_t^*) > 0 \qquad a.s. \tag{3.50}$$

(i) *If $-1 \leq a < 1$, then for all $i \notin I$,*

$$\theta_{t,i} \to \bar{\theta}_i \qquad a.s.\ on \qquad \mathcal{B}(I) \cap \mathcal{C}(I). \tag{3.51}$$

(ii) *If $a < -1$, then for all $i \notin I$,*

$$\theta_{t,i} \to \bar{\theta}_i \quad a.s.\ on \quad \mathcal{B}(I) \cap \mathcal{C}(I) \cap \left[\limsup_{t\to\infty} \lambda_t < \frac{2}{1-a}\right]. \tag{3.52}$$

Proof
We can follow the lines of the proof of Theorem 3.1 up to (3.38) without any change. We thus have $\tilde{Z}_T(\theta_{T+1} - \bar{\theta}) \to 0$ a.s. on (3.18). On the event $\mathcal{B}(I)$ we have

$$\|\tilde{Z}_T(\theta_{T+1} - \bar{\theta})\| = \|Z_T^*(\theta_{T+1}^* - \bar{\theta}^*)\| + o(1) \tag{3.53}$$

where $\theta_t^*, \bar{\theta}^*$ denote the vectors $\theta_t, \bar{\theta}$, resp., with the ith component removed for all $i \in I$. Hence $\|Z_T^*(\theta_{T+1} - \bar{\theta})\| \to 0$ a.s. on $\mathcal{B}(I)$. On the event $C(I)$ we have

$$\|Z_T^*(\theta_{T+1}^* - \bar{\theta}^*)\| \geq \lambda_{min}(Z_T^*)\|\theta_{T+1}^* - \bar{\theta}^*\| \geq \epsilon\|\theta_{T+1}^* - \bar{\theta}^*\| \tag{3.54}$$

with some (possibly path-dependent) $\epsilon > 0$ for T sufficiently large. But this implies $\|\theta_{T+1}^* - \bar{\theta}^*\| \to 0$. ∎

3.4 Condition Analysis

In this section we determine the order of $\lambda_{max}(Z_t)$ and $\lambda_{min}(Z_t)$ and thus obtain an upper bound for the condition number of the matrix Z_t, defined as $c(Z_t) = \|Z_t\|\|Z_t^{-1}\|$, since $c(Z_t) \leq \lambda_{max}(Z_t)/\lambda_{min}(Z_t)$. While the order of $\lambda_{max}(Z_t)$ is easily obtained since

$$\lambda_{max}(Z_t) \leq tr(Z_t) \leq n\lambda_{max}(Z_t) \tag{3.55}$$

the determination of the (minimum) order of $\lambda_{min}(\boldsymbol{Z}_t)$ is much more complicated and requires a technical result on asymptotic properties of certain projections. Of course, only if the model (3.1) is autoregressive the determination of the maximum and minimum eigenvalues causes a problem. Otherwise the order of the eigenvalues is given exogenously.

3.4.1 Determination of $\lambda_{max}(\boldsymbol{Z}_t)$

Let $p \geq 1$ and suppose that the Assumptions (A.1) and (A.2) hold. Using the identity $\boldsymbol{\phi} + a\bar{\boldsymbol{\theta}} = \bar{\boldsymbol{\theta}}$ we can rewrite the model (3.10) as

$$y_{t+1} = \bar{\boldsymbol{\theta}}'\boldsymbol{z}_t + a(\boldsymbol{\theta}_t - \bar{\boldsymbol{\theta}})'\boldsymbol{z}_t + w_{t+1}. \tag{3.56}$$

Thus y_{t+1} can be decomposed into a (fixed parameter) RE part, $\bar{\boldsymbol{\theta}}'\boldsymbol{z}_t$, a PE part, $a(\boldsymbol{\theta}_t - \bar{\boldsymbol{\theta}})'\boldsymbol{z}_t$, and the disturbance term w_{t+1}. Of course, these parts cannot be considered separately but this decomposition is useful in the following.

It is more convenient to write (3.56) in vector notation

$$\boldsymbol{y}_{t+1} = \boldsymbol{A}\boldsymbol{y}_t + \boldsymbol{R}_{t+1} \tag{3.57}$$

with

$$\boldsymbol{R}'_{t+1} = \left(a(\boldsymbol{\theta}_t - \bar{\boldsymbol{\theta}})'\boldsymbol{z}_t + \sum_{j=1}^{q} \bar{\theta}_{p+j} x_{t,j} + w_{t+1} \, , \, 0 \, , \ldots , \, 0 \right) \tag{3.58}$$

and $\boldsymbol{A}$ the companion form matrix

$$\boldsymbol{A} = \begin{pmatrix} \bar{\theta}_1 & \cdots & \bar{\theta}_{p-1} & \bar{\theta}_p \\ 1 & & & 0 \\ & \ddots & & \vdots \\ & & 1 & 0 \end{pmatrix}. \tag{3.59}$$

It is well-known that the *characteristic polynomial*

$$\pi(y) = y^p - \bar{\theta}_1 y^{p-1} - \cdots - \bar{\theta}_{p-1} y - \bar{\theta}_p \tag{3.60}$$

plays a central role in the asymptotic behaviour of (constant parameter) autoregressive processes. If it possesses roots only inside the unit circle, then there exists some $0 < \rho < 1$ such that $\|\boldsymbol{A}^t\| = o(\rho^t)$ and a constant parameter autoregressive process given by (3.57) with $\boldsymbol{R}'_t = (w_t, 0, \ldots, 0)$ is stable in the sense that $\sum_1^T y_t^2 = O(T)$ a.s. The following result shows that a similar property holds also in our model. It is a straightforward extension of Lemma 4 of LAI/WEI (1982b).

Lemma 3.4.1
Suppose that (A.1) and (A.2) are satisfied and that the exogenous variables $\{x_t\}$ *satisfy*

$$\|x_t\|^2 = o(t^\beta) \quad a.s. \tag{3.61}$$

and

$$\sum_{t=1}^{T} \|x_t\|^2 = O(T^\gamma) \quad a.s. \tag{3.62}$$

for some $\beta \geq 0, \gamma \geq 0$. *Suppose furthermore that the characteristic polynomial (3.60) possesses roots only inside the unit circle. Then*

$$\|y_t\|^2 = o(t^\mu) + O\left(\sum_{s=0}^{t-1}[z_s'(\theta_t - \bar{\theta})]^2\right) \quad a.s. \tag{3.63}$$

for every μ *such that* $\mu \geq \beta$ *and* $\mu > 2/(2+\delta)$, *with* $\delta > 0$ *given by (A.2), and*

$$\sum_{t=1}^{T} \|y_t\|^2 = O(T^\nu) + O\left(\sum_{s=0}^{T-1}[z_s'(\theta_t - \bar{\theta})]^2\right) \quad a.s. \tag{3.64}$$

with $\nu = \max\{1, \gamma\}$.

Notice that Lemma 4.1 includes the purely autoregressive case since in that case we can set $\beta = \gamma = 0$.

Proof
Iteration of (3.57) leads to

$$y_t = A^t y_0 + \sum_{s=1}^{t} A^{t-s} R_s. \tag{3.65}$$

With the C_r-inequality and the Cauchy-Schwarz inequality we obtain

$$\begin{aligned} \|y_t\|^2 &\leq 2\|A^t\|^2\|y_0\|^2 + 2\left(\sum_{s=1}^{t} \|A^{t-s}\|\|R_s\|\right)^2 \\ &\leq 2\|A^t\|^2\|y_0\|^2 + 2\sum_{s=1}^{t}\|A^{t-s}\|\sum_{s=1}^{t}\|A^{t-s}\|\|R_s\|^2. \end{aligned} \tag{3.66}$$

Since $||A^t|| = o(\rho^t)$ with some $0 < \rho < 1$, (3.66) implies

$$\begin{aligned} ||y_t||^2 &= o(\rho^{2t}) + O\left(\sum_{s=1}^{t} \rho^{t-s} \sum_{s=1}^{t} \rho^{t-s} ||R_s||^2\right) \\ &= o(\rho^{2t}) + O\left(\sum_{s=0}^{t-1} \rho^{t-s} ||x_s||^2\right) + O\left(\sum_{s=0}^{t-1} \rho^{t-s} [z_s'(\theta_s - \bar{\theta})]^2\right) \\ &\quad + O\left(\sum_{s=1}^{t} \rho^{t-s} w_s^2\right) \qquad (3.67) \\ &= o(t^\beta) + O\left(\sum_{s=0}^{t-1} [z_s'(\theta_s - \bar{\theta})]^2\right) + o(t^{2\alpha}) \qquad \text{a.s.} \end{aligned}$$

with $\alpha > 1/(2+\delta)$. The last line follows from (3.61) and, since

$$\text{(3.68)} \qquad \mathrm{P}\left[|w_t| > t^\alpha \middle| \mathcal{F}_{t-1}\right] \le \frac{1}{t^{\alpha(2+\delta)}} \mathrm{E}\left[|w_t|^{2+\delta} \middle| \mathcal{F}_{t-1}\right],$$

from the conditional Borel–Cantelli lemma (see, e.g., STOUT (1974), p. 55) which implies $|w_t| = o(t^\alpha)$ a.s. for all $\alpha > 1/(2+\delta)$. Hence (3.63) is shown.

Summation of (3.66) leads to

$$\begin{aligned} \sum_{t=1}^{T} ||y_t||^2 &\le 2||y_0||^2 \sum_{t=1}^{T} ||A^t||^2 + 2\sum_{t=1}^{T}\left(\sum_{s=1}^{t} ||A^{t-s}|| \sum_{s=1}^{t} ||A^{t-s}|| ||R_s||^2\right) \\ &= O(1) + O\left(\sum_{t=1}^{T}\sum_{s=1}^{t} \rho^{t-s} \sum_{s=1}^{t} \rho^{t-s} ||R_s||^2\right) \\ &= O\left(\left(\sum_{t=0}^{\infty} \rho^t\right) \sum_{t=1}^{T}\sum_{s=1}^{t} \rho^{t-s} ||R_s||^2\right) \qquad (3.69) \\ &= O\left(\left(\sum_{t=0}^{\infty} \rho^t\right)^2 \sum_{t=1}^{T} ||R_t||^2\right) \\ &= O\left(\sum_{t=0}^{T-1} ||x_t||^2\right) + O\left(\sum_{t=0}^{T-1} [z_t'(\theta_t - \bar{\theta})]^2\right) + O\left(\sum_{t=1}^{T} w_t^2\right). \end{aligned}$$

Hence also (3.64) is shown since $\sum_1^T w_t^2 = O(T)$ a.s. as shown in Lemma A.3 in Appendix A. ■

Under Assumption (A.3) we obtain the following result which determines the order of $\lambda_{max}(Z_t)$ in the stable case.

Theorem 3.4.2
Suppose that (A.1)–(A.3) are satisfied. If the characteristic polynomial (3.60) possesses roots only inside the unit circle, then

$$\lambda_{max}(Z_t) = O(t) \quad a.s. \tag{3.70}$$

if $-1 \leq a < 1$, *and*

$$\lambda_{max}(Z_t) = O(t) \quad a.s.\ on \quad \left[\limsup_{t\to\infty} \lambda_t < \frac{2}{1-a}\right] \tag{3.71}$$

if $a < -1$.

Proof
Let $-1 \leq a < 1$. From (A.3) and Lemma 4.1 we know that

$$\sum_{t=1}^{T} \|y_t\|^2 = O(T) + O\left(\sum_{t=0}^{T-1} [z_t'(\theta_t - \bar{\theta})]^2\right) \quad \text{a.s.} \tag{3.72}$$

Hence

$$tr(Z_T) = O(T) + O\left(\sum_{t=0}^{T-1} [z_t'(\theta_t - \bar{\theta})]^2\right) \quad \text{a.s.} \tag{3.73}$$

Theorem 3.1 and the Kronecker lemma imply

$$\sum_{t=0}^{T} [z_t'(\theta_t - \bar{\theta})]^2 = o(tr(Z_T)) \quad \text{a.s.} \tag{3.74}$$

Hence $tr(Z_T) = O(T)$ a.s. Using the inequality (3.55) we finally obtain (3.70). The proof of (3.71) follows exactly the same lines. ■

3.4.2 Determination of $\lambda_{min}(Z_t)$

As already mentioned the determination of the minimum order of $\lambda_{min}(Z_t)$ is much more complicated. Lai/Wei (1982b) provide the following result.

Lemma 3.4.3 (LAI/WEI (1982b))
Let $Z(t) = (z_1(t), \ldots, z_n(t))$ be a matrix of dimension $t \times n$. Then

$$\begin{aligned} \frac{1}{n} \min_{1 \le j \le n} \|z_j(t) - \hat{z}_j(t)\|^2 &\le \lambda_{min}[Z(t)'Z(t)] \\ &\le n \min_{1 \le j \le n} \|z_j(t) - \hat{z}_j(t)\|^2 \end{aligned} \tag{3.75}$$

where $\hat{z}_j(t)$ denotes the (orthogonal) projection of $z_j(t)$ onto the linear space spanned by $z_1(t), \ldots, z_{j-1}(t), z_{j+1}(t), \ldots, z_n(t)$.

All projections appearing in this chapter apply pointwise (i.e. in an Euclidian space) and should not be confused with the L_2-projections usually applied in the theory of stochastic processes. The following result is the keystone for the determination of $\lambda_{min}(Z_t)$.

Proposition 3.4.4 (LAI/WEI (1982b))
Suppose that (A.2) holds. Let u_t, v_t and $z_{t,1}, \ldots, z_{t,n}$ be $\mathcal{F}_{t-1}$-measurable random variables. Let $Z(t) = (z_{ij})_{1 \le i \le t}^{1 \le j \le n}$, $w_t = (w_1, \ldots, w_t)'$, $u_t = (u_1, \ldots, u_t)'$ and $v_t = (v_1, \ldots, v_t)'$. Let $\hat{w}_t, \hat{u}_t, \hat{v}_t$ denote the projections of w_t, u_t, v_t onto $L[Z(t)]$, the linear space spanned by the column vectors of $Z(t)$. Furthermore, let $\hat{\hat{u}}_t$ denote the projection of u_t onto $L[Z(t), v_t + w_t]$ and let v_t^* denote the projection of v_t onto $L[Z(t), w_t]$. Suppose that

$$\max\left\{0, \log\left(\sum_{i=1}^{n}\sum_{j=1}^{t} z_{ij}^2 + \sum_{s=1}^{t} u_s^2\right)\right\} = o(t) \qquad a.s. \tag{3.76}$$

Then

$$\|w_t\|^2 = O(t) \quad a.s. \quad \text{and} \quad \liminf_{t \to \infty} \frac{1}{t}\|w_t - \hat{w}_t\|^2 > 0 \quad a.s. \tag{3.77}$$

and with probability one

$$\left\|u_t - \hat{\hat{u}}_t\right\|^2 = \left(\frac{\|v_t - v_t^*\|^2 + \|w_t - \hat{w}_t\|^2}{\|v_t - \hat{v}_t\|^2 + \|w_t - \hat{w}_t\|^2} + o(1)\right)\|u_t - \hat{u}_t\|^2 . \tag{3.78}$$

With the aid of Proposition 4.4 we can prove the following result which determines the minimum order of the minimum eigenvalue in the stable case.

Theorem 3.4.5
Suppose that (A.1)-(A.3) are satisfied and $tr(Z_t) = O(t)$ a.s.

(i) *If $-1 \leq a < 1$, then*

$$\liminf_{t\to\infty} \frac{1}{t}\lambda_{min}(Z_t) > 0 \qquad a.s. \tag{3.79}$$

(ii) *If $a < -1$, then (3.79) holds on the event*

$$\left[\lambda_{max}(Z_t) = O(t)\ ,\ \limsup_{t\to\infty} \lambda_t < \frac{2}{1-a}\right]. \tag{3.80}$$

Proof
We imitate the proof of Corollary 2 of LAI/WEI (1982b). In order to maintain comparability we try to use their notation wherever possible. Define

$$\begin{aligned}
\boldsymbol{y}_t(\nu) &= (y_{p+1-\nu},\ldots,y_{t-\nu})', & \nu &= 0,\ldots,2p,\\
\boldsymbol{w}_t(\nu) &= (w_{p+1-\nu},\ldots,w_{t-\nu})', & \nu &= 0,\ldots,p,\\
\boldsymbol{x}_{t,i}(\nu) &= (x_{p+1-\nu,i},\ldots,x_{t-\nu,i})', & \nu &= 1,\ldots,p+1,\ i=1,\ldots,n,\\
\boldsymbol{\eta}_t(\nu) &= (\eta_{p+1-\nu},\ldots,\eta_{t-\nu})', & \nu &= 1,\ldots,p+1,
\end{aligned} \tag{3.81}$$

with $\eta_{t-\nu} = a(\boldsymbol{\theta}_{t-\nu} - \bar{\boldsymbol{\theta}})'\boldsymbol{z}_{t-\nu}$. Then (3.56) implies for all $t \geq p+1$ and every $\nu = 0,\ldots,p$

$$\begin{aligned}
\boldsymbol{y}_t(\nu) &= \bar{\theta}_1\boldsymbol{y}_t(\nu+1) + \cdots + \bar{\theta}_p\boldsymbol{y}_t(\nu+p) + \bar{\theta}_{p+1}\boldsymbol{x}_{t,1}(\nu+1)\\
&\quad + \bar{\theta}_n\boldsymbol{x}_{t,q}(\nu+1) + \boldsymbol{\eta}_t(\nu+1) + \boldsymbol{w}_t(\nu).
\end{aligned} \tag{3.82}$$

Notice that $\boldsymbol{y}_t(\nu), \boldsymbol{x}_{t,i}(\nu), \boldsymbol{\eta}_t(\nu)$ and $\boldsymbol{w}_t(\nu)$ are all $\mathcal{F}_{t-\nu}$-measurable. Define furthermore matrices $\boldsymbol{X}(t)$ and $\boldsymbol{Z}(t)$ by

$$\boldsymbol{X}(t) = (\boldsymbol{x}_{t,1}(1),\ldots,\boldsymbol{x}_{t,q}(1)) \tag{3.83}$$

and

$$\boldsymbol{Z}(t) = (\boldsymbol{z}_1(t),\ldots,\boldsymbol{z}_n(t)) := (\boldsymbol{y}_t(1),\ldots,\boldsymbol{y}_t(p),\boldsymbol{X}(t)). \tag{3.84}$$

Now let $|a| \leq 1$. By assumption we have $tr(Z_t) = O(t)$ a.s. Then Theorem 3.1 implies $\|\eta_t(\nu)\|^2 = o(t)$ a.s. Since by construction we have $Z(t)'Z(t) = Z_{t-1} - Z_{p-1}$ it therefore suffices to show $\liminf_{t\to\infty} \frac{1}{t}\lambda_{min}[Z(t)'Z(t)] > 0$ a.s. in order to show (3.79). In view of (3.75) this is equivalent to showing that

$$\liminf_{t\to\infty} \frac{1}{t} \|z_j(t) - \hat{z}_j(t)\|^2 > 0 \quad \text{a.s.} \tag{3.85}$$

for all $j = 1, \ldots, n$ with $\hat{z}_j(t)$ the projection of $z_j(t)$ onto $L_j^*[Z(t)]$, the linear space spanned by $z_1(t), \ldots, z_{j-1}(t), z_{j+1}(t), \ldots, z_n(t)$.

In the sequel we will repeatedly apply Proposition 4.4. Notice that the assumption $tr(Z_t) = O(t)$ implies that condition (3.76) is fulfilled whenever we apply Proposition 4.4 to the time series of our model.

Step 1: If $q \geq 1$, thus if z_t includes exogenous variables, consider a column vector u_t of $X(t)$ and denote by $X^*(t)$ the matrix $X(t)$ with the vector u_t removed and by $\hat{u}_t$ the projection of u_t onto $L[X^*(t)]$. (If $q = 0$ we can proceed immediately to Step 2.) From Assumption (A.3) and (3.75) with $X(t)$ playing the role of $Z(t)$ we can infer that

$$\liminf_{t\to\infty} \frac{1}{t}\|u_t - \hat{u}_t\|^2 > 0 \quad \text{a.s.} \tag{3.86}$$

Now put $Z(t) = X^*(t)$ in Proposition 4.4 and let $\hat{u}_{t,p}$ be the projection of u_t onto $L[X^*(t), y_t(p)]$. From (3.82) with $\nu = p$ we obtain

$$y_t(p) = v_t(p) + w_t(p) \tag{3.87}$$

with some $v_t(p) = (v_{p+1}, \ldots, v_t)'$ such that, for all $\tau \in \{p+1, \ldots, t\}$, v_τ is $\mathcal{F}_{\tau-p-1}$-measurable. Then Proposition 4.4 (with $\hat{u}_{t,p}$ playing the role of $\hat{\hat{u}}_t$ in (3.78)) gives

$$\|u_t - \hat{u}_{t,p}\|^2 \geq \left(\frac{\|w_t(p) - \hat{w}_t(p)\|^2}{\|v_t(p) - \hat{v}_t(p)\|^2 + \|w_t(p) - \hat{w}_t(p)\|^2} + o(1)\right) \times \cdots$$
$$\cdots \times \|u_t - \hat{u}_t\|^2 \quad \text{a.s.} \tag{3.88}$$

with $\hat{v}_t(p), \hat{w}_t(p)$ the projections of $v_t(p), w_t(p)$, resp., onto $L[X^*(t)]$. Since, by assumption, $\|v_t(p)\|^2 = O(t)$ a.s. and $\liminf_{t\to\infty} \frac{1}{t}\|w_t(p) - \hat{w}_t(t)\|^2 > 0$ a.s. by Proposition 4.4 it follows that

$$\liminf_{t\to\infty} \frac{1}{t}\|u_t - \hat{u}_{t,p}\|^2 > 0 \quad \text{a.s.} \tag{3.89}$$

Now let $\widehat{u}_{t,p-1}$ be the projection of u_t onto $L[X^*(t), y_t(p), y_t(p-1)]$. Using a similar argument as above we obtain $\liminf_{t\to\infty} \frac{1}{t}\|u_t - \widehat{u}_{t,p-1}\|^2 > 0$ a.s. Proceeding inductively in this way we finally obtain

$$\liminf_{t\to\infty} \frac{1}{t}\|u_t - \widehat{u}_{t,1}\|^2 > 0 \qquad \text{a.s.} \tag{3.90}$$

with $\widehat{u}_{t,1}$ the projection of u_t onto $L[X^*(t), y_t(p), \ldots, y_t(1)]$. Hence we have shown (3.85) for all vectors $z_j(t)$ with $j \geq p+1$.

Step 2: To proceed (or if z_t includes no exogenous variables) consider a column vector $y_t(\nu)$, $\nu = 1, \ldots, p$, of $Z(t)$. Define the matrices $X_t(\nu)$ and $Z_t(\nu)$ by

$$\begin{aligned} X_t(\nu) &= (x_{t,1}(\nu), \ldots, x_{t,q}(\nu)), \\ Z_t(\nu) &= (y_t(\nu+1), \ldots, y_t(\nu+p), X_t(\nu+1), \ldots, X_t(1)). \end{aligned} \tag{3.91}$$

Notice that Assumption (A.2) implies that the matrix $Z_t(\nu)$ is $\mathcal{F}_{t-\nu-1}$-measurable[4]. Then define the matrix $Z^*(t)$ as the matrix $Z(t)$ with the column vector $y_t(\nu)$ removed. Let $y_t^*(\nu)$ be the projection of $y_t(\nu)$ onto $L[Z^*(t)]$ and $\widehat{y}_t(\nu)$ the projection of $y_t(\nu)$ onto $L[y_t(1), \ldots, y_t(\nu-1), Z_t(\nu)]$. We want to show that $\liminf_{t\to\infty} \frac{1}{t}\|y_t(\nu) - y_t^*(\nu)\|^2 > 0$ a.s. Since $L[Z^*(t)] \subset L[y_t(1), \ldots, y_t(\nu-1), Z_t(\nu)]$ implies that

$$\|y_t(\nu) - y_t^*(\nu)\|^2 \geq \|y_t(\nu) - \widehat{y}_t(\nu)\|^2 \tag{3.92}$$

it is sufficient to show that $\liminf_{t\to\infty} \frac{1}{t}\|y_t(\nu) - \widehat{y}_t(\nu)\|^2 > 0$ a.s.

By construction $y_t(\nu)$ is the sum of a linear combination of some column vectors of $Z_t(\nu)$ and the vector $w_t(\nu)$. Let $\pi_{0,t}$ be the projection of $y_t(\nu)$ onto $L[Z_t(\nu)]$. Then, since $y_t(\nu) - \pi_{0,t} = w_t - \widehat{w}_t$, Proposition 4.4 gives

$$\liminf_{t\to\infty} \frac{1}{t}\|y_t(\nu) - \pi_{0,t}\|^2 > 0 \qquad \text{a.s.} \tag{3.93}$$

Now let $\pi_{1,t}$ be the projection of $y_t(\nu)$ onto $L[Z_t(\nu), y_t(\nu-1)]$. Since

$$L\left[Z_t(\nu), y_t(\nu-1)\right] = L\left[Z_t(\nu), \bar{\theta}_1 y_t(\nu) + \eta_t(\nu) + w_t(\nu-1)\right] \tag{3.94}$$

and letting $v_t = \bar{\theta}_1 y_t(\nu) + \eta_t(\nu)$ Proposition 4.4 implies

$$\begin{aligned} \|y_t(\nu) - \pi_{1,t}\|^2 = {} & \left(\frac{\|v_t - v_t^*\|^2 + \|w_t(\nu-1) - \widehat{w}_t(\nu-1)\|^2}{\|v_t - \widehat{v}_t\|^2 + \|w_t(\nu-1) - \widehat{w}_t(\nu-1)\|^2} + o(1) \right) \times \\ & \cdots \times \|y_t(\nu) - \pi_{0,t}\|^2 \qquad \text{a.s.} \end{aligned} \tag{3.95}$$

[4]This is the only place where we need this measurability condition.

with $\widehat{\boldsymbol{v}}_t$, $\boldsymbol{v}_t^*$, resp., the projections of $\boldsymbol{v}_t$ onto $L[\boldsymbol{Z}_t(\nu)]$, $L[\boldsymbol{Z}_t(\nu), \boldsymbol{w}_t(\nu-1)]$, resp. By assumption we have $\|\boldsymbol{v}_t\|^2 = O(t)$ a.s., hence Proposition 4.4 implies

$$\liminf_{t\to\infty} \frac{1}{t}\|\boldsymbol{y}_t(\nu) - \boldsymbol{\pi}_{1,t}\|^2 > 0 \qquad \text{a.s.} \tag{3.96}$$

Proceeding inductively in this way we finally obtain

$$\liminf_{t\to\infty} \frac{1}{t}\|\boldsymbol{y}_t(\nu) - \boldsymbol{\pi}_{\nu-1,t}\|^2 > 0 \qquad \text{a.s.} \tag{3.97}$$

with $\boldsymbol{\pi}_{\nu-1,t}$ the projection of $\boldsymbol{y}_t(\nu)$ onto $L[\boldsymbol{Z}_t(\nu), \boldsymbol{y}_t(\nu-1), \ldots, \boldsymbol{y}_t(1)]$. Since $\boldsymbol{\pi}_{\nu-1,t} = \boldsymbol{y}_t^*(\nu)$ by construction Theorem 4.5 is shown for $|a| \leq 1$.

The proof for the case $a < -1$ is completely analogous except that all considerations hold on the event (3.80). ∎

3.5 Convergence Results

In this section we apply the results of the preceding sections in order to show some convergence results.

3.5.1 Non-Autoregressive Models

For non-autoregressive models, thus if $p = 0$ in model (3.1), the situation is quite simple since all assumptions ensuring convergence of the estimates $\{\boldsymbol{\theta}_t\}$ can be formulated as exogenous.

Theorem 3.5.1
Suppose that $p = 0$ and that the assumptions (A.1) and (A.2) are satisfied. Suppose furthermore that

$$\frac{\lambda_{max}(\boldsymbol{X}_t)}{\lambda_{min}(\boldsymbol{X}_t)} = O(1) \quad a.s. \quad and \quad tr(\boldsymbol{X}_t) \to \infty \quad a.s. \tag{3.98}$$

with $\boldsymbol{X}_t = \sum_{t=0}^{T} \boldsymbol{x}_t \boldsymbol{x}_t'$.

(i) *If $-1 \leq a < 1$, then $\boldsymbol{\theta}_t \to \bar{\boldsymbol{\theta}}$ a.s.*

(ii) *If $a < -1$, then $\boldsymbol{\theta}_t \to \bar{\boldsymbol{\theta}}$ a.s. on the event where*

$$\limsup_{t\to\infty} \frac{\boldsymbol{x}_t'\boldsymbol{x}_t}{tr(\boldsymbol{X}_t)} < \frac{2}{1-a}. \tag{3.99}$$

Theorem 5.1 is an immediate consequence of Theorem 3.1, hence we can omit a proof. As a corollary we obtain

Corollary 3.5.2
Suppose that $p = 0$ and the assumptions (A.1) and (A.2) are satisfied. Suppose furthermore that

$$\frac{1}{T}\sum_{t=1}^{T} \boldsymbol{x}_t \boldsymbol{x}_t' \longrightarrow \boldsymbol{X} \qquad a.s. \tag{3.100}$$

with some positive definite (possibly random) matrix $\boldsymbol{X}$. If $a < 1$, then $\boldsymbol{\theta}_t \to \bar{\boldsymbol{\theta}}$ a.s.

Proof
Since (3.100) clearly implies (3.98) we only have to verify condition (3.99) for arbitrary $a < 1$. Obviously this is equivalent to showing $\lambda_t = \boldsymbol{x}_t'\boldsymbol{x}_t / \sum_0^t \boldsymbol{x}_s'\boldsymbol{x}_s \to 0$ a.s. Since

$$1 - \lambda_t = \frac{tr(\sum_{s=0}^{t-1} \boldsymbol{x}_s\boldsymbol{x}_s')}{tr(\sum_{s=0}^{t} \boldsymbol{x}_s\boldsymbol{x}_s')} = \frac{t-1}{t}\frac{tr(\frac{1}{t-1}\boldsymbol{X}_{t-1})}{tr(\frac{1}{t}\boldsymbol{X}_t)} \tag{3.101}$$

$\lambda_t \to 0$ a.s. is immediate from (3.100). ■

Notice that condition (3.100) and hence (3.98) is fulfilled whenever $\{\boldsymbol{x}_t\}$ is a covariance stationary and ergodic stochastic process with a non-singular variance-covariance matrix, thus for a large class of stochastic processes. Apart from the study of FOURGEAUD ET AL. (1986), (3.100) is the assumption usually employed for the exogenous variables in models with forecast feedback.

Notice that Theorem 5.1 is more general since it applies, on the one hand, for processes $\{\boldsymbol{x}_t\}$ with a time-varying covariance structure as long as the PEC is satisfied and the trace of the matrix of moments diverges a.s. to infinity. On the other hand it applies also for integrated processes $\{\boldsymbol{x}_t\}$ as long as the PEC holds. Notice, however, that if $\boldsymbol{z}_t$ contains two integrated processes which are cointegrated the PEC fails to hold. (For details see Example 4.5 in the following chapter.)

Since $\lambda_t \to 0$ a.s. under condition (3.100) it is worthwhile to ask whether condition (3.99) can be dispensed with under more general conditions than (3.100). The following example shows that this is, in general, not possible. Hence the PEC does not necessarily imply $\lambda_t \to 0$ a.s.

Example 3.5.3
Consider the (deterministic) process x_t given by

$$x_t = \begin{cases} \sqrt{\frac{9}{10}t} & \text{if } t = 10^m, m \in \mathbb{N}, \\ 0 & \text{otherwise.} \end{cases} \tag{3.102}$$

It is easy to see that

$$\limsup_{t\to\infty} \lambda_t = \frac{9}{10} \quad \text{and} \quad \frac{1}{T}\sum_{t=0}^{T} x_t^2 \in \left[\frac{1}{10}, \frac{9}{10}\right]. \tag{3.103}$$

Obviously, the PEC holds but $\lambda_t \not\to 0$. Nevertheless, Theorem 5.1 implies that $\theta_t \to \bar{\theta}$ if $-11/9 < a < 1$. To our knowledge, no other approach employed in the literature is able to give a convergence result in this situation.

3.5.2 Autoregressive Models – The Stable Case

For autoregressive models, thus if $p \geq 1$ in (3.1), we obtain the following result.

Theorem 3.5.4
Suppose that $p \geq 1$ and (A.1)–(A.3) are satisfied. Suppose furthermore that the characteristic polynomial (3.60) possesses roots only inside the unit circle.

(i) *If $-1 \leq a < 1$, then $\boldsymbol{\theta}_t \to \bar{\boldsymbol{\theta}}$ a.s.*

(ii) *If $a < -1$, then $\boldsymbol{\theta}_t \to \bar{\boldsymbol{\theta}}$ a.s. on the event where*

$$\limsup_{t\to\infty} \lambda_t < \frac{2}{1-a}. \tag{3.104}$$

Proof

Firstly, notice that the event (3.104) is a.s. in the case of $-1 \leq a < 1$. We therefore omit the distinction between the cases (i) and (ii) in the following. Theorem 4.2 implies $\lambda_{max}(\boldsymbol{Z}_t) = O(t)$ a.s. on (3.104) and Theorem 4.5 implies $\liminf_{t\to\infty} t^{-1}\lambda_{min}(\boldsymbol{Z}_t) > 0$ a.s. on (3.104). Hence the PEC holds true on (3.104) and Theorem 3.1 applies to give the desired results. ■

Theorem 5.4 is the central result of this chapter. It states that if the influence of the forecast feedback is limited and the REE is a stable ARX process, then agents following the SG learning procedure cannot destabilize the system in the sense that the PEC fails to hold and can eventually learn to form rational expectations with probability one. In particular, agents do not learn to believe in sun-spots.

If $n = 1$ this result corresponds to the convergence results in Chapter 2 (cf. Example 2.6.5) and to the convergence result of KOTTMANN/-KULIBERDA (1990). (Notice that $n = 1$ implies that the SG algorithm and the OLS algorithm coincide.) If $n > 1$, however, this result is, to our knowledge, the first global convergence result in the dynamic case which does not rely on a projection facility.

3.5.3 Autoregressive Models – The Unstable Case

Now we consider the case that the characteristic polynomial possesses roots on or outside the unit circle. Hence the REE is an unstable ARX process. This implies, apart from special cases, that the PEC is not satisfied; and in view of Theorem 3.2 we can expect to obtain convergence only for some components of $\boldsymbol{\theta}_t$. Since this kind of convergence is less satisfactory and additional technical difficulties arise we shall omit formal proofs. We only outline briefly how the respective proofs could be given.

Let $\mu_1, \ldots, \mu_k$ be the roots of the characteristic polynomial (3.60) and $m_1, \ldots, m_k$ the respective algebraic multiplicities. Define

$$(3.105) \qquad \bar{\mu} = \max_{1\leq i\leq k} |\mu_i| \qquad \text{and} \qquad M = \max_{|\mu_j|=\bar{\mu}} \{m_j\}.$$

It is well-known (cf. LAI/WEI (1985, p. 378)) that there exists a positive constant c such that

$$(3.106) \qquad ||\boldsymbol{A}^t|| \approx ct^{M-1}\bar{\mu}^t \qquad \text{as } t \to \infty$$

with $\boldsymbol{A}$ the companion form matrix defined in (3.59).

Now suppose that (A.1), (A.2), and $-1 \leq |a| < 1$ hold. Then, using the same technique as in the proof of Lemma 4.1, it is possible to show that under the assumptions (3.61) and (3.62)

$$tr(\boldsymbol{Z}_t) = O(t^{\nu}) \quad \text{a.s.} \tag{3.107}$$

for some $\nu \geq 2$ if $\bar{\mu} = 1$, and

$$tr(\boldsymbol{Z}_t) = O\left(t^{2(M-1)}\bar{\mu}^{2t}\right) \quad \text{a.s.} \tag{3.108}$$

if $\bar{\mu} > 1$. Moreover, it can be shown that $\frac{1}{t}\lambda_{max}(\boldsymbol{Z}_t) \to \infty$ a.s. in both cases.

Now suppose that the model (3.1) with $\bar{\mu} \geq 1$ includes some exogenous variables which satisfy (A.3). Since

$$\lambda_{min}(\boldsymbol{Z}_t) \leq \lambda_{min}(\boldsymbol{X}_t) \leq \lambda_{max}(\boldsymbol{X}_t) \leq \lambda_{max}(\boldsymbol{Z}_t) \tag{3.109}$$

we face the situation that $\lambda_{min}(\boldsymbol{Z}_t)$ and $\lambda_{max}(\boldsymbol{Z}_t)$ are of different order and the PEC fails to hold. The same happens if the characteristic polynomial possesses roots also inside the unit circle (cf. LAI/WEI (1985)). We therefore cannot apply Theorem 3.1. In order to show consistency for at least some components of $\boldsymbol{\theta}_t$ we can apply Theorem 3.2.

If $p = 1$, thus if $\boldsymbol{z}_t$ is autoregressive of first order, the characteristic polynomial is $\pi(y) = y - \bar{\theta}_1$ which possesses only one root, $y^* = (1-a)^{-1}\phi_1$. This root is unstable whenever $|\phi_1| \geq |1-a|$. In that case Theorem 3.2 implies $\theta_{t,1} \to \bar{\theta}_1$ a.s. if $-1 \leq a < 1$.

Hence the first component of the REE parameter $\bar{\boldsymbol{\theta}}$ (corresponding to the fastest growing component in $\boldsymbol{z}_t$) will be identified properly by the SG algorithm. For the remaining components of $\boldsymbol{\theta}_t$ we only know that they remain bounded a.s. The limit expectations of agents may thus be non-rational but, since $z_{t,1}$ dominates the whole vector $\boldsymbol{z}_t$ and $\theta_{t,1} \to \bar{\theta}_1$ a.s., the predictions $\boldsymbol{\theta}_t{}'\boldsymbol{z}_t$ are close to the 'rational predictions' $\bar{\boldsymbol{\theta}}'\boldsymbol{z}_t$ in relative terms, i.e. $||\boldsymbol{z}_t||^{-2}[(\boldsymbol{\theta}_t - \bar{\boldsymbol{\theta}})'\boldsymbol{z}_t]^2$ is small.

If $p > 1$ and the characteristic polynomial possesses roots on or outside the unit circle the situation is even more complicated. In order to apply Theorem 3.2 we have to determine first the matrices $\boldsymbol{Z}_t^*$. Generally, we have $\boldsymbol{Z}_t^* = r_t^{-1}\sum_0^t \boldsymbol{y}_s \boldsymbol{y}_s'$, since all components of $\boldsymbol{y}_t$ are unstable while $\boldsymbol{x}_t$ is stable by (A.3). But unless to the case that all roots of $\pi(y)$ are equal in modulus we always have $\lambda_{min}(Z_t^*) \to 0$ a.s. Hence Theorem 3.2 applies only for a set of parameter values $a, \phi_1, \ldots, \phi_p$ of Lebesgue measure zero.

3.6 An Example

We come back to the example in Section 2.9. The structural equations (2.96) in that example are formulated in terms of deviations from equilibrium values. Although such a formulation is common in economic theory it is problematic whenever the structural equations include expectations terms since it requires that agents think (and predict) in terms of deviations from equilibrium values. This is only possible if agents know these equilibrium values. But, of course, in that case learning is obsolete. We therefore restate this model in a proper form using the same notation as in Section 2.9.

3.6.1 The Model

The market equations take the form

$$\begin{aligned} D_t &= d_1 - \beta p_t && \text{(Demand)} \\ S_t &= d_2 + \alpha p_{t+1}^e + u_t && \text{(Supply)} \\ D_t &= S_t && \text{(Market equilibrium)} \end{aligned} \tag{3.110}$$

with $d_1 - d_2 > 0$, $\alpha > 0$, and $\beta > 0$. The reduced form equation of this model is

$$p_{t+1} = \frac{d_1 - d_2}{\beta} - \frac{\alpha}{\beta} p_{t+1}^e - \frac{1}{\beta} u_t. \tag{3.111}$$

As in Section 2.9 we assume that there are two different types of agents (or firms) in the market, the one predicting p_{t+1} by p_t, and the other by $\boldsymbol{\theta}_t' \boldsymbol{z}_t$ with $\boldsymbol{z}_t' = (p_t, 1)$ and $\boldsymbol{\theta}_t$ given by the SG algorithm. With a_1 and a_2 we denote the fractions of the respective type of agents. Hence $a_1, a_2 \geq 0$ and $a_1 + a_2 = 1$.

Under this assumption the reduced form equation can be rewritten as

$$\begin{aligned} p_{t+1} &= \frac{d_1 - d_2 - \alpha a_2 \theta_{t,2}}{\beta} - \frac{\alpha(a_1 + a_2 \theta_{t,1})}{\beta} p_t - \frac{1}{\beta} u_t \\ &= (\boldsymbol{\phi} + a\boldsymbol{\theta}_t)' \boldsymbol{z}_t + w_{t+1} \end{aligned} \tag{3.112}$$

with $w_{t+1} = -\beta^{-1} u_t$ and

$$(3.113) \qquad a = -a_2 \frac{\alpha}{\beta} \quad \text{and} \quad \phi' = \left(-\frac{a_1 \alpha}{\beta}, \frac{d_1 - d_2}{\beta} \right).$$

The REE parameter $\bar{\theta}$ is easily calculated as

$$(3.114) \qquad \bar{\theta}' = \left(-\frac{a_1 \alpha}{\beta + a_2 \alpha}, \frac{d_1 - d_2}{\beta + a_2 \alpha} \right).$$

Notice that under the above parameter restrictions a is always negative, hence rational expectations exist no matter of the exact values of α, β, and a_2. Notice furthermore that the first component of $\bar{\theta}$ coincides with the REE parameter of the model in Section 2.9 (cf. (2.101)).

3.6.2 Convergence Results

First we determine which parameter configurations lead to a stable REE. Since the characteristic polynomial is $\pi(y) = y - \bar{\theta}_1$, which has only one root $y^* = \bar{\theta}_1$, the REE is stable if, and only if, $|\bar{\theta}_1| < 1$. (Notice that the REE is stable under exactly the same parameter conditions as the REE of the model in Section 2.9.)

For notational convenience we define constants c_1, c_2 by

$$(3.115) \qquad c_1 = \frac{\beta}{\alpha} \quad \text{and} \quad c_2 = \frac{1}{2}\left(1 - \frac{\beta}{\alpha}\right).$$

It is easy to see that

$$(3.116) \qquad \begin{aligned} -1 \leq a < 1 \quad &\Longleftrightarrow \quad a_2 \leq c_1, \text{ and} \\ |\bar{\theta}_1| < 1 \quad &\Longleftrightarrow \quad a_2 > c_2. \end{aligned}$$

In view of Theorem 5.4 and Theorem 3.2 we obtain the following convergence result.

Suppose that for the model given above (A.1) and (A.2) are satisfied.

(i) If $\alpha \leq \beta$, then $-1 \leq a < 1$ and $|\bar{\theta}_1| < 1$. Consequently, $\theta_t \to \bar{\theta}$ a.s.

	$\beta < \alpha < 3\beta$	$\alpha \geq 3\beta$
$a_2 \leq c_2$	$\theta_{t,1} \to \bar{\theta}_1$ a.s.	
$c_2 < a_2 \leq c_1$	$\boldsymbol{\theta}_t \to \bar{\boldsymbol{\theta}}$ a.s.	
$c_1 < a_2$	$\boldsymbol{\theta}_t \to \bar{\boldsymbol{\theta}}$ a.s. on (*)	
$a_2 \leq c_1$		$\theta_{t,1} \to \bar{\theta}_1$ a.s.
$c_1 < a_2 \leq c_2$		$\theta_{t,1} \to \bar{\theta}_1$ a.s. on (*)
$c_2 < a_2$		$\boldsymbol{\theta}_t \to \bar{\boldsymbol{\theta}}$ a.s. on (*)

Table 3.1

(ii) If $\alpha > \beta$, denote by (*) the event where

$$\limsup_{t\to\infty} \lambda_t < \frac{2}{1-a} = \frac{2\beta}{a_2\alpha + \beta} \tag{3.117}$$

holds. Then the convergence results reported in Table 3.1 hold.

This result can be interpreted economically in the same way as the result in Section 2.9. (Notice that the stability result for this model and the model in Section 2.9 are similar. To appreciate this point compare Table 3.1 with Table 2.2.1.) Firstly, under the usual cobweb stability condition, $\alpha \leq \beta$, the price process is stable and agents employing the SG procedure eventually learn to form rational expectations with probability one.

Secondly, the learning firms have a stabilizing effect in the sense that even for parameter configurations which induce an unstable market situation, i.e., if $\alpha > \beta$, the resulting price process can be stable. In particular, if the fraction of learning agents is sufficiently large, i.e., $a_2 > c_2$, then the REE is stable.

On the other hand, the learning firms have also a destabilizing effect. If the fraction of learning firms is too large, i.e. $a_2 > c_1$, then the risk of explosion occurs[5]. This means that convergence takes place

[5]We carried out some computer simulations for this model and observed that whenever there exists a risk of explosion, indicated by the addition "on (*)" in Table 3.1, such an explosion occurs with positive but not unit probability.

only on the event (*) which may be a strict subset of the underlying probability space. Hence the success of learning can be understood as an insider effect. If too many agents are learning, then then the success of learning can get lost[6].

Finally, we want to remark that in an REE neither the market prediction nor the predictions of the 'classical' or myopic agents are rational. Only the predictions of the learning agents may be rational in the limit. Hence the 'classical' agents do not participate in the success of the learning agents while the learning agents implicitly learn about the irrational behaviour of the 'classical' agents without solving the problem of infinite regress of expectations.

3.7 Simulation Results

Although the convergence results of Section 5 are satisfactory from the mathematical point of view it is worthwhile to consider the performance of the SG algorithm in practice. We carried out some computer simulations and it turned out that the performance of the SG algorithm is not as convincing as the theory suggests[7].

In the literature on recursive identification and control (see, e.g., GRAUPE (1984, Chapter 7)) it is well-known that, in practice, the SG algorithm has the following shortcomings:

- A slow rate of convergence
- Non-robustness to non-stationary time series
- Dependence on initial values

[6]This finding corresponds in some weak sense to the impossibility of an informationally efficient market as shown by GROSSMANN/STIGLITZ (1980). But while GROSSMANN/STIGLITZ show that the value of private information decreases if this information becomes more and more public, hence the incentive to gather these (costly) information decreases, we face the situation that if too many agents are learning, then learning may become worthless.

[7]MARCET/SARGENT (1989b) claim that boundedly rational learning procedures can be employed to calculate rational expectations in complex models for which an analytical determination of the REE is very difficult. In view of the findings presented in this section this assertion should be treated with care although the performance of the OLS procedure considered by MARCET/SARGENT is, generally, better than the one of the SG procedure.

Besides these features we observed also some strange kind of long-term behaviour which we like to report.

In order to keep the programming efforts as low as possible most of the computer simulation runs were carried out for the simplest non-trivial ARX model[8], i.e. the model (3.1) with $\boldsymbol{z}_t' = (y_t, x_t)$ where either $x_t \equiv 1$ or $\{x_t\}$ a stable ARMA(2,3) process with Gaussian innovations. As disturbance terms we employed i.i.d. random variables, either $N(0,1)$-distributed or $U(-1,1)$-distributed. The initial values $\boldsymbol{\theta}_0$ were chosen to be deterministic.

We observed that the qualitative long-term behaviour of the dynamical system $(y_t, \boldsymbol{\theta}_t)$ is affected neither by the type of the exogenous variable nor by the choice of the disturbance terms.

3.7.1 Slow Rate of Convergence

It is well-known that the rate of convergence of the SG algorithm is quite slow. CHEN/GUO (1991) show for the case of no forecast feedback that under the PEC $\|\boldsymbol{\theta}_t - \bar{\boldsymbol{\theta}}\| = O(r_t^{-\mu})$ a.s. with some small constant $\mu > 0$. The existence of this constant is ensured by the theory but it is difficult to determine in practice (see their Theorem 4.6 with proof). This theoretical result coincides with our findings. We observed that the trajectories of the SG algorithm are generally smooth and that convergence proceeds very slowly.

In practice it is possible to improve the rate of convergence by replacing, after a few periods, the term r_t^{-1} in equation (3.4) by a term which decreases at a slower rate, for example, $r_t^{-\nu}$ with some $1/2 < \nu < 1$. Since (see Lemma 2.2.2)

$$(3.118) \qquad \sum_{t=0}^{\infty} \frac{\|\boldsymbol{z}_t\|^2}{r_t^{\nu}} = \infty \quad \text{a.s.} \quad \text{and} \quad \sum_{t=0}^{\infty} \frac{\|\boldsymbol{z}_t\|^2}{r_t^{2\nu}} < \infty \quad \text{a.s.}$$

this replacement does not alter the qualitative long-term behaviour of the estimation process. (Notice that the proof of Theorem 3.1 requires that (3.118) holds.)

[8]We started our Monte-Carlo study with this model. Later on we analyzed also higher-dimensional models but the qualitative properties were the same. The calculations for the simple model were performed using the statistical environment XLISPSTAT as described in TIERNY (1988). For the calculations of higher-dimensional models we employed a program written in the language C. We are grateful to THOMAS SIWIK for writing this program.

3.7.2 Non-Robustness to Non-Stationary Time Series

In Section 3 we have shown convergence of the SG algorithm only under the PEC. For the case of no forecast feedback CHEN/GUO (1991) show convergence under the slightly more general condition that $r_t \to \infty$ a.s. and

$$
\begin{aligned}
\frac{r_t}{r_{t-1}} &= O((\log r_{t-1})^{\delta}) \qquad \text{a.s.,} \\
\frac{\lambda_{max}(Z_t)}{\lambda_{min}(Z_t)} &= O\left((\log r_t)^{\frac{1}{4}-\delta}\right) \qquad \text{a.s.}
\end{aligned}
\tag{3.119}
$$

with some $\delta \in [0, 1/4]$. (In that case the rate of convergence is $\|\theta_t - \bar{\theta}\| = O((\log r_t)^{-\nu})$ a.s. for some $\nu > 0$.) The scope of this generalization is, however, limited since it covers neither the case of unit roots of the characteristic polynomial nor the case of integrated processes or polynomial trends among the exogenous variables. To our knowledge, no considerably more general results exist in the literature.

Consistency of the SG algorithm thus depends crucially on system stability, i.e. on the PEC. Nevertheless, as Theorem 3.2 shows, if the PEC is violated, then the SG algorithm can still give 'good' predictions. We observed in case of roots of the characteristic polynomial on or outside the unit circle that $\|y_t - y_t^e\| = O(1)$ a.s. Hence the PE remains bounded and, generally, the RPE converges to zero.

3.7.3 Dependence on Initial Values

We observed that, in practice, the SG algorithm depends on the initial values chosen. If these values are far-away from the REE parameter, then the SG algorithm seems to converge to some biased value. This finding seems to contradict the results of Section 5 but this apparent contradiction is due to the slow rate of convergence and to round-off errors. Nevertheless, real economic agents basing their predictions on the SG estimates may be led to biased limit expectations since at least round-off errors cannot be avoided in practice.

In order to overcome this shortcoming one can use a rolling sample technique, i.e., only the last M observations are used for the calculation of the estimates with some appropriate M. Of course, the convergence results of Section 5 do not apply for such a modification.

3.7.4 Strange Behaviour

For some parameter values and initial values the dynamical system (y_t, θ_t) shows a strange behaviour — see Figure 3.1 to Figure 3.3.

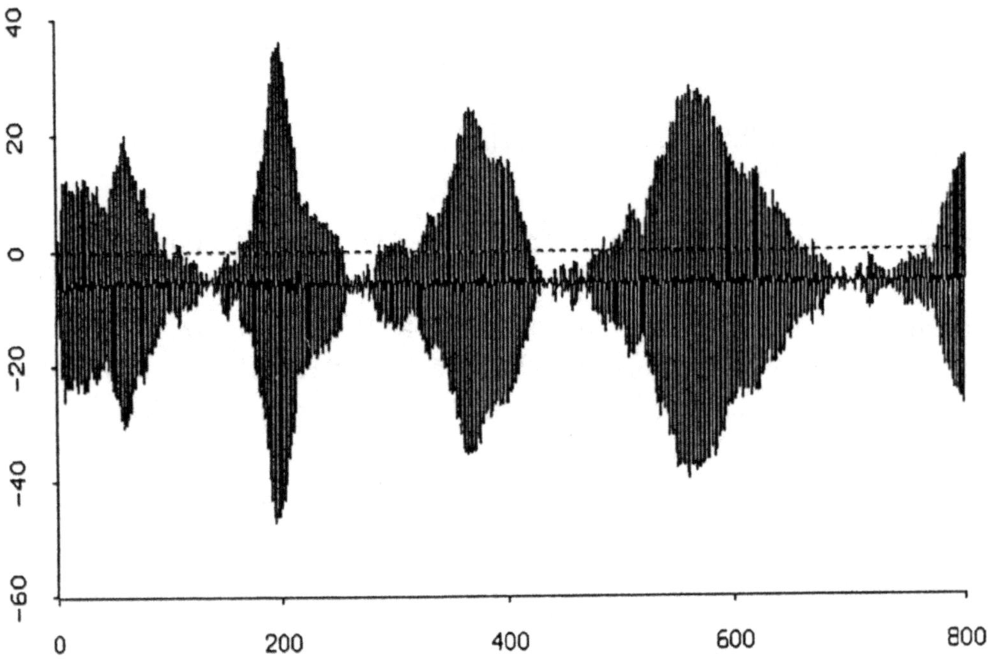

Figure 3.1: The evolution of y_t under SG learning

The three figures show the evolution of the endogenous variable and the two parameter estimates. The underlying parameter configuration is

$$
\begin{aligned}
a &= -0.8, \\
\phi' &= (-1.6, -10), \\
\bar{\theta} &= (-8/9, -50/9), \\
\theta_0' &= (-0.5, 2), \\
x_t &\equiv 1.
\end{aligned}
\tag{3.120}
$$

The three time series show a quite strange behaviour. While the estimates for the second component of $\bar{\theta}$ (Figure 3.3.) seem to converge to some value far off the equilibrium value the endogenous variable shows a kind of chaotic pattern (Figure 3.1) and the estimates $\theta_{t,1}$ cycle slowly in some range (Figure 3.2).

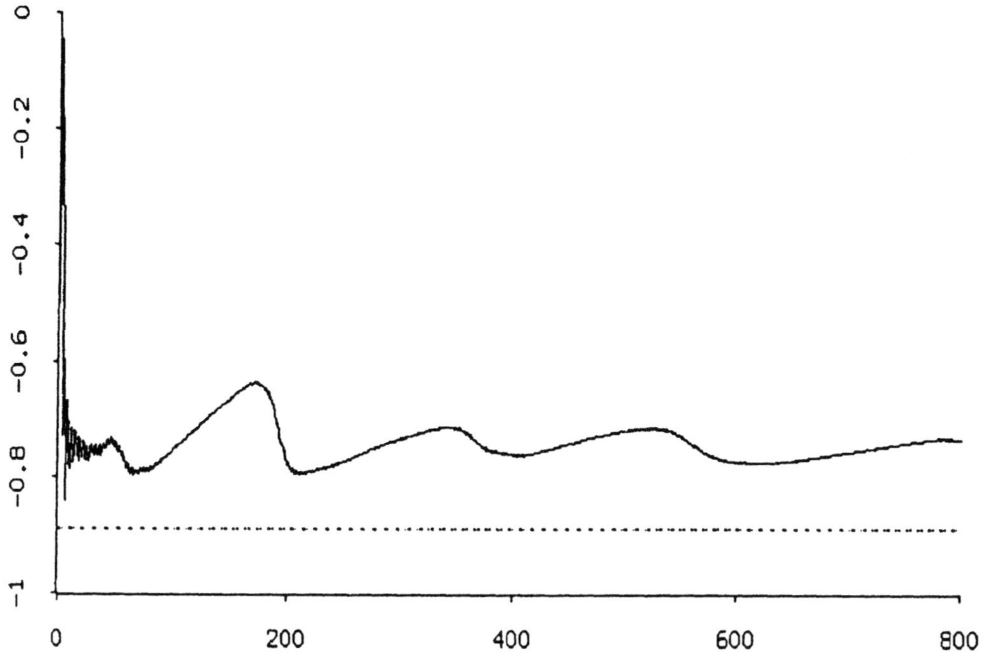

Figure 3.2: The evolution of $\theta_{t,1}$

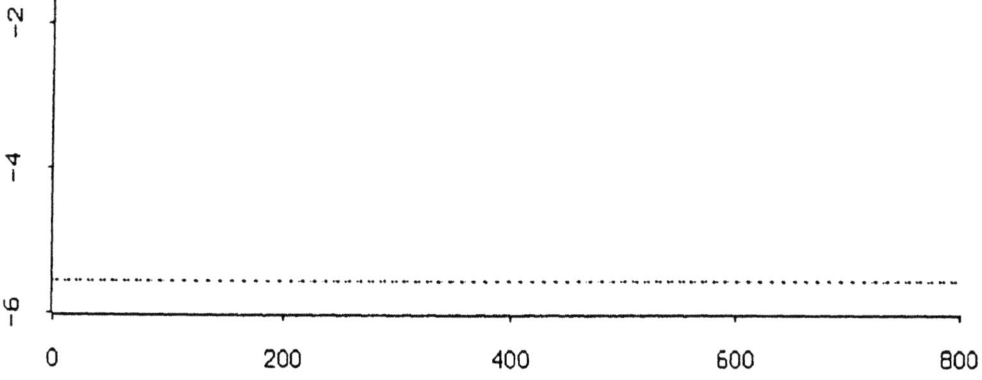

Figure 3.3: The evolution of $\theta_{t,2}$

To understand this strange behaviour remember that the SG algorithm splits up the (univariate) prediction error to give the adjustments of $\theta_{t,1}$ and $\theta_{t,2}$. Since

$$\begin{aligned} y_{t+1} - y^e_{t+1} &= (\phi_1 + a\theta_{t,1})y_t + (\phi_2 + a\theta_{t,2})x_t - \theta_{t,1}y_t - \theta_{t,2}x_t + w_{t+1} \\ &= (a-1)(\theta_{t,1} - \bar{\theta}_1)y_t + (a-1)(\theta_{t,2} - \bar{\theta}_2)x_t + w_{t+1} \end{aligned} \tag{3.121}$$

the PE depends on five different terms; the two estimation errors $\theta_{t,i} - \bar{\theta}_i$, the current endogenous variable y_t, the current exogenous variable x_t, and the disturbance term w_{t+1}. While the evolution of the two latter terms is exogenously given the evolution of the former three terms is linked in a complex way. (This is a consequence of the forecast feedback.) We shall explain how the interaction between the first three terms leads to the strange behaviour as shown in the figures.

Firstly, notice that the trajectories of the estimates are smooth after a short transient phase. This is a consequence of the fact that the endogenous variable is relatively large in that phase, hence the scaling factor r_t^{-1} becomes small quite rapidly.

Secondly, notice that the initial value $\theta_{0,2} = 2$ is larger than $\bar{\theta}_2$ (indicated by the dotted line in Figure 3.3). This implies, jointly with $x_t \equiv 1$ and $a < 1$, that the estimation error in the second component contributes a persisting negative amount to the PE.

Next, notice that if the endogenous variable is large in modulus, the PE due to the estimation error in the first component is likely to dominate the whole PE. As the second line of

$$\begin{aligned} \theta_{t+1,1} &= \theta_{t,1} + \frac{y_t}{r_t}(y_{t+1} - y^e_{t+1}) \\ &= \theta_{t,1} - (1-a)\frac{y_t^2}{r_t}(\theta_{t,1} - \bar{\theta}_1) - (1-a)\frac{y_t}{r_t}(\theta_{t,2} - \bar{\theta}_2 + w_{t+1}), \qquad (3.122) \\ \theta_{t+1,2} &= \theta_{t,2} + \frac{1}{r_t}(y_{t+1} - y^e_{t+1}). \end{aligned}$$

indicates, in that case $\theta_{t,1}$ will be adjusted in the proper direction, this means in the direction of $\bar{\theta}_1$. In fact, this is exactly what Figure 3.1 and Figure 3.2 show, most concisely for the time range $180 \le t \le 200$. During these periods the endogenous variable is large in modulus and the estimates are adjusted in the proper direction. This reasoning explains the downward movements of the estimates $\theta_{t,1}$.

In order to explain the upward movements, thus the repeated adjustments in the wrong direction, notice that if $|y_t|$ is relatively small (approximately $|y_t| \leq 20$ due to the choice of the initial value $\theta_{0,2}$ for the trajectory under consideration), then the PE due to the estimation error in the second component dominates the whole PE. Since $\theta_{t,2} > \bar{\theta}_2$ (see Figure 3.3) the PE is then negative.

As (3.122) shows, if the PE is negative, the estimate $\theta_{t,1}$ is adjusted upwards only if y_t is negative. Figure 3.1 shows that y_t is more likely to realize in the negative numbers than in the positive numbers. Hence the estimate $\theta_{t,1}$ is more likely to be adjusted upwards than downwards. In addition, if $|y_t|$ is large, then $\theta_{t,1}$ is adjusted by a relatively large amount. All this together explains why the estimates $\theta_{t,1}$ show a tendency to increase if $|y_t|$ is large, but not too large. (If $|y_t|$ is too large, the PE will be dominated by the PE due to the estimation error in the first component, hence $y_t(y_{t+1} - y^e_{t+1}$ will be negative, and $\theta_{t,1}$ will be adjusted downwards.)

The recursive representation (3.122) also explains why the estimates $\theta_{t,2}$ do not vary by much. This is a consequence of the fact that the scaling factor for the second component of $\boldsymbol{\theta}_t$, $1/r_t = x_t/r_t$, is small after a few periods and converges quite rapidly to zero. (Notice that the scaling factor y_t/r_t of the first component is larger for most t, in particular during a 'bubble' of the endogenous variable.)

To understand the strange fluctuation of the endogenous variable notice that $\theta_{t,1} \geq -0.75$ implies $\phi_1 + a\theta_{t,1} \leq -1$. Hence if $\theta_{t,1}$ exceeds -0.75, then the actual law of motion is unstable and the endogenous variable is likely to explode. In fact, as Figure 3.1 and Figure 3.2 show, this is exactly what happens, for example from period 100 to period 180. The estimates $\theta_{t,1}$ increase slowly beyond the boundary -0.75 and, after some 'reaction time', the endogenous variables begin to explode. On the other hand, as explained above, if the endogenous variables explode, the estimates $\theta_{t,1}$ will be adjusted into the proper direction. Hence if the estimates $\theta_{t,1}$ grow beyond the boundary -0.75, then, after some 'reaction time', they will be pushed back in direction of $\bar{\theta}_1$. Since the RE law of motion, $\bar{\theta}_1 = -8/9$, is stable the 'bubble' of the data process $\{y_t\}$ disappears when $\theta_{t,1}$ approaches $\bar{\theta}_1$.

However, $\theta_{t,1}$ does not get really close to $\bar{\theta}_1$. This is a consequence of the fact that if these estimates enter the parameter region which implies a stable law of motion, then the endogenous variables become small. Hence the scale of the adjustments becomes small and the estimates $\theta_{t,1}$ tend to stay in that region. This in turn implies that the PE is likely dominated by the PE due to the persistent bias of

$\theta_{t,2}$. Hence, as explained above, the estimates $\theta_{t,1}$ are likely to be adjusted upwards, hence are forced to leave the stability region, and a new 'bubble' begins.

Since the gains of the SG algorithm decrease rapidly (especially during a 'bubble') the feedback mechanism described above takes place 'in slow motion'. Moreover, it persists for a long time. We carried out simulation runs with a time horizon of 10,000 periods and at the end the same pattern was still present, although damped due to the large values of r_t. This finding indicates that a theoretical convergence result like Theorem 3.1 does not necessarily ensures a good performance of the learning procedure in practice.

Finally, we want to remark that the strange behaviour of the SG algorithm is (locally) stable in the sense that we can alter slightly the parameters and the initial values without changing the qualitative long-term behaviour of the dynamical system. We can also change the type of the exogenous inputs. For example, if $\{x_t\}$ is a stable ARMA process, then the same pattern occurs, however, not as concise as in the case $x_t \equiv 1$.

Chapter 4

Univariate Non-Stationary Models

4.1 Introduction

Generally, the subject of 'learning to become rational' is attached to stationary economic environments; and nearly all studies on this subject are restricted to the case that at least the exogenous variables entering the model are stationary and ergodic processes. Apart from questions of mathematical convenience this point of view is based on the idea that learning, as a repeated trial-and-error mechanism, requires a stable, or stationary, environment in order to be successful. How should agents learn something in a non-stationary environment?

As already mentioned in Chapter 1 this point of view falls short of a proper understanding of the basic problem. In the models usually considered agents do not learn about absolute (equilibrium) values or probabilities; rather they learn about the law of motion which governs the endogenous variable. In linear models this law of motion can be represented by a finite dimensional parameter and statistical parameter estimation procedures like the OLS algorithm or the SG algorithm can be employed as learning procedures. Of course, the use of these learning procedures makes sense only if the REE possesses a time-invariant law of motion[1], thus only if the *law of motion* is stationary.

[1]If the law of motion is time-varying other learning procedures have to be considered. BULLARD (1992), for example, considers a learning procedure based on the Kalman filter. He assumes that agents believe in an auxiliary model with time-

The involved time series themselves, however, do not have to be stationary processes. Moreover, sometimes it is easier to detect the law of motion if the involved time series are non-stationary. (As shown in Section 2.8 the rate of convergence is much higher in such a case.) In statistics this property is well-known, at least for the OLS algorithm, and the 'classical' case (stationary and ergodicity of all involved time series) is nowadays often treated only as a special case.

In this chapter we analyze whether these findings carry over to models with forecast feedback. It turns out that this is, in fact, the case if the influence of the forecast feedback is limited. The convergence analysis employed in this chapter differs from the one in the preceding chapters since it does not rely on the study of the evolution of the estimates directly; instead we consider the evolution of an associated stochastic Lyapunov function. Unfortunately, we did not fully succeed since we failed in verifying the conditions necessary to ensure convergence of the OLS estimates in the dynamic case. Hence our convergence results are restricted to the static case although computer simulations suggest that they hold as well in the dynamic case.

The remainder of this chapter is structured as follows. The basic assumptions are introduced in Section 2. Section 3 is devoted to the convergence analysis. In Section 4 we derive some convergence results in verifying the conditions of the results of Section 3 for some examples. It turns out that we can allow as exogenous variables beside the 'classical' ones all kinds of polynomial trends, autoregressive processes with unit roots, integrated and co-integrated processes, and combinations of them. This considerably extends the class of models the boundedly rational learning approach applies to. Since the performance of the OLS procedure in autoregressive models is not yet

---

varying parameters and, consequently, adopt a learning procedure which takes into account the time-varying nature of the parameters. Of course, one cannot expect this learning procedure to converge towards a REE since it is not designed to give consistent parameter estimates. Nevertheless, BULLARD argues that "if agents correctly view parameters as time-varying, however, the local convergence properties of least squares are, in general, overturned" (p. 166).

Notice that in his model the parameters are time-varying for the only reason that agents' predictions are time-varying during the learning phase. Hence the agents in his model are not actually 'more rational', as BULLARD claims. Although they recognize that parameters are time-varying they do not understand *why* parameters are time-varying. If they would really understand the time-varying nature of the parameters, they would not apply the Kalman filter learning procedure.

explored analytically in a satisfactory manner we finally present in Section 5 the findings of a Monte–Carlo study.

4.2 Basic Assumptions

We consider the same model as in Chapter 3

$$y_{t+1} = \phi' z_t + a y^e_{t+1} + w_{t+1}, \qquad t \geq 0, \tag{4.1}$$

with a few modifications. The meaning and the dimensions of the respective variables are the same as in Chapter 3 and are therefore not discussed any further. Our analysis relies on the following set of assumptions.

Assumption (A.1) (Behavioural Assumption)
Agents' predictions y^e_{t+1} are given as

$$y^e_{t+1} = \theta_t{}' z_t, \qquad t \geq 0, \tag{4.2}$$

with some initial value θ_0 and

$$\theta_t = \left(\sum_{s=0}^{t-1} z_s z_s' \right)^{-1} \sum_{s=0}^{t-1} z_s y_{s+1} \tag{4.3}$$

for $t \geq 1$ where our convention throughout this chapter is that stochastic inverses are defined as Moore–Penrose inverses, $Z^{-1}(\omega) = (Z(\omega))^+$.

Assumption (A.2) (Probabilistic Assumption)
The disturbance terms $\{w_t\}_{t \geq 1}$ form a MDS w.r.t. a filtration $\{\mathcal{F}_t\}_{t \geq 0}$ such that

$$\sup_{t \geq 0} \mathrm{E}\left[|w_{t+1}|^{2+\delta} \middle| \mathcal{F}_t \right] < \infty \qquad \text{a.s.} \tag{4.4}$$

for some fixed $\delta > 0$. The initial value θ_0 is assumed to be $\mathcal{F}_0$-measurable.

Assumption (A.3)
The random variables z_t are $\mathcal{F}_t$-measurable for all $t \geq 0$ and satisfy

$$\sum_{t=0}^{\infty} \|z_t\|^2 = \infty \qquad \text{a.s.} \tag{4.5}$$

and

$$T^* = \inf\{t \in I\!N \mid Z_t \text{ is nonsingular }\} < \infty \qquad \text{a.s.} \tag{4.6}$$

where Z_T is defined as $Z_T = \sum_{t=0}^{T} z_t z_t'$.

Again, Assumption (A.1) specifies the learning procedure agents follow. In this chapter we assume that agents employ the OLS learning procedure. Notice that with (4.3) we assume that agents know which time series determine the endogenous variable. Agents' predictions are thus based on the information set $I_t = \{y_t, z_t, \ldots, y_1, z_1, z_0, \theta_0\}$, where we assume that all time t variables are observable and known by agents at time t. As in Chapter 3 the vector z_t may contain sun-spot variables.

Since the matrix Z_t is singular for all $t < n - 1$ and may be so even for larger t we agree on the convention that the stochastic inverse is given as the Moore–Penrose inverse in order to ensure that θ_t is always well-defined and measurable on the full ω–space. In practice other conventions might be more convenient, such as replacing the matrix Z_t in (4.3) by $\epsilon I + Z_t$ with some small $\epsilon > 0$ for all $t \geq 0$. The resulting estimates, known as *recursive least squares (RLS) estimates*, differ slighly from the OLS estimates but the asymptotic behaviour is the same[2].

Assumption (A.2) is the same as in Chapter 2 and Chapter 3. As already mentioned in Chapter 2, the reason why we require w_t to have slightly more than bounded second (conditional) moments is, more or less, a didactical one. The slightly stronger assumption enables us to obtain slightly stronger convergence results and reduces the notational complexity in some proofs. The technique used to show convergence

[2]The RLS estimates are usually employed in Monte–Carlo studies to avoid the problems associated with singular matrices Z_t. In particular, the RLS estimates can be calculated recursively without any explicit matrix inversion. This considerably speeds up the calculation of the estimates.

applies also under the weaker assumption of bounded second (conditional) moments. But in that case we need slightly stronger assumptions on the variables z_t. This tradeoff will be described in more detail in Section 3.

Assumption (A.3) is a minimum assumption for the variables z_t. It should be noted that it is not sufficient for our convergence results to hold. But since the additional assumptions ensuring convergence arise quite naturally in the course of the convergence analysis in Section 3 we decided to introduce them later on. The conditions (4.5) and (4.6) are very weak in that they only require z_t not to vanish too rapidly as $t \to \infty$ and that there are no exact linear dependencies among the variables contained in z_t. Notice that the random time T^* is a stopping time w.r.t. $\{\mathcal{F}_t\}$.

Assumption (A.3) does not explicitly require the variables z_t to be exogenous. As it will become clear in the sequel the convergence analysis of this chapter relies, apart from measurability conditions, only upon algebraic properties of the time series $\{z_t\}$. Consequently, the convergence results will be stated in terms of these properties only. Of course, if z_t contains lagged endogenous variables these properties are endogenous. Unfortunately, and unlike to the preceding chapter, we are not able to verify these properties in the dynamic case. For that reason the z_t's should be regarded as exogenous in the sequel.

As in Chapter 3 rational expectations are unique in this model and determined by the parameter

$$\bar{\theta} = \frac{1}{1-a}\phi \tag{4.7}$$

provided that $a \neq 1$. We assume throughout this chapter that $a \neq 1$ holds.

4.3 Convergence Analysis

The main result of this section is

Theorem 4.3.1
Suppose that (A.1)–(A.3) are satisfied and $a < 1/2$. For $t \geq 0$ define

$$\lambda_t = z_t' Z_t^{-1} z_t. \tag{4.8}$$

If

$$\limsup_{t\to\infty} \lambda_t < \frac{1-2a}{(1-a)^2} \quad a.s., \tag{4.9}$$

then

$$\|\theta_{t+1} - \bar{\theta}\|^2 = O\left(\frac{\log \lambda_{max}(Z_t)}{\lambda_{min}(Z_t)}\right) \quad a.s.. \tag{4.10}$$

Hence Theorem 3.1 determines the order of convergence or divergence of the OLS estimates. Notice that $a < 1/2$ is necessary for condition (4.9) to make sense. The following corollary is obvious.

Corollary 4.3.2
Suppose that (A.1)–(A.3) are satisfied and $a < 1/2$. If the condition (4.9) holds, for example if $\lambda_t \to 0$ a.s., and

$$\log \lambda_{max}(Z_t) = o(\lambda_{min}(Z_t)) \quad a.s., \tag{4.11}$$

then $\theta_t \to \bar{\theta}$ a.s.

The proof of Theorem 3.1 is based on the analysis of the quadratic form

$$V_t = (\theta_t - \bar{\theta})' Z_{t-1} (\theta_t - \bar{\theta}). \tag{4.12}$$

We show that V_t is an extended stochastic Lyapunov function in the sense of LAI (1989), i.e. we show that V_t has some kind of 'almost-supermartingale' property. This enables us to apply a refinement of the almost-supermartingale convergence theorem of ROBBINS/SIEGMUND (1971) in order to show $V_{t+1} = O(\log \lambda_{max}(Z_t))$ a.s.

Proposition 4.3.3 (LAI (1989))
Let $\{w_t\}$ be a MDS w.r.t. some filtration $\{\mathcal{F}_t\}$ s.t. $\sup_{t\geq 0} \mathrm{E}[w_{t+1}^2|\mathcal{F}_t] < \infty$ a.s. Let V_t, α_t, β_t, η_t, and u_t be non-negative $\mathcal{F}_t$-measurable random variables such that $\sum_{t=0}^{\infty} \alpha_t < \infty$ a.s. Suppose that for $t \geq 0$

$$V_{t+1} \leq (1+\alpha_t)V_t + \beta_{t+1} - \eta_{t+1} + u_t w_{t+1} \qquad a.s. \tag{4.13}$$

(i) *On the event where $\sum_{t=1}^{\infty} \mathrm{E}[\beta_t|\mathcal{F}_{t-1}] < \infty$ holds true V_t converges a.s. and $\sum_{t=1}^{\infty} \mathrm{E}[\eta_t|\mathcal{F}_{t-1}] < \infty$ a.s.*

(ii) *For every $\alpha > 0$*

$$\max\left\{V_T, \sum_{t=1}^{T} \eta_t\right\} = O\left(\sum_{t=1}^{T} \beta_t + \left(\sum_{t=0}^{T-1} u_t^2\right)^{\frac{1}{2}+\alpha}\right) \qquad a.s. \tag{4.14}$$

We need some more auxiliary results. The following result is based on the local convergence theorem for martingales of CHOW (1965) and provides, jointly with Lemma 2.3.2, a kind of deterministic reduction for weighted sums of martingale difference sequences.

Lemma 4.3.4 (LAI/WEI (1982a))
Let $\{w_t\}$ be a MDS w.r.t. some filtration $\{\mathcal{F}_t\}$ s.t. $\sup_{t\geq 0} \mathrm{E}[w_{t+1}^2|\mathcal{F}_t] < \infty$ a.s. and let $\{u_t\}$ be a sequence of $\mathcal{F}_t$-adapted random variables. Then

$$\text{(i)} \quad \sum_{t=0}^{\infty} |u_t| w_{t+1}^2 < \infty \quad a.s. \text{ on the event } \left[\sum_{t=0}^{\infty} |u_t| < \infty\right],$$

$$\text{(ii)} \quad \sum_{t=0}^{T} |u_t| w_{t+1}^2 = o\left(\sum_{t=0}^{T} |u_t|\right)^{1+\alpha} \quad a.s. \text{ on } \left[\sum_{t=0}^{\infty} |u_t| = \infty\right] \quad \forall \alpha > 0.$$

If $\{w_t\}$ satisfies also $\sup_{t\geq 0} \mathrm{E}[|w_{t+1}|^{2+\delta}|\mathcal{F}_t] < \infty$ a.s. for some $\delta > 0$, then

$$\text{(iii)} \quad \sum_{t=0}^{T} |u_t| w_{t+1}^2 = O\left(\sum_{t=0}^{T} |u_t|\right) \quad a.s. \text{ on } \left[\sup_{t\geq 0} |u_t| < \infty, \sum_{t=0}^{\infty} |u_t| = \infty\right].$$

The next auxiliary result concerns the quadratic form λ_t. Notice that it is purely algebraic.

Lemma 4.3.5 (LAI/WEI (1982a))
Let (z_t) be a sequence of n-dimensional vectors. Let Z_t and T^* be defined as in Assumption (A.3) and λ_t by (4.8), resp. Suppose that $T^* < \infty$. Then

(4.15) $$\lambda_t = \frac{|Z_t| - |Z_{t-1}|}{|Z_t|} \qquad \text{for} \qquad t \geq T^*$$

and

(4.16) $$\sum_{t=0}^{T} \lambda_t = O\left(\log |Z_T|\right) = O\left(\log \lambda_{max}(Z_T)\right).$$

The following lemma shows that $\sum_{t=0}^{\infty} \lambda_t$ is a.s. unbounded under Assumption (A.3).

Lemma 4.3.6
Let $\{z_t\}$ be a sequence of random vectors in $I\!R^n$ such that (A.3) is satisfied. Then

(4.17) $$\sum_{t=0}^{\infty} z_t' Z_t^{-1} z_t = \infty \qquad a.s.$$

Proof
We argue pathwise. Since $T^* < \infty$ a.s. by Assumption (A.3) it is sufficient to show (4.17) with the sum starting at $t = T^*$. Let $t \geq T^*$. Since Z_t is symmetric and positive definite we know that

(4.18) $$z_t' Z_t^{-1} z_t \geq z_t' z_t \lambda_{min}(Z_t^{-1}) = \frac{z_t' z_t}{\lambda_{max}(Z_t)}$$

and since $\lambda_{max}(Z_t) \leq tr(Z_t)$ we obtain

(4.19) $$\sum_{t=T^*}^{\infty} z_t' Z_t^{-1} z_t \geq \sum_{t=T^*}^{\infty} \frac{z_t' z_t}{\sum_{s=0}^{t} z_s' z_s} = \infty.$$

The equality follows from the theorem of ABEL/DINI (Lemma 2.2.2) which can be applied since (4.5) holds. ■

Proof of Theorem 3.1

We argue pathwise separately for regular and singular Z_t. For fixed t let $t \geq T^*$. Then we have the following recursive representation for the OLS estimates (cf. (1.13))

$$\theta_{t+1} = \theta_t - (1-a)Z_t^{-1} z_t z_t'(\theta_t - \bar{\theta}) + Z_t^{-1} z_t w_{t+1}. \tag{4.20}$$

Hence

$$\theta_{t+1} - \bar{\theta} = \left[I - (1-a)Z_t^{-1} z_t z_t'\right](\theta_t - \bar{\theta}) + Z_t^{-1} z_t w_{t+1}. \tag{4.21}$$

Define

$$V_t = (\theta_t - \bar{\theta})' Z_{t-1} (\theta_t - \bar{\theta}). \tag{4.22}$$

Then we obtain

$$\begin{aligned} V_{t+1} &= (\theta_{t+1} - \bar{\theta})' Z_t (\theta_{t+1} - \bar{\theta}) \\ &= V_t + (\theta_t - \bar{\theta})' z_t z_t' (\theta_t - \bar{\theta}) + \lambda_t w_{t+1}^2 + u_t w_{t+1} \\ &\quad -(\theta_t - \bar{\theta})' \left[2(1-a) z_t z_t' - (1-a)^2 \lambda_t z_t z_t'\right](\theta_t - \bar{\theta}) \\ &= V_t + \lambda_t w_{t+1}^2 + u_t w_{t+1} \\ &\quad - \left[1 - 2a - (1-a)^2 \lambda_t\right] [z_t(\theta_t - \bar{\theta})]^2 \end{aligned} \tag{4.23}$$

with

$$u_t = 2[1 - (1-a)\lambda_t](\theta_t - \bar{\theta})' z_t. \tag{4.24}$$

Furthermore define

$$\begin{aligned} \tilde{\eta}_{t+1} &= [1 - 2a - (1-a)^2 \lambda_t][z_t'(\theta_t - \bar{\theta})]^2, \\ \eta_{t+1} &= (\tilde{\eta}_{t+1})^+, \quad \text{and} \\ \beta_{t+1} &= \lambda_t w_{t+1}^2 + (-\tilde{\eta}_{t+1})^+ \end{aligned} \tag{4.25}$$

to obtain

$$V_{t+1} = V_t + \beta_{t+1} - \eta_{t+1} + u_t w_{t+1} \tag{4.26}$$

on the event $[t \geq T^*]$.

If $0 \leq t < T^*$ we define V_{t+1} by (4.22) and set $\beta_{t+1} = V_{t+1}$, $\eta_{t+1} = V_t$, and $u_t = 0$. Also set $V_0 = 0$ for all ω. Then V_t, β_{t+1}, η_{t+1}, and u_t are well-defined random variables satisfying (4.26) and the measurability assumption of Proposition 3.3.

In order to verify the assumptions of Proposition 3.3 we remark first that $\tilde{\eta}_t(\omega) < 0$ only for finitely many t for almost all $\omega \in \Omega$. This is easily seen because

$$\tilde{\eta}_{t+1} \geq 0 \quad \Longleftrightarrow \quad \lambda_t \leq \frac{1-2a}{(1-a)^2}. \tag{4.27}$$

Hence in view of (4.9) we can infer that $\tilde{\eta}_t < 0$ only for finitely many t. This implies

$$\sum_{t=1}^{T} \beta_t = O\left(\sum_{t=0}^{T-1} \lambda_t w_{t+1}^2\right) + O(1) \qquad \text{a.s.} \tag{4.28}$$

From Lemma 3.6 we know that $\sum_0^\infty \lambda_t = \infty$ a.s. Hence, since $\lambda_t \leq n$, Lemma 3.4 (iii) and Lemma 3.5 jointly imply that

$$\sum_{t=1}^{T} \beta_t = O\left(\log \lambda_{max}(Z_{T-1})\right) \qquad \text{a.s.} \tag{4.29}$$

Now we determine the order of $\sum_0^T u_t^2$. Assumption (4.9) ensures that there exists a positive constant $\epsilon = \epsilon(\omega)$ such that $1 - 2a - (1 - a)^2\lambda_t > \epsilon$ for all but finitely many t. This implies that $u_t^2 \leq C\eta_{t+1}$ for all but finitely many t with some positive constant C. Hence

$$\sum_{t=0}^{T-1} u_t^2 = O\left(\sum_{t=1}^{T} \eta_t\right) \qquad \text{a.s.} \tag{4.30}$$

Now we can apply Proposition 3.3. We obtain

$$\max\left\{V_T, \sum_{t=1}^{T} \eta_t\right\} = O\left(\sum_{t=1}^{T} \beta_t + \left(\sum_{t=1}^{T} u_t^2\right)^{\frac{1}{2}+\alpha}\right) \qquad \text{a.s.} \tag{4.31}$$

for every $\alpha > 0$. Hence, in view of (4.29) and (4.30) with some $\alpha < 1/2$

$$\max\left\{V_T, \sum_{t=1}^{T} \eta_t\right\} = O\left(\log \lambda_{max}(Z_{T-1})\right) \qquad \text{a.s.} \tag{4.32}$$

Since

$$V_{T+1} = \left\| Z_T^{1/2}(\theta_{T+1} - \bar{\theta})\right\|^2 \geq \lambda_{min}(Z_T)\|\theta_{T+1} - \bar{\theta}\|^2 \tag{4.33}$$

we finally obtain

$$\|\theta_{T+1} - \bar{\theta}\|^2 = O\left(\frac{\log \lambda_{max}(Z_T)}{\lambda_{min}(Z_T)}\right) \qquad \text{a.s.} \tag{4.34}$$

and the proof is complete. ■

Since the proof of Theorem 3.1 applies in a pathwise manner we can formulate Theorem 3.1 also in the following way.

Theorem 4.3.7
Suppose that (A.1)–(A.3) are satisfied and $a < 1/2$. Then $\boldsymbol{\theta}_t \to \bar{\boldsymbol{\theta}}$ a.s. on the event where

$$(4.35)\quad \limsup_{t\to\infty} \lambda_t < \frac{1-2a}{(1-a)^2} \quad a.s. \quad and \quad \frac{\log \lambda_{max}(\boldsymbol{Z}_t)}{\lambda_{min}(\boldsymbol{Z}_t)} = o(1) \quad a.s.$$

Notice that Theorem 3.1 and Theorem 3.7 apply for any choice of random variables $\boldsymbol{z}_t$ such that Assumption (A.3) is satisfied. If $\boldsymbol{z}_t$ contains lagged endogenous variables the measurability condition of (A.3) is generically satisfied (provided that $\boldsymbol{y}_0$ is $\mathcal{F}_0$-measurable) and condition (4.5) is satisfied in view of Theorem A.7 in Appendix A. Usually, also condition (4.6) is satisfied. Nevertheless, Theorem 3.7 cannot be applied directly since the condition (4.35) is endogenous and has to be verified first. Unfortunately, we see no way in which this can be done. If $\boldsymbol{\theta}_t$ is already close to $\bar{\boldsymbol{\theta}}$ and the REE is a non-exploding ARX process it is possible to show that (4.35) holds true. Convergence of $\{\boldsymbol{\theta}_t\}$ is thus possible. Indeed, the computer simulations reported in Section 5 show that convergence actually occurs but a formal proof is still outstanding.

Remark
As already mentioned, there exists a tradeoff between the assumptions imposed on the disturbance terms and the order of $\boldsymbol{\theta}_t - \bar{\boldsymbol{\theta}}$. If we relax Assumption (A.2) and only require

$$(4.36)\qquad \sup_{t\geq 0} \mathrm{E}[w_{t+1}^2|\mathcal{F}_t] < \infty \qquad \text{a.s.}$$

we obtain by the same reasoning as in the proof of Theorem 3.1, but with Lemma 3.5 (ii) instead of (iii), the slightly weaker result

$$(4.37)\qquad ||\boldsymbol{\theta}_{T+1} - \bar{\boldsymbol{\theta}}||^2 = O\left(\frac{(\log \lambda_{max}(\boldsymbol{Z}_T))^{1+\delta}}{\lambda_{min}(\boldsymbol{Z}_T)}\right) \qquad \text{a.s.}$$

for every $\delta > 0$. Hence we can relax Assumption (A.2) only at the cost of imposing more restrictive conditions upon the variables $\boldsymbol{z}_t$.

4.4 Convergence Results

Although the convergence results of the preceding section are satisfactory from the mathematical point of view it is not yet clear which kind of time series $\{z_t\}$ satisfy the conditions of Theorem 3.1 and Corollary 3.2. In particular, it is not at all clear which time series imply the condition (4.9) for the quadratic form λ_t to hold. In this section we present some examples for which $\lambda_t \to 0$ a.s.

Corollary 4.4.1
Suppose that (A.1)-(A.3) are satisfied and $a < 1/2$. If

$$\frac{1}{T}\sum_{t=1}^{T} z_t z_t' \longrightarrow Z^* \qquad a.s. \tag{4.38}$$

with Z^* a (possibly path-dependent) positive definite matrix, then we have $\theta_t \to \bar{\theta}$ a.s.

Proof
We show first that $\lambda_t \to 0$ a.s. From Lemma 3.5 we know that for t sufficiently large

$$\lambda_t = z_t' Z_t^{-1} z_t = 1 - \frac{|Z_{t-1}|}{|Z_t|} = 1 - \left(\frac{t-1}{t}\right)^n \frac{|\frac{1}{t-1}Z_{t-1}|}{|\frac{1}{t}Z_t|}. \tag{4.39}$$

Hence in view of (4.38), $\lambda_t \to 0$ a.s. and condition (4.9) holds true. Moreover, (4.38) also implies $\lambda_{max}(Z_t) = O(\lambda_{min}(Z_t))$ a.s. Hence condition (4.11) is met and Corollary 3.2. applies. ■

Corollary 4.1 gives a result which is somewhat weaker than the results obtained by BRAY/SAVIN (1986) and KOTTMANN (1990) who show a.s. convergence under the parameter condition $a < 1$. This indicates that the approach proposed in this chapter is not optimal for this class of processes. Theorem 3.1, however, gives a slightly stronger result for the rate of convergence than the result $||\theta_t - \bar{\theta}||^2 = o(t^{-\pi})$ for every $\pi < 1$ obtained by KOTTMANN (1990).

As already mentioned in Chapter 3 the assumption of a stationary and ergodic environment considerably simplifies the analysis. In that case the property $\lambda_t \to 0$ a.s. ensures that the condition (4.9) of Theorem 3.1 is satisfied whenever $a < 1/2$. The property $\lambda_t \to 0$ a.s., however, relies crucially on the assumption (4.38) as shown in Example 3.5.3. If we dispense with this assumption and only require $\lambda_{max}(Z_t) = O(\lambda_{min}(Z_t))$ a.s. we can get lost of it.

But the property $\lambda_t \to 0$ a.s. does not necessarily get lost if we dispense with the assumption of stationarity and ergodicity. In the remainder of this section we show in some examples that weaker assumptions still imply $\lambda_t \to 0$ a.s.

First, notice that

$$\frac{\|z_t\|^2}{\lambda_{max}(Z_t)} \leq \lambda_t \leq \frac{\|z_t\|^2}{\lambda_{min}(Z_t)}. \tag{4.40}$$

Hence, if $\lambda_{max}(Z_t) = O(\lambda_{min}(Z_t))$ a.s., $\lambda_t \to 0$ a.s. holds true if, and only if, $\|z_t\|^2 = o(tr(Z_t))$ a.s. In the sequel we call processes satisfying this condition and condition (4.40) *stable processes.*

Next, consider the case that $\lambda_{max}(Z_t)$ and $\lambda_{min}(Z_t)$ are of different orders. If $\lambda_{max}(Z_t)$ grows a.s. at a geometrical rate, for instance if a component of z_t is an explosive autoregression, then $\|z_t\|^2/tr(Z_t) \not\to 0$ a.s. Hence $\lambda_t \not\to 0$ a.s. in that case.

Finally, notice that the condition $\|z_t\|^2 = o(\lambda_{min}(Z_t))$ a.s. is sufficient for $\lambda_t \to 0$ a.s. But this condition is not only difficult to verify in general (cf. Section 3.4) but it is also unnecessarily restrictive[3]. In the sequel we shall derive weaker conditions for $\lambda_t \to 0$ a.s. Our analysis relies on the following partitioning.

Suppose that there exists a partition $z_t' = (z_t^{1'}, \ldots, z_t^{m'})$ where z_t^i is $q_i \times 1$ and $\sum_1^m q_i = n$. For $i = 0, \ldots, m-1$ define $u_t^{i'} = (z_t^{i+1'}, \ldots, z_t^{m'})$

[3]The convergence result for the OLS procedure given by FOURGEAUD ET AL. (1986) relies heavily on that condition. Apart from this condition they assume that $a < 1/2$, $\lambda_{max}(Z_t) = O(\lambda_{min}(Z_t))$ a.s., and $E[z_t w_{t+1}] = 0$.

It is interesting that also FOURGEAUD ET AL. need the parameter condition $a < 1/2$ while the studies of BRAY/SAVIN (1986) and KOTTMANN (1990) only require $a < 1$. (However, since the latter studies rely crucially on the assumption of stationarity and ergodicity the result of FOURGEAUD ET AL. is not covered in its full scope by the results of the other authors.) The coincidence that FOURGEAUD ET AL. and we both need $a < 1/2$ possibly stems from the fact that their convergence analysis, as well as ours, relies only on algebraic properties of the involved time series.

and

$$Q_T^i = \sum_{t=0}^{T} u_t^i u_t^{i\prime}. \tag{4.41}$$

Also define

$$P_T^i = \sum_{t=0}^{T} z_t^i z_t^{i\prime} \tag{4.42}$$

for $i = 1, \ldots, m$.

Provided that the matrix Z_t can be partitioned in an appropriate way the following result shows that the behaviour of the quadratic form λ_t is determined by the behaviour of the same kind of quadratic forms involving only the subvectors u_t^i, z_t^i and the submatrices P_t^i, Q_t^i.

Theorem 4.4.2
Let $\{z_t\}$ be a sequence of n-dimensional random vectors. Suppose that the vectors z_t and the matrices Z_t can be partitioned as above such that

(i) $\lambda_{max}(P_t^i) = O\left(\lambda_{min}(Q_t^{i-1})\right)$ *a.s. for $i = 1, \ldots, m-1$,*

(ii) $\|z_t^i\|^2 = o\left(tr(P_t^i)\right)$ *a.s. for $i = 1, \ldots, m$, and*

(iii) $z_t^{m\prime}(P_t^m)^{-1} z_t^m \longrightarrow 0$ *a.s.*

Then $\lambda_t \to 0$ a.s.

The proof of Theorem 4.2 relies on the following result.

Lemma 4.4.3 (LAI/WEI (1983a))
Let A be a positive definite symmetric $n \times n$ matrix. Let A be partitioned as

$$A = \begin{pmatrix} P & H \\ H' & Q \end{pmatrix} \tag{4.43}$$

where P, Q are $p \times p$ and $q \times q$ matrices such that $n = p + q$. Then, for every $u \in \mathbb{R}^q$,

$$\begin{pmatrix} 0 \\ u \end{pmatrix}' A^{-1} \begin{pmatrix} 0 \\ u \end{pmatrix} \le u' Q^{-1} u \left(1 + \|A\|^{-1} tr(P)\right). \tag{4.44}$$

Proof of Theorem 4.2

Let u_t^i, z_t^i, P_t^i, and Q_t^i be defined as above. Then

$$\begin{aligned} z_t' Z_t^{-1} z_t &= \begin{pmatrix} z_t^1 \\ u_t^1 \end{pmatrix}' Z_t^{-1} \begin{pmatrix} z_t^1 \\ u_T^1 \end{pmatrix} \\ &\leq 2\begin{pmatrix} z_t^1 \\ \mathbf{o} \end{pmatrix}' (Q_t^0)^{-1} \begin{pmatrix} z_t^1 \\ \mathbf{o} \end{pmatrix} + 2\begin{pmatrix} \mathbf{o} \\ u_t^1 \end{pmatrix}' (Q_t^0)^{-1} \begin{pmatrix} \mathbf{o} \\ u_t^1 \end{pmatrix} \qquad (4.45) \end{aligned}$$

since $Z_t = Q_t^0$. For the first quadratic form we obtain using (i) and (ii)

$$\begin{aligned} \begin{pmatrix} z_t^1 \\ \mathbf{o} \end{pmatrix}' (Q_t^0)^{-1} \begin{pmatrix} z_t^1 \\ \mathbf{o} \end{pmatrix} &\leq \frac{\|z_t^1\|^2}{\lambda_{min}(Q_t^0)} \\ &= O\left(\frac{\|z_t^1\|^2}{tr(P_t^1)} \frac{\lambda_{max}(P_t^1)}{\lambda_{min}(Q_t^0)} \right) \qquad (4.46) \\ &= o(1) \qquad \text{a.s.} \end{aligned}$$

since $\lambda_{max}(P_t^1) \leq tr(P_t^1) \leq q_1 \lambda_{max}(P_t^1)$. Since

$$Q_t^0 = \begin{pmatrix} P_t^1 & H_t^1 \\ H_t^{1\prime} & Q_t^1 \end{pmatrix} \qquad (4.47)$$

with some matrix H_t^1 Lemma 4.3 implies for the second quadratic form in (4.45)

$$\begin{aligned} \begin{pmatrix} \mathbf{o} \\ u_t^1 \end{pmatrix}' (Q_t^0)^{-1} \begin{pmatrix} \mathbf{o} \\ u_t^1 \end{pmatrix} &\leq u_t^{1\prime} (Q_t^1)^{-1} u_t^1 \left(1 + \|Q_t^0\|^{-1} tr(P_t^1) \right) \\ &= O\left(u_t^{1\prime} (Q_t^1)^{-1} u_t^1 \left(1 + \frac{\lambda_{max}(P_t^1)}{\lambda_{min}(Q_t^0)} \right) \right) \qquad (4.48) \\ &= O\left(u_t^{1\prime} (Q_t^1)^{-1} u_t^1 \right) \qquad \text{a.s.} \end{aligned}$$

Because $u_t^{1\prime} = (z_t^{2\prime}, u_t^{2\prime})$ and Q_t^1 can be partitioned in the same manner as in (4.47) we can proceed inductively in the same way and finally obtain

$$z_t' Z_t^{-1} z_t = O\left(z_t^{m\prime} (P_t^m)^{-1} z_T^m \right) + o(1) \qquad \text{a.s.} \qquad (4.49)$$

Then condition (iii) implies the desired result. ∎

A first application of Theorem 4.2 is given in

Example 4.4.4
Let $\{x_t\}$ be a real valued stochastic process such that

$$\bar{x}_T := \frac{1}{T}\sum_{t=1}^{T} x_t \longrightarrow \mu \qquad \text{a.s.} \tag{4.50}$$

and

$$\frac{1}{T}\sum_{t=1}^{T}(x_t - \bar{x}_T)^2 \longrightarrow \sigma^2 \qquad \text{a.s.} \tag{4.51}$$

with some fixed $\mu \in \mathbb{R}$ and $\sigma^2 > 0$. Set $\boldsymbol{z}_t' = (x_t, t, t^2)$. Thus $\boldsymbol{z}_t$ contains a stationary and ergodic component x_t, a linear trend, and a quadratic trend. We partition $\boldsymbol{z}_t$ as $\boldsymbol{z}_t' = (z_t^1, z_t^2, z_t^3)$ with $z_t^1 = x_t$, $z_t^2 = t$, and $z_t^3 = t^2$. Hence $\boldsymbol{P}_T^1 = \sum_1^T x_t^2$, $\boldsymbol{P}_T^2 = \sum_1^T t^2$, $\boldsymbol{P}_T^3 = \sum_1^T t^4$, and $\boldsymbol{Q}_T^i$ is given as in (4.41). In view of Theorem 4.2 we have to verify the following conditions.

(i) $\sum_{t=1}^{T} x_t^2 = O(\lambda_{min}(\boldsymbol{Z}_T))$ a.s.,

(ii) $\sum_{t=1}^{T} t^2 = O(\lambda_{min}(\boldsymbol{Q}_T^1))$ a.s.,

(iii) $x_T^2 = o\left(\sum_{t=1}^{T} x_t^2\right)$ a.s.,

(iv) $T^2 = o\left(\sum_{t=1}^{T} t^2\right)$, and

(v) $T^4 = o\left(\sum_{t=1}^{T} t^4\right)$.

Since

$$\sum_{t=1}^{T} t^{\pi} = \left(\frac{1}{\pi+1} + o(1)\right) T^{\pi+1} \tag{4.52}$$

for every $\pi \geq 0$ the conditions (iv) and (v) are obvious. Since $\{x_t\}$ is stationary and ergodic (iii) holds. Hence only (i) and (ii) have to be verified. To show (i) define

$$D_T = \begin{pmatrix} T & 0 & 0 \\ 0 & T^3 & 0 \\ 0 & 0 & T^5 \end{pmatrix}. \tag{4.53}$$

We shall show that

$$D_T^{-1/2} Z_T D_T^{-1/2} \longrightarrow Z^* \tag{4.54}$$

with some positive definite matrix Z^*. Hence we show that $\lambda_{min}(Z_T)$ and $\lambda_{min}(D_T) = T$ are of the same order such that (i) follows.

Next, we calculate the entries of the matrix $D_T^{-1/2} Z_T D_T^{-1/2}$. In view of (4.52) only three terms have to be calculated. In ZENNER (1995) it is shown that

$$\sum_{t=1}^{T} x_t^2 = \left(\sigma^2 + \mu^2 + o(1)\right) T \qquad \text{a.s.} \tag{4.55}$$

and

$$\sum_{t=1}^{T} t x_t = \left(\frac{\mu}{2} + o(1)\right) T^2 \qquad \text{a.s.} \tag{4.56}$$

Using these results it is easy to show via partial summation that

$$\sum_{t=1}^{T} t^2 x_t = \left(\frac{\mu}{3} + o(1)\right) T^3 \qquad \text{a.s.} \tag{4.57}$$

Hence

$$D_T^{-1/2} Z_T D_T^{-1/2} = \begin{pmatrix} \sigma^2 + \mu^2 & \mu/2 & \mu/3 \\ \mu/2 & 1/3 & 1/4 \\ \mu/3 & 1/4 & 1/5 \end{pmatrix} + o(1) \qquad \text{a.s.} \tag{4.58}$$

With some elementary calculations it is readily shown that the determinant of this matrix is positive (although very small). Hence $\lambda_{min}(D_t^{-1/2} Z_T D_T^{-1/2}) > 0$ a.s. and (i) follows. To show (ii) remove the first row and the first column of Z_t and D_T and proceed in the same manner as above.

Then Theorem 4.2. gives $\lambda_t \to 0$ a.s. Since

$$\frac{\log \lambda_{max}(\boldsymbol{Z}_T)}{\lambda_{min}(\boldsymbol{Z}_T)} = O\left(\frac{\log T^5}{T}\right) = o(1) \qquad \text{a.s.} \tag{4.59}$$

Corollary 3.2 implies $\boldsymbol{\theta}_t \to \bar{\boldsymbol{\theta}}$ a.s. if $a < 1/2$.

We like to remark that Example 4.4 can be generalized in order to allow $\boldsymbol{x}_t$ to be multivariate under conditions analogous to (4.50) and (4.51). Of course, the verification of the conditions (i)–(iii) of Theorem 4.2 requires some additional (matrix) techniques. Instead of going into those details we want to give some other examples. The first one concerns co-integrated processes.

Example 4.4.5
Suppose that $\boldsymbol{z}_t' = (z_{t,1}, z_{t,2})$ where $z_{t,1}$, $z_{t,2}$ are integrated and co-integrated. For convenience we assume that $z_{t,1}$, $z_{t,2}$ are first order integrated, hence $z_{t,1} - \alpha z_{t,2}$ is a stationary (and ergodic) process for some $\alpha \neq 0$. Using Lemma 3.4.3 it is easy to show that

$$\liminf_{T\to\infty} \frac{1}{T}\lambda_{min}(\boldsymbol{Z}_T) > 0 \quad \text{a.s. and} \quad \lambda_{max}(\boldsymbol{Z}_T) = O(T^2) \quad \text{a.s.} \tag{4.60}$$

In order to apply Theorem 4.2 we have to transform the time series $\{\boldsymbol{z}_t\}$ in a suitable manner since Theorem 4.2 cannot be applied directly. Define $\tilde{\boldsymbol{z}}_t$ by $\tilde{\boldsymbol{z}}_t = \boldsymbol{C}\boldsymbol{z}_t$ with

$$\boldsymbol{C} = \begin{pmatrix} 1 & -\alpha \\ 0 & 1 \end{pmatrix}. \tag{4.61}$$

Then it is obvious that $\tilde{z}_{t,1} = z_{t,1} - \alpha z_{t,2}$ is stationary and ergodic while $\tilde{z}_{t,2}$ is first order integrated. In order to apply Theorem 4.2 we have to verify the conditions (i)–(iii). Since $\tilde{z}_{t,1}$ is stationary and ergodic and in view of (4.60) the conditions (i) and (ii) are evidently satisfied. Using well-known properties of integrated processes (see, e.g., BANERJEE ET AL. (1993)) it is not difficult to show (iii). Then we can apply Theorem 4.2 and obtain

$$\tilde{\boldsymbol{z}}_T' \left(\sum_{t=0}^{T} \tilde{\boldsymbol{z}}_t \tilde{\boldsymbol{z}}_t'\right)^{-1} \tilde{\boldsymbol{z}}_T \longrightarrow 0 \qquad \text{a.s.} \tag{4.62}$$

Clearly, this is equivalent to $\lambda_t \to 0$ a.s. If $a < 1/2$, then $\boldsymbol{\theta}_t \to \bar{\boldsymbol{\theta}}$ a.s. follows from Corollary 3.2.

Notice that also this example can be generalized to multivariate co-integrated processes and to co-integrated processes of different orders provided that multi-collinearities can be ruled out.

Another class of stochastic processes popular in economics, especially in macro-economics, are unit root autoregressive processes. We show in the following example that also these processes satisfy the assumptions of Corollary 3.2.

Example 4.4.6
Let $\{x_t\}$ be a real valued *AR(p)* process driven by a MDS which is independent of $\{\mathcal{F}_t\}$ and satisfies an assumption analogous to (A.2). Suppose furthermore that the characteristic polynomial of this process possesses roots inside and on the unit circle. Let ρ be the largest multiplicity of all the distinct roots on the unit circle and set $\boldsymbol{z}_t{}' = (x_t, \ldots, x_{t-p+1})$. Then it is well-known (cf. LAI/WEI (1985)) that

$$\lambda_{max}(Z_T) = O\left(T^{2\rho} \log\log T\right) \quad \text{a.s.} \tag{4.63}$$

and

$$\liminf_{T\to\infty} \frac{1}{T}\lambda_{min}(Z_T) > 0 \quad \text{a.s.} \tag{4.64}$$

Moreover, it is well-known that also $\lambda_t \to 0$ a.s. in that case. Hence Corollary 3.2 gives $\boldsymbol{\theta}_t \to \bar{\boldsymbol{\theta}}$ a.s. if $a < 1/2$.

We like to remark that Example 4.6 can be generalized to allow x_t to be a multivariate autoregressive process.

These three examples suggest that the convergence analysis of Section 3 applies for a large class of (stochastic) processes $\{\boldsymbol{z}_t\}$. It is not our aim to determine the scope of this analysis in all detail but we believe that it applies for any time series $\{\boldsymbol{z}_t\}$ consisting of stable processes, integrated processes, co-integrated processes, and polynomial trends as long as there are no linear dependencies among the components of $\boldsymbol{z}_t$ and, in case of various co-integrated processes and in view of Example 4.4.5, among the components of $\tilde{\boldsymbol{z}}_t$.

4.5 Simulation Results

As already mentioned several times the main shortcoming of the convergence analysis in this chapter is that it does not apply properly to autoregressive models. For these models we only know from Theorem 3.7 that $\boldsymbol{\theta}_t \to \bar{\boldsymbol{\theta}}$ a.s. on the event where

$$(4.65) \quad \frac{\log \lambda_{max}(Z_t)}{\lambda_{min}(Z_t)} = o(1) \quad \text{a.s. and} \quad \limsup_{t\to\infty} \lambda_t < \frac{1-2a}{(1-a)^2} \quad \text{a.s.}$$

Since the probability of this event is endogenously determined and we have no results how to determine this probability this result is not yet satisfactory.

In Chapter 3 we faced a similar kind of problem. The main convergence result, Theorem 3.3.1, incorporated as a central requirement the PEC to hold. With the condition analysis in Section 3.4 we verified that the PEC holds under suitable parameter conditions. Unfortunately, this condition analysis does not carry over to the case that the estimates are given by the OLS procedure. A reexamination of the respective proofs in Section 3.3 and 3.4 shows that the convergence analysis as well as the condition analysis for the SG algorithm relies crucially on the property

$$(4.66) \qquad \sum_{t=0}^{\infty} \frac{[(\boldsymbol{\theta}_t - \bar{\boldsymbol{\theta}})' \boldsymbol{z}_t]^2}{r_t} < \infty \qquad \text{a.s.}$$

which is provided by the almost-supermartingale convergence theorem. If there were a way to show this property also for the OLS algorithm in autoregressive models, then at least the condition analysis of Section 3.4 would carry over without any change. But, unfortunately, the process $\{||\boldsymbol{\theta}_t - \bar{\boldsymbol{\theta}}||^2\}$ does not possess the almost-supermartingale property if the estimates are given by the OLS procedure, and we see no other way to show (4.66). We therefore carried out some computer simulations to explore which parameter conditions ensure the event (4.65) to be a.s. In this section we present our findings.

4.5.1 The Model

In order to gain some intuition and not to obscure the fundamental properties of the dynamical system $(y_t, \boldsymbol{\theta}_t)$ with too much complexity we started our simulations with the simplest ARX model where

$z_t' = (y_t, x_t)$ with x_t a univariate exogenous variable. As exogenous variable we employed either stable stochastic processes (stable ARMA processes or i.i.d. sequences) or deterministic series (a constant or a polynomial trend). As disturbance terms we employed i.i.d. sequences, either $N(0,1)$-distributed or $U(-1,1)$-distributed. The initial values y_0, θ_0 were chosen to be deterministic.

In order to check our findings for the simple model we also carried out simulations for higher-dimensional models (where z_t includes several lagged endogenous variables and multivariate exogenous variables). It turned out that the simple model already exhibits all important kinds of long-term behaviour.

4.5.2 The Calculations

For the simple model the calculations were performed using a XLISP-program within the statistical environment XLISPSTAT. In order to speed up the calculations for the higher-dimensional models we employed a program[4] written in the language C. The calculations of the inverse matrix Z_t^{-1} were performed in two different ways. For the simple model we employed two initial values θ_0 and θ_1 and calculated the inverse of Z_1 (which is generically regular) using the inversion subroutine contained in XLISPSTAT. For the higher-dimensional models we used the Kalman filter representation

$$Z_t^{-1} = Z_{t-1}^{-1} - \frac{1}{1 + z_t' Z_{t-1}^{-1} z_t} Z_{t-1}^{-1} z_t z_t' Z_{t-1}^{-1} \tag{4.67}$$

to compute the inverse recursively without any explicit matrix inversion. We started the recursion with an initial value $Z_{-1}^{-1} = \beta I$ with some $\beta > 0$. This kind of calculation has proved to be favourable for the higher-dimensional models since it is quick and does not rely on any inversion algorithm.

4.5.3 Preliminary Results

We observed that the qualitative long-term behaviour of the dynamical system (y_t, θ_t) is not affected by the distribution of the disturbance terms and the type of the calculation of the inverse. In addition, the

[4] We are grateful to THOMAS SIWIK for writing this program.

qualitative long-term behaviour is also independent of the choice of $\beta > 0$ if the inverse matrix is calculated recursively. Large values of β, however, generally improve the performance of the OLS algorithm[5].

Furthermore, the performance of the OLS algorithm depends on the exogenous variables only via algebraic properties. More precisely, we observed that the same long-term behaviour for the choices $x_t \equiv 1$, $\{x_t\}$ i.i.d., and $\{x_t\}$ a stable ARMA process. But the performance is altered if the exogenous variables are chosen to be non-stationary, i.e. $x_t = t^\mu$ with some $\mu > 0$ (see the results below).

4.5.4 Convergence Results

Since autoregressive models show very different long-term behaviour depending on whether the roots of the characteristic polynomial lie inside, on, or outside the unit circle and, in addition, non-stationary exogenous variables affect the long-term behaviour sometimes in a crucial way we have to distinguish several cases. Before going into details, we mention the features which are common to all the different cases.

Firstly, if $a > 1$ both the estimation process $\{\theta_t\}$ and the data process $\{y_t\}$ explode with increasing speed. This finding coincides with findings in the static case reported by BRAY/SAVIN (1986).

Secondly, if $a \leq -1$ there is always the *risk of explosion* as described in Chapter 2. We observed, for the same initial values and the same realizations of the exogenous variables, as well convergent as divergent trajectories of the estimation process. It thus depends on the respective trajectory of the disturbance process whether the estimates converge or diverge.

If $-a$ or $||\theta_0 - \bar{\theta}||$ is increased, then the risk of explosion increases. More precisely, if one of these values was increased, we observed more and more exploding trajectories. In order to gain some intuition we want to quote that for $a < -4$ we always observed exposions, even if $\theta_0 = \bar{\theta}$. For $a = -4$, however, we observed some convergent trajectories.

[5] As mentioned by GRAUPE (1984, p. 73), "β should be sufficiently below the square root of the maximum computer word. In pactice, the identification algorithms are not too sensitive to a choice of β which may range from $\beta = 5$ to 10,000. There is little point to go beyond $\beta = 100$".

Now we turn to the different cases. Since the long-term behaviour is already described for the cases $a > 1$ and $a \leq -1$ the following considerations all concern the case $|a| < 1$.

The Case of Stable Roots

If the characteristic polynomial possesses roots only inside the unit circle we observed the following.

- If the vector z_t contains no exogenous variables or only stable exogenous variables in the sense that

$$(4.68)\quad \lambda_{max}\left(\sum_{t=0}^{T} x_t x_t'\right) = O\left(\lambda_{min}\left(\sum_{t=0}^{T} x_t x_t'\right)\right) = O(T) \quad \text{a.s.}$$

  and

$$(4.69)\qquad \frac{\|x_T\|^2}{\sum_{t=0}^{T}\|x_t\|^2} = o(1) \qquad \text{a.s.,}$$

  then $\theta_t \to \bar{\theta}$ seems to hold with probability one regardless of the initial values chosen.

  If $a < 1/2$, convergence proceeds quite rapidly, i.e., as suggested by Theorem 3.1, $\|\theta_t - \bar{\theta}\| = O(\log t/t)$. If $a \geq 1/2$, the rate of convergence is much slower and it is not always obvious whether the estimation process actually converges, especially if the initial values are chosen far-off the REE parameter (see Figure 4.1). This finding coincides, again, with the findings for the static case reported by BRAY/SAVIN (1986) for which it is known that $\|\theta_t - \bar{\theta}\| = O(1/t^{1-a})$. Hence, if a is close to one, then the rate of convergence is very slow. We believe that the same rate of convergence holds for the stable dynamic case (see Theorem 2.8.4 for the special case of an univariate first order autoregression).

- If z_t includes non-stationary exogenous variables, for example polynomial trends, then the restriction $a < 1/2$ is quite decisive. More precisely, only for the case $a < 1/2$ we observed convergence of the estimation process. Again, convergence is not affected by the choice of the initial values. As determined by Theorem 3.1 the rate of convergence is $\|\theta_t - \bar{\theta}\| = O(\log t/t)$, provided that the exogenous variables grow at most at a polynomial rate.

If $a \geq 1/2$, then the estimates do not seem to converge. But they do not explode either. Mostly, the estimates seem to converge to some biased value. But we also observed both estimates moving slowly away from the REE parameters (see Figure 4.2).

- In the case of convergence we always observed $|y_t - y_t^e| = O(1)$.

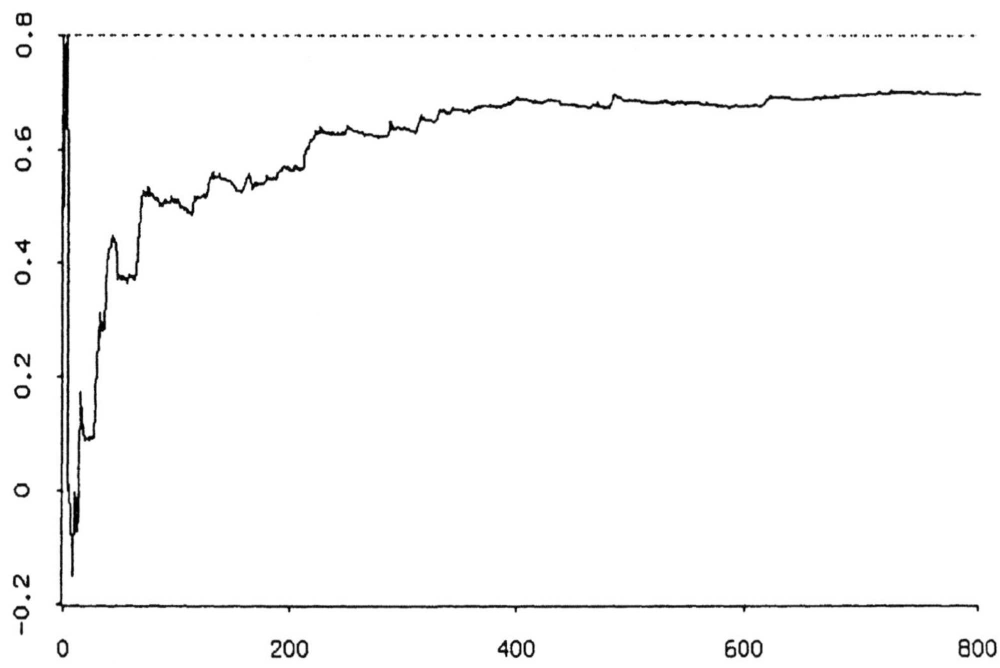

Figure 4.1: The evolution of $\theta_{t,1}$ with $a = 0.75$ and $\{x_t\}$ a stable ARMA process

The Case of Unit Roots

If the characteristic polynomial possesses roots inside and/or on the unit circle we observed the following.

- If $a < 1/2$, then convergence takes place regardless of the initial values chosen and of the exogenous variables, provided that they grow at most at a polynomial rate. If $a \geq 1/2$, then at least some components of $\boldsymbol{\theta}_t$ do not converge to the respective REE parameter values. These components seem either to converge to some biased value or even diverge very slowly.

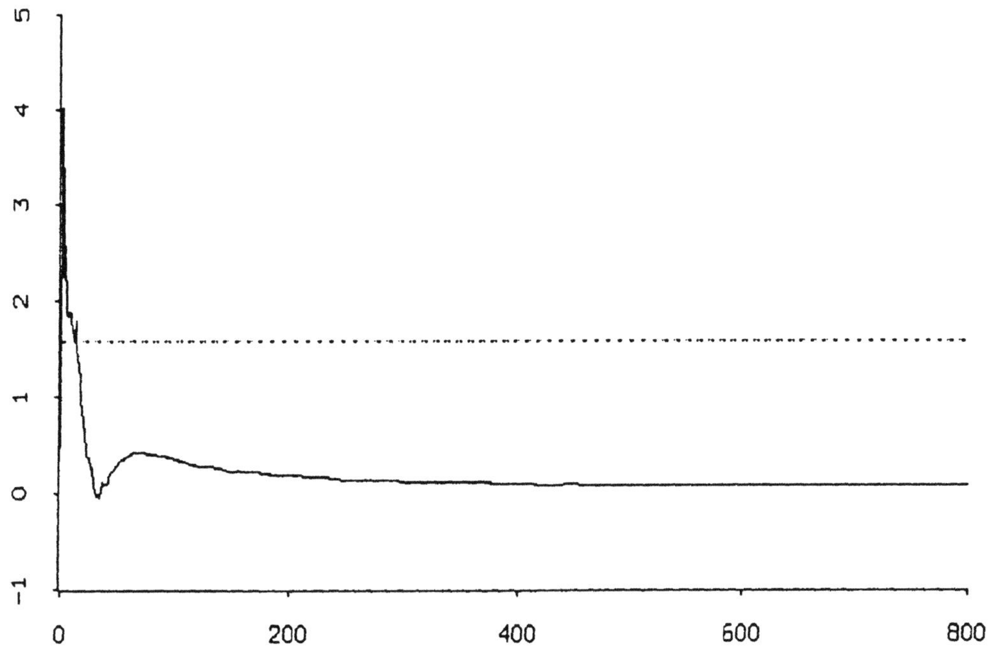

Figure 4.2: The evolution of $\theta_{t,2}$ with $a = 0.75$ and $x_t = \sqrt{t}$

- The rate of convergence differs for several subcases. If the exogenous variables grow at most at a polynomial rate, we have $\lambda_{max}(Z_t) = O(t^\nu)$ with some $\nu \geq 1$, hence $\log(\lambda_{max}(Z_t)) = O(\log t)$. If either the characteristic polynomial possesses roots inside the unit circle or z_t contains stable exogenous variables, then the minimum order of $\lambda_{min}(Z_t)$ is $O(t)$. Hence $\|\theta_t - \bar{\theta}\| = O(\log t/t)$ by Theorem 3.1. Otherwise the order of $\lambda_{min}(Z_t)$ is larger and convergence proceeds more quickly.

  This theoretical reasoning coincides with our observations. Figure 4.3 and Figure 4.4. show two typical trajectories of $\{\theta_{t,2}\}$ for the simple model with $x_t = 1$ and with $x_t = \sqrt{t}$, resp. It is obvious that in the latter case the estimates converge more rapidly.

- In the case of convergence we always observed $|y_t - y_t^e| = O(1)$. The PE thus remains bounded. This is a remarkable fact since the data process $\{y_t\}$ is not stable in case of unit roots.

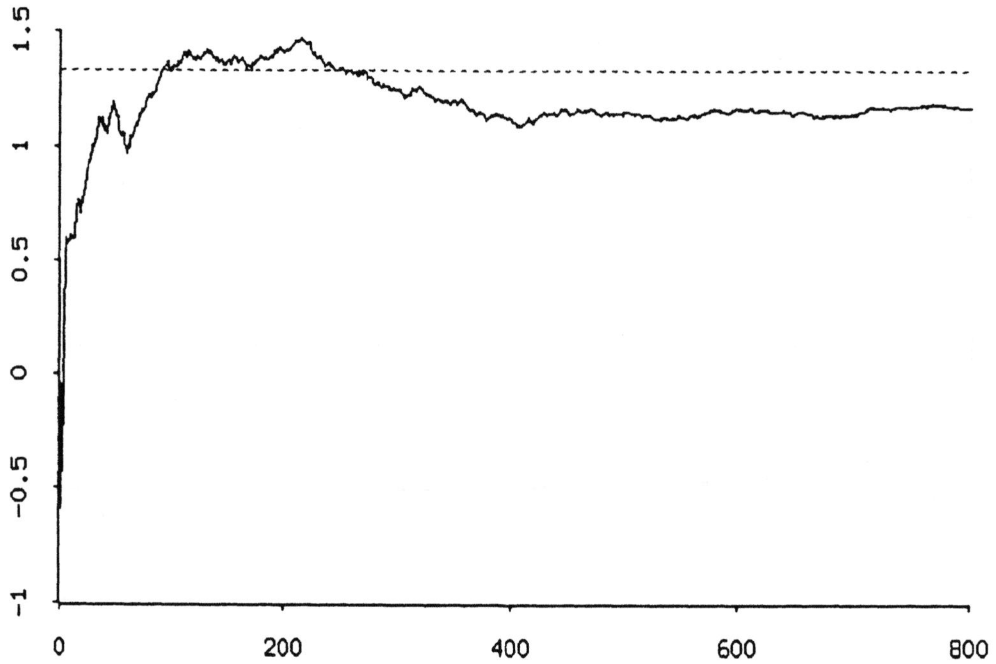

Figure 4.3: The evolution of $\theta_{t,2}$ with $a = 0.25$ and $x_t = 1$

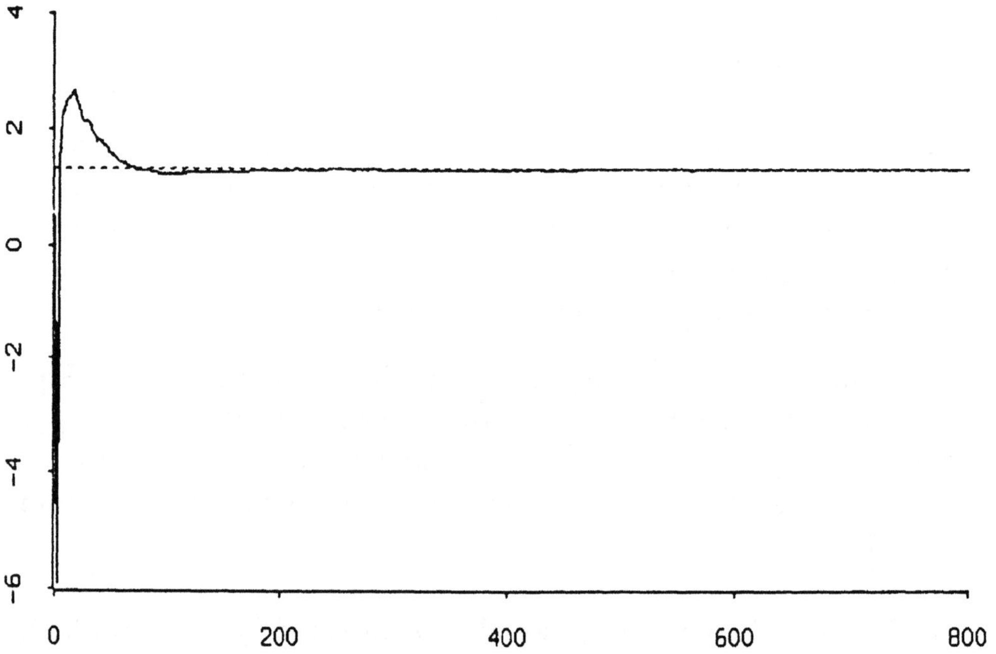

Figure 4.4: The evolution of $\theta_{t,2}$ with $a = 0.25$ and $x_t = \sqrt{t}$

The Case of Explosive Roots

If the characteristic polynomial possesses roots outside the unit circle we observed the following.

- The restriction $a < 1/2$ is crucial in this case. Moreover, the condition (4.9) takes effect. If it is violated, then at least some components of $\boldsymbol{\theta}_t$ do not converge.

  For the simple model with $\boldsymbol{z}_t' = (y_t, x_t)$ and $\{x_t\}$ satisfying $x_t^2 = o(\sum_0^t x_\tau^2)$ condition (4.9) is equivalent to

  $$\frac{\bar{\theta}_1^2 - 1}{\bar{\theta}_1^2} < \frac{1-2a}{(1-a)^2} \tag{4.70}$$

  with $|\bar{\theta}_1| > 1$ where $\bar{\theta}_1$ is the only root of the characteristic polynomial. To see that λ_t converges to the l.h.s. of (4.70) on the event $[\boldsymbol{\theta}_t \to \bar{\boldsymbol{\theta}}]$ notice that, firstly, using the decomposition technique of Theorem 4.2 it is possible to show that $\lambda_t = y_t^2 / \sum_0^t y_\tau^2 + o(1)$. Secondly, since the influence of the exogenous variable x_t becomes negligible as t increases the process $\{y_t\}$ behaves like an exploding univariate autoregression as considered in Appendix A, and Theorem A.13 implies that the l.h.s. of (4.70) is the limit point of $y_t^2 / \sum_0^t y_\tau^2$.

  Again, this theoretical reasoning coincides exactly with our observations for the simple model. Whenever condition (4.70) was violated we observed divergent trajectories of $\{\theta_{t,2}\}$. Notice, however, that $|a| < 1$ seems to imply that $\theta_{t,1}$ always converges towards the REE parameter.

- If condition (4.70) is satisfied, then $\boldsymbol{\theta}_t \to \bar{\boldsymbol{\theta}}$ seems to hold with probability one regardless of the type of exogenous variables, provided that they increase at most at a polynomial rate. This is somewhat surprising if $\{x_t\}$ is a stable process since then $\lambda_{min}(\boldsymbol{Z}_t)$ is of order $O(t)$ and Theorem 3.1 only gives $\|\boldsymbol{\theta}_t - \bar{\boldsymbol{\theta}}\| = O(1)$. Indeed, in this case the rate of convergence of $\theta_{t,2}$ is quite slow. On the other hand, it is well-known (cf. LAI/WEI (1983a)) that the OLS estimates are strongly consistent in autoregressive models without forecast feedback no matter of the roots of the characteristic polynomial. If there are roots inside and outside the unit circle, then $\log \lambda_{max}(\boldsymbol{Z}_t)$ and $\lambda_{min}(\boldsymbol{Z}_t)$ are of the same order $O(t)$ and also in this case Theorem 3.1 only gives

$||\theta_t - \bar{\theta}||^2 = O(1)$ a.s. (Notice that Theorem 3.1 covers the case of no forecast feedback, $a = 0$.)

- If the exogenous variable x_t is a polynomial trend, the rate of convergence is better. Of course, this is what Theorem 3.1 suggests since $\lambda_{min}(Z_t)$ is of higher order than $O(t)$.
- Again, in case of convergence we always observed $|y_t - y_t^e| = O(1)$. This finding is much more remarkable than in the preceding case since in case of roots outside the unit circle the data process $\{y_t\}$ diverges at a geometrical rate. The RPE thus converges at a geometrical rate.

The computer simulations show that the static case and the dynamic case differ in some important features. Firstly, the risk of explosion, thus convergence with positive but not unit probability, is exclusive to the dynamical case. Hence the forcast feedback *can* destabilize the whole system but it *need not.* In order to avoid the risk of explosion we have to restrict the influence of the forecast feedback to $|a| < 1$ in the stable dynamic case.

In the unstable dynamic case (thus if the REE is an autoregressive process with roots on or outside the unit circle or the exogenous variables are non-stationary) the influence of the forecast feedback has to be even smaller in order to ensure a.s. convergence of the OLS learning procedure. More precisely, if the REE is unstable and the components of z_t grow at different rates, then we need at least $-1 < a < 1/2$.

In the explosive case the influence of the forecast feedback has to be even smaller. For first order autoregressive processes condition (4.70) seems to be necessary and sufficient for convergence. For higher order autoregressive processes the l.h.s. of (4.70) has to be replaced by the respective limit point of $\bar{\lambda}_t$ with $\bar{\lambda}_t$ defined as in (4.8) with z_t replaced by the respective REE $\bar{z}_t$. This limit point is usually difficult to determine but, based on the simulation results, we conjecture that it is given by (4.70) with θ_1 the absolute value of the largest root of the characteristic polynomial.

In order to conclude this chapter we like to remark that the parameter condition $a < 1/2$, which is, first of all, a consequence of the Lyapunov function approach, is actually a necessary condition in several cases. Hence, understanding the parameter a as the derivative of the feedback function, the idea that if the feedback is damped in the sense that $|a| < 1$, then agents eventually learn the REE parameter with probability one is misleading in the non-stationary case.

Chapter 5

Multivariate ARX Models

5.1 Introduction

Fairly realistic economic models usually have to explain the outcome of more than one variable. In these models the evolution of several endogenous variables is described simultaneously by a set of equations. Here and in the following chapter we consider such multivariate, or simultaneous equations, models and analyze whether agents, following an appropriate learning procedure, can eventually learn the parameters of a REE. Since our analysis is based on the reduced form equation we assume that these models are complete such that a transition to the reduced form is possible.

The multivariate stable static case has already been analyzed by KOTTMANN (1990) and MOHR (1990). In this chapter we therefore consider the multivariate dynamic case. This case has been analyzed by MARCET/SARGENT (1989a,b) and KUAN/WHITE (1994) but, as already mentioned in Chapter 1, only in the local sense. In order to obtain global convergence results we generalize the results of Chapter 3 and consider as learning procedure a multivariate version of the SG algorithm.

It turns out that the generalization is essentially straightforward and requires only little additional considerations. The notation, however, is more cumbersome than in Chapter 3 since agents have to learn a parameter matrix instead of a parameter vector. Most results of Chapter 3 carry over more or less directly to the multivariate case. We therefore omit formal proofs wherever they are straightforward.

This chapter is arranged analogously to Chapter 3. After introducing the basic assumptions in Section 2 we develop the convergence analysis in Section 3. Since the convergence results rely on the PEC we continue with the condition analysis in Section 4. Section 5 then provides the convergence results and in Section 6 we present as an application a macroeconomic example.

5.2 Basic Assumptions

We consider the multivariate version of the model (3.1) given by its reduced form equation

$$y_{t+1} = \Phi z_t + A y^e_{t+1} + w_{t+1}, \qquad t \geq 0, \tag{5.1}$$

where the random variables and parameters have the following dimensions.

- y_t is $k \times 1$,
- z_t is $n \times 1$,
- w_t is $k \times 1$,
- Φ is $k \times n$, and
- A is $k \times k$

with $k \geq 1$ and $n \geq 1$. The respective variables have the same meaning as in Chapter 3 and are therefore not discussed any further. The vector z_t may contain lagged endogenous variables as well as exogenous variables, i.e.

$$z'_t = (y'_t, \ldots, y'_{t-p+1}, x'_t) \in \mathbb{R}^{pk+q} \tag{5.2}$$

with $p \geq 0$, $q \geq 0$, and $kp + q = n$. In order to rule out linear dependencies among the components of z_t we assume that y_t contains no lagged endogenous variables. Finally, we allow z_t to contain sunspot variables.

Assumption (A.1)
Agents' predictions y^e_{t+1} are componentwise given as

$$y^e_{t+1,i} = z_t'\theta^i_t, \qquad i = 1, \ldots, k, \qquad t \geq 0, \tag{5.3}$$

where the estimates θ^i_t are recursively given by

$$\theta^i_{t+1} = \theta^i_t + \frac{1}{r_t} z_t (y_{t+1,i} - y^e_{t+1,i}), \qquad i = 1, \ldots, k, \quad t \geq 0, \tag{5.4}$$

with $r_t = \sum_{s=0}^t z_s' z_s$. The initial values $\theta^1_0, \ldots, \theta^k_0$ may be random.

Assumption (A.2)
The disturbance terms $\{w_t\}_{t \geq 1}$ form a k-dimensional MDS w.r.t. a filtration $\{\mathcal{F}_t\}_{t \geq 0}$ such that

$$\sup_{t \geq 0} \mathrm{E}\left[\|w_{t+1}\|^{2+\delta} \middle| \mathcal{F}_t \right] < \infty \qquad \text{a.s.} \tag{5.5}$$

with some fixed $\delta > 0$ and

$$\liminf_{T \to \infty} \lambda_{min} \left(\frac{1}{T} \sum_{t=0}^{T} \mathrm{E}\left[w_{t+1} w_{t+1}' \middle| \mathcal{F}_t \right] \right) > 0 \qquad \text{a.s.} \tag{5.6}$$

We assume furthermore that $\theta^1_0, \ldots, \theta^k_0$ and y_0 are $\mathcal{F}_0$-measurable and that x_t is $\mathcal{F}_{t-p-1}$-measurable for all $t \geq p+1$ and $\mathcal{F}_0$-measurable otherwise.

Assumption (A.3)
The exogenous variables $x_t = (x_{t,1}, \ldots, x_{t,q})'$ satisfy

$$tr \left(\sum_{t=0}^{T} x_t x_t' \right) = O(T) \qquad \text{a.s.} \tag{5.7}$$

and

$$\liminf_{T \to \infty} \lambda_{min} \left(\frac{1}{T} \sum_{t=0}^{T} x_t x_t' \right) > 0 \qquad \text{a.s.} \tag{5.8}$$

These three assumptions are either straightforward multivariate generalizations of the respective assumptions in Chapter 3 or even coincide with them. Nevertheless, we want to discuss Assumption (A.1) a little further.

In view of (5.3) and (5.4) we assume that agents predict y_{t+1} componentwise by applying the SG learning procedure to each equation in (5.1) separately. It is tempting to conclude that we can consider the behaviour of the respective estimates θ_t^i separately. But this is only possible if the *feedback matrix* $A = (a_{ij})_{1\le i\le k}^{1\le j\le k}$ is diagonal. Otherwise the evolutions of the respective estimates θ_t^i, $i = 1, \ldots, k$, are linked by the matrix A and we have to consider them simultaneously.

The special case of A being a diagonal matrix is not very interesting since it states that, for $i \neq j$, the prediction $y_{t+1,i}^e$ does not affect the realization of $y_{t+1,j}$. Clearly, the outcomes of real economic variables are affected by the predictions of agents only via the actions chosen by agents. Since agents are assumed to be rational in the sense that they behave in their own best interest these actions will generally rely on the full prediction vector y_{t+1}^e, and not only on one of its components. Hence, if a component of y_{t+1} is affected by agents' behaviour, then it is, in general, affected by the whole prediction vector. Consequently, the matrix A (which is determined by the underlying economic model) is not diagonal. See Section 6 for an example.

Unfortunately we need some more notation. Define the $k \times n$ matrices Θ_t by

$$\Theta_t' = (\theta_t^1, \ldots, \theta_t^k). \tag{5.9}$$

Then we can rewrite (5.4) as

$$\Theta_{t+1} = \Theta_t + \frac{1}{r_t}(y_{t+1} - \Theta_t z_t)z_t', \qquad t \geq 0. \tag{5.10}$$

Under (A.1)–(A.3) equation (5.1) can be rewritten as

$$y_{t+1} = \Phi z_t + A\Theta_t z_t + w_{t+1}. \tag{5.11}$$

Now suppose that $\Theta_t \equiv \bar{\Theta}$ with some fixed $k \times n$ matrix $\bar{\Theta}$. Hence $y_{t+1}^e = \bar{\Theta} z_t$. Then agents form rational expectations, i.e., $y_{t+1}^e = \mathrm{E}[y_{t+1}|\mathcal{F}_t]$ a.s., if, and only if,

$$(I - A)\bar{\Theta} = \Phi. \tag{5.12}$$

Hence, provided that $\boldsymbol{I}-\boldsymbol{A}$ is regular, rational expectations in this model exist and are uniquely determined by the parameter matrix

$$\bar{\Theta}=(I-A)^{-1}\Phi. \tag{5.13}$$

Since it is more convenient to work with vectors instead of matrices we transform the matrix recursion (5.10) into a vector recursion. Define

$$\boldsymbol{\theta}_t = vec(\Theta_t{}') \qquad \text{and} \qquad \bar{\boldsymbol{\theta}} = vec(\bar{\Theta}'), \tag{5.14}$$

thus $\boldsymbol{\theta}_t$ is the $kn\times 1$ vector consisting of the stagged vectors $\boldsymbol{\theta}_t{}^1,\ldots,\boldsymbol{\theta}_t{}^k$. Define furthermore $\bar{\boldsymbol{\theta}}^i$ as the ith column of $\bar{\Theta}'$. Then (5.1) can be rewritten as

$$\begin{aligned} \boldsymbol{y}_{t+1} &= \boldsymbol{\Phi z}_t + \boldsymbol{A y}^e_{t+1} + \boldsymbol{w}_{t+1} \\ &= (\boldsymbol{I}-\boldsymbol{A})\bar{\Theta}\boldsymbol{z}_t + \boldsymbol{A}\Theta_t\boldsymbol{z}_t + \boldsymbol{w}_{t+1} \\ &= (\boldsymbol{I}-\boldsymbol{A})(\boldsymbol{I}\otimes\boldsymbol{z}_t')\bar{\boldsymbol{\theta}} + \boldsymbol{A}(\boldsymbol{I}\otimes\boldsymbol{z}_t')\boldsymbol{\theta}_t + \boldsymbol{w}_{t+1} \\ &= (\boldsymbol{I}\otimes\boldsymbol{z}_t')\bar{\boldsymbol{\theta}} + (\boldsymbol{A}\otimes\boldsymbol{z}_t')(\boldsymbol{\theta}_t-\bar{\boldsymbol{\theta}}) + \boldsymbol{w}_{t+1}. \end{aligned} \tag{5.15}$$

Consequently (5.10) turns out to be

$$\begin{aligned} \boldsymbol{\theta}_{t+1} &= \boldsymbol{\theta}_t + r_t^{-1}(\boldsymbol{I}\otimes\boldsymbol{z}_t)(\boldsymbol{y}_{t+1}-\boldsymbol{y}^e_{t+1}) \\ &= \boldsymbol{\theta}_t + r_t^{-1}(\boldsymbol{I}\otimes\boldsymbol{z}_t)\left[(\boldsymbol{I}\otimes\boldsymbol{z}_t')\bar{\boldsymbol{\theta}} + (\boldsymbol{A}\otimes\boldsymbol{z}_t')(\boldsymbol{\theta}_t-\bar{\boldsymbol{\theta}})\right. \\ &\qquad \left. - (\boldsymbol{I}\otimes\boldsymbol{z}_t')\boldsymbol{\theta}_t + \boldsymbol{w}_{t+1}\right] \\ &= \boldsymbol{\theta}_t + r_t^{-1}(\boldsymbol{I}\otimes\boldsymbol{z}_t)\left[(\boldsymbol{I}\otimes\boldsymbol{z}_t')(\bar{\boldsymbol{\theta}}-\boldsymbol{\theta}_t) + (\boldsymbol{A}\otimes\boldsymbol{z}_t')(\boldsymbol{\theta}_t-\bar{\boldsymbol{\theta}})\right] \\ &\qquad + r_t^{-1}(\boldsymbol{I}\otimes\boldsymbol{z}_t)\boldsymbol{w}_{t+1} \\ &= \boldsymbol{\theta}_t - r_t^{-1}(\boldsymbol{I}\otimes\boldsymbol{z}_t)\left[(\boldsymbol{I}-\boldsymbol{A})\otimes\boldsymbol{z}_t'\right](\boldsymbol{\theta}_t-\bar{\boldsymbol{\theta}}) + r_t^{-1}(\boldsymbol{I}\otimes\boldsymbol{z}_t)\boldsymbol{w}_{t+1} \\ &= \boldsymbol{\theta}_t - r_t^{-1}\left[(\boldsymbol{I}-\boldsymbol{A})\otimes\boldsymbol{z}_t\boldsymbol{z}_t'\right](\boldsymbol{\theta}_t-\bar{\boldsymbol{\theta}}) + r_t^{-1}(\boldsymbol{I}\otimes\boldsymbol{z}_t)\boldsymbol{w}_{t+1}. \end{aligned} \tag{5.16}$$

Hence we have obtained a recursive representation of the estimates $\boldsymbol{\theta}_t$ similar to the one in Chapter 3.

As in Chapter 3 the disturbance terms introduce persistent stochastic fluctuation into the model. This is made explicit in the following lemma. The proof follows the same lines as the proof of Theorem A.7 in Appendix A and is therefore omitted.

Lemma 5.2.1
Suppose that (A.1)-(A.3) are satisfied. Then

$$\liminf_{T\to\infty} \frac{1}{T}\sum_{t=0}^{T} y_{t,i}^2 > 0 \qquad a.s. \qquad i = 1,\ldots,k. \tag{5.17}$$

5.3 Convergence Analysis

Although we have a recursive representation of the estimates $\boldsymbol{\theta}_t$ similar to the one in Chapter 3 we cannot directly apply the results of that chapter unless $\boldsymbol{A}$ is a diagonal matrix. But it is not difficult to derive a multivariate generalization of the first part of Theorem 3.3.1.

Theorem 5.3.1
Suppose that (A.1) and (A.2) are satisfied and $\boldsymbol{I} - \boldsymbol{A}$ is regular. If $q \geq 1$, thus if the model includes exogenous variables, suppose that

$$\sum_{t=0}^{\infty} \boldsymbol{x}_t'\boldsymbol{x}_t = \infty \quad a.s. \quad and \quad \limsup_{t\to\infty} \frac{\boldsymbol{x}_t'\boldsymbol{x}_t}{\sum_{\tau=0}^{t} \boldsymbol{x}_\tau\boldsymbol{x}_\tau'} < 1 \quad a.s. \tag{5.18}$$

If $||\boldsymbol{A}||^2 = \lambda_{max}(\boldsymbol{A}'\boldsymbol{A}) < 1$, *then*

$$||\boldsymbol{\theta}_t - \bar{\boldsymbol{\theta}}||^2 \qquad converges\ a.s.,\ and \tag{5.19}$$

$$\sum_{t=0}^{T} \frac{[z_t'(\theta_t^i - \bar{\theta}^i)]^2}{r_t} < \infty \qquad a.s., \qquad i = 1,\ldots,k. \tag{5.20}$$

Furthermore

$$\boldsymbol{\theta}_t \longrightarrow \bar{\boldsymbol{\theta}} \qquad a.s.\ on \qquad \left[\frac{\lambda_{max}(\boldsymbol{Z}_t)}{\lambda_{min}(\boldsymbol{Z}_t)} = O(1)\right]. \tag{5.21}$$

Proof
For the estimates θ_t we have the recursion

$$\begin{aligned}\theta_{t+1} - \bar{\theta} &= \left[I - \frac{1}{r_t}((I - A) \otimes z_t z_t')\right](\theta_t - \bar{\theta}) \\ &\quad + \frac{1}{r_t}(I \otimes z_t) w_{t+1}. \end{aligned} \tag{5.22}$$

Define the matrix

$$C_t = I - r_t^{-1}\left((I - A) \otimes z_t z_t'\right). \tag{5.23}$$

Then

$$\begin{aligned} C_t'C_t &= I - \frac{1}{r_t}[(I - A) \otimes z_t z_t' + (I - A)' \otimes z_t z_t'] \\ &\quad + \frac{1}{r_t^2}(I - A)'(I - A) \otimes z_t z_t' z_t z_t' \\ &= I - \frac{1}{r_t}[(I - A) + (I - A)' - \lambda_t (I - A)'(I - A)] \otimes z_t z_t' \end{aligned} \tag{5.24}$$

with $\lambda_t = \|z_t\|^2 / r_t$. Now define $V_t = \|\theta_t - \bar{\theta}\|^2$ and

$$D_t = \left[(I - A) + (I - A)' - \lambda_t (I - A)'(I - A)\right] \otimes z_t z_t'. \tag{5.25}$$

Then

$$\begin{aligned} \mathrm{E}\left[V_{t+1} \mid \mathcal{F}_t\right] &= V_t - \frac{1}{r_t}(\theta_t - \bar{\theta})' D_t (\theta_t - \bar{\theta}) \\ &\quad + \frac{z_t' z_t}{r_t^2} \mathrm{E}\left[\|w_{t+1}\|^2 \middle| \mathcal{F}_t\right]. \end{aligned} \tag{5.26}$$

Now we show that D_t is non-negative definite a.s. Since D_t is symmetric this is equivalent to showing $\lambda_{min}(D_t) \geq 0$ a.s. It is well-known that the eigenvalues of a Kronecker product $R \otimes S$ are the products of the respective eigenvalues of R and S. Since $z_t z_t'$ is non-negative definite and symmetric, thus possesses only non-negative eigenvalues, it remains to show that the matrix on the l.h.s. of the Kronecker symbol in (5.25) is non-negative definite. Notice that this matrix is symmetric, hence it sufficies to show that it has only non-negative eigenvalues.

Since, by assumption, $\|A\| < 1$ and, by construction, $0 \leq \lambda_t \leq 1$ we obtain

$$\lambda_{min}\left[I - A + (I - A)' - \lambda_t (I - A)'(I - A)\right]$$

$$\begin{aligned}
&\geq \lambda_{min}\left[2I - A - A' - (I - A)'(I - A)\right] \\
&= \lambda_{min}\left(I - A'A\right) \qquad (5.27)\\
&\geq \epsilon
\end{aligned}$$

with some $\epsilon > 0$. Then Proposition 2.5.1 implies that $\{||\theta_t - \bar{\theta}||^2\}$ converges a.s., hence (5.19) is shown.

Moreover, (5.27) implies that

$$\begin{aligned}
(\theta_t - \bar{\theta})' D_t (\theta_t - \bar{\theta}) &\geq (\theta_t - \bar{\theta})' \left((I - A'A) \otimes z_t z_t'\right)(\theta_t - \bar{\theta}) \\
&\geq (\theta_t - \bar{\theta})' \left(\epsilon I \otimes z_t z_t'\right)(\theta_t - \bar{\theta}) \qquad (5.28)\\
&= \epsilon \sum_{i=1}^{k} \left[z_t'(\theta_t^i - \bar{\theta}^i)\right]^2 .
\end{aligned}$$

Hence Proposition 2.5.1 implies that (5.20) holds.

In order to show (5.21) we can follow the lines of the proof of Theorem 3.3.1. Without any change in the argumentation we obtain

$$(5.29) \qquad Z_T(\theta_{T+1}^i - \bar{\theta}^i) = \sum_{t=0}^{T} Z_t(\theta_{t+1}^i - \theta_t^i) + o(r_T) \qquad \text{a.s.}$$

for every $i = 1, \ldots, k$. Since

$$(5.30) \qquad (\theta_{t+1}^i - \theta_t^i) = \frac{1}{r_t} z_t (y_{t+1,i} - y_{t+1,i}^e)$$

and

$$(5.31) \quad y_{t+1,i} - y_{t+1,i}^e = \sum_{j=1}^{k} a_{ij} z_t'(\theta_t^j - \bar{\theta}^j) - z_t'(\theta_t^i - \bar{\theta}^i) + w_{t+1,i}$$

we obtain, analogously to (3.37),

$$\begin{aligned}
\sum_{t=0}^{T} Z_t(\theta_{t+1}^i - \theta_t^i) &= \sum_{t=0}^{T}\sum_{j=1}^{k} a_{ij} \widetilde{Z}_t z_t z_t'(\theta_t^j - \bar{\theta}^j) \\
&\quad - \sum_{t=0}^{T} \widetilde{Z}_t z_t z_t'(\theta_t^i - \bar{\theta}^i) + \sum_{t=0}^{T} \widetilde{Z}_t z_t w_{t+1,i} \qquad (5.32)\\
&= o(r_T) \qquad \text{a.s.}
\end{aligned}$$

with $\widetilde{Z}_t = r_t^{-1} Z_t$. Then we can again follow the lines of the proof of Theorem 3.3.1 and obtain

$$(5.33) \quad \|\theta_t - \bar{\theta}\| \to 0 \quad \text{a.s. on} \quad \left[\limsup_{t\to\infty} \frac{\lambda_{max}(Z_t)}{\lambda_{min}(Z_t)} = O(1)\right] \quad \text{a.s.}$$

This completes the proof. ■

Theorem 3.1 is the multivariate version of part (i) of Theorem 3.3.1. The following result generalizes a special case of Theorem 3.3.1 (ii). Since this is the most interesting special case we omit a full generalization of Theorem 3.3.1 (ii).

Theorem 5.3.2
Suppose that the assumptions of Theorem 3.1 are met. If $I - \frac{1}{2}(A + A')$ is positive definite then (5.19)-(5.21) hold on the event $[\lambda_t \to 0]$.

Proof
We can follow the preceding proof up to (5.26). Then we have to argue pathwise. Since $2I - (A + A')$ is positive definite there exists some $\epsilon = \epsilon(\omega)$ and some $T = T(\epsilon, \omega)$ such that on the event $[\lambda_t \to 0]$

$$(5.34) \qquad (I - A) + (I - A)' - \lambda_t (I - A)'(I - A) \geq \epsilon I$$

for all $t \geq T$ in the sense of the Löwner ordering. Then we can again follow the lines of the proof of Theorem 3.1 since all considerations are of a pathwise nature as explained in detail in the proof of Theorem 3.3.1. ■

We want to remark that it is also possible to generalize Theorem 3.3.2 which gives partial convergence in case of the PEC being violated. We decided to disregard this generalization since it gives only little additional gain.

5.4 Condition Analysis

In this section we generalize the results of Section 3.4. Again, this generalization is straightforward and we omit formal proofs wherever possible.

5.4.1 Determination of $\lambda_{max}(Z_t)$

Let $p \geq 1$ and suppose that the Assumptions (A.1) and (A.2) are satisfied. Using the equality $\Phi + A\bar{\Theta} = \bar{\Theta}$ we can rewrite the model (5.11) as

$$y_{t+1} = \bar{\Theta} z_t + A(\Theta_t - \bar{\Theta}) z_t + w_{t+1}. \tag{5.35}$$

If we decompose the $k \times n$ matrix $\bar{\Theta}$ as

$$\bar{\Theta} = (\bar{\Theta}_1, \ldots, \bar{\Theta}_p, \bar{\Theta}_{p+1}) \tag{5.36}$$

with $\bar{\Theta}_i$ $k \times k$ matrices for $i = 1, \ldots, p$, and $\bar{\Theta}_{p+1}$ a $k \times q$ matrix, then we can rewrite (5.35) as

$$y_{t+1} = \bar{\Theta}_1 y_t + \cdots + \bar{\Theta}_p y_{t-p+1} + \bar{\Theta}_{p+1} x_t + A(\Theta_t - \bar{\Theta}) z_t + w_{t+1}. \tag{5.37}$$

We write (5.37) as a first order supermodel. Define $kp \times 1$ vectors ψ_t and φ_t by

$$\begin{aligned} \psi_t' &= (y_t', \ldots, y_{t-p+1}'), \\ \varphi_{t+1}' &= \left([\bar{\Theta}_{p+1} x_t + A(\Theta_t - \bar{\Theta}) z_t + w_{t+1}]', 0, \ldots, 0 \right), \end{aligned} \tag{5.38}$$

and the $kp \times kp$ companion form matrix

$$\Pi = \begin{pmatrix} \bar{\Theta}_1 & \cdots & \bar{\Theta}_{p-1} & \bar{\Theta}_p \\ I_k & & & 0 \\ & \ddots & & \vdots \\ & & I_k & 0 \end{pmatrix}. \tag{5.39}$$

Then (5.37) can be written as

$$\psi_{t+1} = \Pi \psi_t + \varphi_{t+1}. \tag{5.40}$$

The characteristic polynomial π of Π is given as

$$\pi(y) = I y^p - \bar{\Theta}_1 y^{p-1} - \cdots - \bar{\Theta}_{p-1} y - \bar{\Theta}_p \tag{5.41}$$

and its roots are defined as the solutions of the determinantal equation $|\pi(y)| = 0$. If these roots all lie inside the unit circle we obtain $\|\Pi^t\| = o(\rho^t)$ with some $0 < \rho < 1$ and the process $\{\psi_t\}$ is stable.

Under Assumption (A.3) we obtain the following result which determines the order of $\lambda_{max}(Z_t)$ in the stable case.

Theorem 5.4.1
Suppose that (A.1)-(A.3) are satisfied and $I - A$ is regular. Suppose furthermore that the characteristic polynomial (5.41) possesses roots only inside the unit circle.

(i) *If* $\|A\| < 1$, *then* $\lambda_{max}(Z_t) = O(t)$ *a.s.*

(ii) *If* $I - \frac{1}{2}(A + A')$ *is positive definite, then* $\lambda_{max}(Z_t) = O(t)$ *a.s. on the event* $[\lambda_t \to 0]$.

The proof follows exactly the same lines as in Chapter 3 and is therefore omitted.

5.4.2 Determination of $\lambda_{min}(Z_t)$

Analogously to Chapter 3 we obtain

Theorem 5.4.2
Suppose that (A.1)-(A.3) are satisfied and $I - A$ is regular. Suppose furthermore that $\lambda_{max}(Z_t) = O(t)$ *a.s. Then*

(i) *If* $\|A\| < 1$, *then*

$$\liminf_{T\to\infty} \frac{1}{T}\lambda_{min}(Z_T) > 0 \qquad a.s. \tag{5.42}$$

(ii) *If* $I - \frac{1}{2}(A + A')$ *is positive definite, then (5.42) holds on* $[\lambda_t \to 0]$.

This result can be shown in a way similar to Theorem 3.4.5. Since the notation in the proof of that result is already complicated and cumbersome we want to omit this tedious generalization. Nevertheless, we want to explain why the generalization is possible.

An examination of the proof of Theorem 3.4.5 shows that (5.42) holds since the disturbance terms introduce persistent stochastic fluctuation into the model in the sense that, using for the moment the notation of Chapter 3,

$$\liminf_{T\to\infty} \frac{1}{T}\sum_{t=0}^{T} w_{t+1}^2 > 0 \qquad \text{a.s.} \tag{5.43}$$

Moreover, this stochastic fluctuation cannot be exactly predicted in the sense that

$$\liminf_{T\to\infty} \frac{1}{T}\sum_{t=0}^{T}(y_{t+1} - \tilde{y}_{t+1})^2 > 0 \qquad \text{a.s.} \tag{5.44}$$

for any linear prediction $\tilde{y}_{t+1}$ of y_{t+1} based solely on information available at time t.

These findings were applied to infer that a column vector of the regressor matrix $Z(t)$ cannot be orthogonally projected onto the linear space spanned by the other column vectors without obtaining a residuum which grows at the minimum order $O(t)$ as $t \to \infty$. In view of Lemma 3.4.3 this property is equivalent to (5.42).

Since Assumption (A.2) of this chapter generalizes the required property of the disturbance terms we can infer that (5.44) holds also in the multivariate model. Notice that Assumption (A.2) ensures that (5.44) holds componentwise in the sense that the prediction $\tilde{y}_{t+1,i}$ may be based also on the knowledge of $w_{t+1,j}$ for $j \neq i$. (This is easily seen by applying Lemma 3.4.3 to the empirical covariance matrix of the disturbance terms.) Hence for the multivariate model the keypoint of the proof of Theorem 3.4.5 is fulfilled. The remaining considerations then carry over more or less directly.

5.5 Convergence Results

We obtain the following convergence results.

Theorem 5.5.1
Suppose that $p = 0$ and the Assumptions (A.1) and (A.3) are satisfied. Suppose furthermore that $I - A$ is regular and the exogenous variables satisfy the PEC and

$$tr(X_t) \longrightarrow \infty \quad a.s. \quad and \quad \frac{\|x_t\|^2}{tr(X_t)} \longrightarrow 0 \qquad a.s. \tag{5.45}$$

with $X_t = \sum_0^t x_s x_s'$. If $I - \frac{1}{2}(A + A')$ is positive definite, then $\theta_t \to \bar{\theta}$ a.s. In particular, $\theta_t \to \bar{\theta}$ a.s. if $\|A\| < 1$.

Theorem 5.1 is restricted to the case that z_t contains only exogenous variables which satisfy the PEC and it follows directly from Theorem 3.1 and Theorem 3.2. Notice that the second condition in (5.45) ensures that $\lambda_t \to 0$ a.s.

Theorem 5.1 is closely related to some convergence results for the OLS algorithm. For example, BRAY (1983) shows convergence if $z_t \equiv 1$ and KOTTMANN (1990) shows convergence if $\{z_t\}$ is stationary and ergodic under exactly the same condition on the feedback matrix A as above.

Theorem 5.5.2
Suppose that $p \geq 1$ and (A.1)-(A.3) are satisfied. Suppose furthermore that $I - A$ is regular and the characteristic polynomial (5.41) possesses roots only inside the unit circle.

(i) *If* $\|A\| < 1$, *then* $\theta_t \to \bar{\theta}$ *a.s.*

(ii) *If* $I - \frac{1}{2}(A + A)'$ *is positive definite, then* $\theta_t - \bar{\theta}$ *a.s. on the event* $[\lambda_t \to 0]$.

Theorem 5.2 is the multivariate version of Theorem 3.5.4 and, to our knowledge, the first global convergence result in the multivariate dynamic case. It follows from Theorem 3.1, Theorem 3.2, Theorem 4.1, and Theorem 4.2. It shows that, if the influence of the forecast feedback is limited and the REE is a stable ARX process, then also in multivariate models agents following the SG learning procedure cannot destabilize the system but can eventually learn the rational expectations parameter with probability one.

5.6 An Example

The multivariate formulation allows us to consider more sophisticated models than the simple microeconomic model in Section 2.9 and Section 3.6. The following macroeconomic model is a slighly modified version[1] of the model analyzed and estimated by TAYLOR (1979, 1981) under the REH.

The model is assumed to have the reduced form

$$\begin{aligned} y_t &= \beta_1 y_{t-1} + \beta_2 y_{t-2} + \beta_3(m_t - p_t) + \beta_4(m_{t-1} - p_{t-1}) \\ &\quad + \beta_5 \hat{\pi}_t + \beta_0 + u_t \end{aligned} \tag{5.46}$$

and

$$\pi_t = \pi_{t-1} + \gamma_1 \hat{y}_t + \gamma_0 + v_t, \tag{5.47}$$

where

- y_t is the log of real expenditures measured as deviations from trend,
- m_t is the log of money balances during period t,
- p_t is the log of aggregate price level prevailing during period t,
- π_t is the rate of inflation defined as $p_{t+1} - p_t$,
- $\hat{\pi}_t$ is the market prediction of π_t based on information available in period $t-1$,
- $\hat{y}_t$ is the market prediction of y_t based on information available in period $t-1$, and
- u_t, v_t are disturbance terms.

For the derivation of the equations (5.46), (5.47) and for details about the underlying economic ideas we refer to TAYLOR (1979).

Notice that by definition there exists a relationship between prices p_t and the inflation rate π_t. More precisely, also prices are endogenous in this model. Hence the model given by (5.46) and (5.47) does not

[1] We simplify the model of TAYLOR (1979) in two directions. Firstly, we omit a linear trend as explanatory variable to ensure that the REE is stable. This simplification is not too restrictive since a parameter estimation performed by TAYLOR based on aggregate U.S. quarterly data over the period from 1953:I through 1975:IV gives a negligible value for the respective parameter. In a subsequent study TAYLOR (1981) agrees to this simplification.

Secondly, we assume that the disturbance terms form a martingale difference sequence. This assumption rules out the possibility of autocorrelated disturbances as considered by TAYLOR (1979).

yet fit into our setup. As TAYLOR (1979) remarks equation (5.47) implicitly describes the evolution of prices. Since $\pi_t = p_{t+1} - p_t$ we can rewrite (5.47) as

$$p_{t+1} = 2p_t - p_{t-1} + \gamma_1 \hat{y}_t + \gamma_0 + v_t. \tag{5.48}$$

Analogously, since $\hat{\pi}_t = \hat{p}_{t+1} - p_t$, we can rewrite (4.46) as

$$\begin{aligned} y_t &= \beta_1 y_{t-1} + \beta_2 y_{t-2} + \beta_3(m_t - p_t) + \beta_4(m_{t-1} - p_{t-1}) \\ &\quad + \beta_5(\hat{p}_{t+1} - p_t) + \beta_0 + u_t. \end{aligned} \tag{5.49}$$

Since prices are predetermined by (5.47) this formulation causes no problems. As in TAYLOR (1979) we assume that also money balances are predetermined. Then the whole model can be written more compactly as

$$\boldsymbol{y}_{t+1} = \boldsymbol{\Phi} \boldsymbol{z}_t + \boldsymbol{A} \boldsymbol{y}^e_{t+1} + \boldsymbol{w}_{t+1} \tag{5.50}$$

with

$$\begin{aligned} \boldsymbol{y}_t' &= (y_t, p_{t+1}), \\ \boldsymbol{x}_t' &= (m_{t+1}, m_t, 1), \\ \boldsymbol{z}_t' &= (\boldsymbol{y}_t', \boldsymbol{y}_{t-1}', \boldsymbol{x}_t'), \\ \boldsymbol{y}_t^{e\prime} &= (\hat{y}_t, \hat{p}_{t+1}), \\ \boldsymbol{w}_t' &= (u_t, v_t), \end{aligned} \tag{5.51}$$

and

$$\begin{aligned} \boldsymbol{\Phi} &= \begin{pmatrix} \beta_1 & -(\beta_3 + \beta_5) & \beta_2 & -\beta_4 & \beta_3 & \beta_4 & \beta_0 \\ 0 & 2 & 0 & -1 & 0 & 0 & \gamma_0 \end{pmatrix}, \\ \boldsymbol{A} &= \begin{pmatrix} 0 & \beta_5 \\ \gamma_1 & 0 \end{pmatrix}. \end{aligned} \tag{5.52}$$

As in TAYLOR (1979) we assume that $\beta_5\gamma_1 \neq 1$. This implies that $\boldsymbol{I} - \boldsymbol{A}$ is regular. Hence rational expectations exist and are unique. Since

$$\boldsymbol{A}'\boldsymbol{A} = \begin{pmatrix} \gamma_1^2 & 0 \\ 0 & \beta_5^2 \end{pmatrix} \tag{5.53}$$

the condition $\|\boldsymbol{A}\| < 1$ is equivalent to $|\beta_5| < 1$ and $|\gamma_1| < 1$. If only $|\beta_5 + \gamma_1| < 2$ holds then $\boldsymbol{I} - \frac{1}{2}(\boldsymbol{A} + \boldsymbol{A}')$ is positive definite.

In order to obtain a proper convergence result we have to determine first which parameter conditions lead to a stable REE. Firstly, we assume that the exogenous variables satisfy Assumption (A.3). Since

$$(I-A)^{-1} = \frac{1}{1-\beta_5\gamma_1}\begin{pmatrix} 1 & \beta_5 \\ \gamma_1 & 1 \end{pmatrix} \tag{5.54}$$

we obtain

$$\begin{aligned} \bar{\Theta} &= \frac{1}{1-\beta_5\gamma_1}\left(\begin{matrix} \beta_1 & \beta_5-\beta_3 & \beta_2 & \cdots \\ \beta_5\gamma_1 & 2-\gamma_1(\beta_3+\beta_5) & \beta_2\gamma_1 & \cdots \end{matrix}\right. \\ &\qquad \left.\begin{matrix} \cdots & -(\beta_4+\beta_5) & \beta_3 & \beta_4 & \beta_0+\beta_5\gamma_0 \\ \cdots & -(1+\beta_4\gamma_1) & \beta_3\gamma_1 & \beta_4\gamma_1 & \beta_0\gamma_1+\gamma_0 \end{matrix}\right). \end{aligned} \tag{5.55}$$

Let

$$\bar{\Theta}_1 = \frac{1}{1-\beta_5\gamma_1}\begin{pmatrix} \beta_1 & \beta_5-\beta_3 \\ \beta_1\gamma_1 & 2-\gamma_1(\beta_3+\beta_5) \end{pmatrix} \tag{5.56}$$

and

$$\bar{\Theta}_2 = \frac{1}{1-\beta_5\gamma_1}\begin{pmatrix} \beta_2 & -(\beta_4+\beta_5) \\ \beta_2\gamma_1 & -(1+\beta_4\gamma_1) \end{pmatrix}. \tag{5.57}$$

The characteristic polynomial is then

$$\pi(y) = Iy^2 - \bar{\Theta}_1 y - \bar{\Theta}_2. \tag{5.58}$$

Although it is possible to derive a closed form solution for the roots of (5.58) in term of the parameters γ_i, β_j (given as the roots of a polynomial of fourth order) we omit this tedious exercise in calculus since the resulting closed form solution is quite complicated and not very instructive.

Now assume that $\{w_t\}$ is a MDS satisfying Assumption (A.2). Assume furthermore that the roots of (5.58) all lie inside the unit circle and $\beta_5\gamma_1 \neq 1$. If the estimates θ_t are given by Assumption (A.1), then we obtain the following result.

(i) If $|\beta_5| < 1$ and $|\gamma_1| < 1$, then $\theta_t \to \bar{\theta}$ a.s.

(ii) If only $|\beta_5 + \gamma_1| < 2$, then $\theta_t \to \bar{\theta}$ a.s. on $[\lambda_t \to 0]$.

Hence we obtain convergence of the SG estimates $\boldsymbol{\theta}_t$ under quite plausible conditions for the parameters β_5 and γ_1. Notice, however, that these restrictions are only necessary conditions. Since the roots of the characteristic polynomial depend also on these two parameters the assumption that it possesses roots only inside the unit circle implicitely imposes additional restrictions on β_5 and γ_1. Unfortunately, the roots depend in such a complex way on the parameters β_5 and γ_1 that these additional restriction cannot be given in a simple and instructive manner.

Chapter 6

Multivariate Non–Stationary Models

6.1 Introduction

In this chapter we continue the analysis of multivariate models. Since the static case with non-stationary (exogenous) variables is not covered by the studies of MARCET/SARGENT (1989a,b), KOTTMANN (1990), MOHR (1990), and KUAN/WHITE (1994) the results we obtain have, to our knowledge, no counterpart in the literature.

From the mathematical point of view we generalize the results of Chapter 4 to multivariate models. As in the preceding chapter it turns out that this generalization is mostly straightforward and requires only some new ideas. Again, wherever possible, formal proofs are omitted.

The contents of this chapter is arranged analogously to Chapter 4 except that we present no simulation results.

6.2 Basic Assumptions

We consider the same model as in Chapter 5, i.e.

$$y_{t+1} = \Phi z_t + A y^e_{t+1} + w_{t+1}, \qquad t \geq 0, \tag{6.1}$$

where the respective variables and parameters are of the same dimensions as in Chapter 5. Analogously to Chapter 4 the variables z_t are confined to being exogenous.

The following assumptions are straightforward generalizations of the respective assumptions of Chapter 4.

Assumption (A.1)
Agents' predictions y^e_{t+1} are

$$y^e_{t+1} = \Theta_t z_t, \qquad t \geq 0, \tag{6.2}$$

with some initial value Θ_0 and

$$(\theta_t{}^i)' = \left(\sum_{s=0}^{t-1} z_s z_s' \right)^{-1} \sum_{s=0}^{t-1} z_s y_{s+1,i}, \qquad i = 1, \dots, k, \quad t \geq 1, \tag{6.3}$$

where $\theta_t{}^i$ denotes the ith row of the $k \times n$ matrix Θ_t and the stochastic inverse is given as the Moore–Penrose inverse.

Assumption (A.2)
The disturbance terms form a k-dimensional MDS w.r.t. some filtration $\{\mathcal{F}_t\}$ such that

$$\sup_{t \geq 0} \mathrm{E}\left[\|w_{t+1}\|^{2+\delta} \middle| \mathcal{F}_t \right] < \infty \qquad \text{a.s.} \tag{6.4}$$

with some fixed $\delta > 0$. The initial value Θ_0 is assumed to be $\mathcal{F}_0$–measurable.

Assumption (A.3)
The random variables z_t are $\mathcal{F}_t$–measurable for all $t \geq 0$ and satisfy

$$\sum_{t=0}^{\infty} \|z_t\|^2 = \infty \qquad \text{a.s.} \tag{6.5}$$

and

$$T^* = \min\{t \in \mathbb{N} \,|\, Z_t \text{ is non-singular }\} < \infty \qquad \text{a.s.} \tag{6.6}$$

with $Z_t = \sum_0^t z_s z_s'$.

As in the preceding chapter agents predict the endogenous variable componentwise. Here agents are assumed to carry out a linear regression of the components y_t^i onto the explanatory variables z_{t-1}. Of course, these regressions are not unrelated, not even seemingly unrelated whenever the feedback matrix A is not diagonal. Hence we have to analyze the evolution of the estimates $\theta_t{}^i$ simultaneously in $i = 1, \ldots, k$.

Under (A.1)–(A.3) equation (6.1) can be rewritten as

$$y_{t+1} = (\Phi + A\Theta_t)\, z_t + w_{t+1}. \tag{6.7}$$

As shown in Chapter 5, if $I - A$ is regular rational expectations exist and are uniquely determined by the parameter matrix

$$\bar{\Theta} = (I - A)^{-1}\Phi. \tag{6.8}$$

As in Chapter 5 we transform the matrices Θ_t and $\bar{\Theta}$ into vectors by

$$\theta_t = vec(\Theta_t{}') \qquad \text{and} \qquad \bar{\theta} = vec(\bar{\Theta}') \tag{6.9}$$

and obtain the following reduced form equation

$$y_{t+1} = (I \otimes z_t')\bar{\theta} + (A \otimes z_t')(\theta_t - \bar{\theta}) + w_{t+1}. \tag{6.10}$$

It is easy to see that the system of equations (6.3) can be written more compactly as

$$\theta_t = \left(I_k \otimes Z_{t-1}^{-1}\right) \sum_{s=0}^{t-1} (y_{s+1} \otimes z_t). \tag{6.11}$$

6.3 Convergence Analysis

The main result of this section is the multivariate generalization of Theorem 4.3.1.

Theorem 6.3.1
Suppose that (A.1)-(A.3) are satisfied. Suppose furthermore that $I - A$ is regular and $\lambda_{max}(A + A') < 1$. Let $\lambda_t = z_t' Z_t^{-1} z_t$. If

$$\limsup_{t\to\infty} \lambda_t < \frac{1 - \lambda_{max}(A + A')}{\lambda_{max}((I - A)'(I - A))} \qquad a.s., \tag{6.12}$$

then

$$\|\theta_{t+1} - \bar{\theta}\|^2 = O\left(\frac{\log \lambda_{max}(Z_t)}{\lambda_{min}(Z_t)}\right) \qquad a.s. \tag{6.13}$$

Proof
The proof is a straightforward generalization of the proof of Theorem 4.3.1. In a first step we derive a recursive representation of the estimates $\{\theta_t\}$. For fixed $t \geq 0$ let $t \geq T^*$. Using equation (6.11) we can apply the same kind of transformations as in (1.13) to obtain

$$\theta_{t+1} = \theta_t - (I \otimes Z_t^{-1} z_t z_t')\theta_t + (I \otimes Z_t^{-1} z_t) y_{t+1}. \tag{6.14}$$

By (6.10) and since $\Phi = (I - A)\bar{\Theta}$

$$\begin{aligned} \theta_{t+1} - \bar{\theta} &= \theta_t - \bar{\theta} - \left((I - A) \otimes Z_t^{-1} z_t z_t'\right)(\theta_t - \bar{\theta}) \\ &\quad + \left(I \otimes Z_t^{-1} z_t\right) w_{t+1}. \end{aligned} \tag{6.15}$$

Now define the quadratic form V_t by

$$V_t = (\theta_t - \bar{\theta})'(I_k \otimes Z_{t-1})(\theta_t - \bar{\theta}). \tag{6.16}$$

It is easy to see that V_t possesses the recursive representation

$$\begin{aligned} V_{t+1} &= V_t + \lambda_t \|w_{t+1}\|^2 + (\theta_t - \bar{\theta})' \times \cdots \\ &\quad \cdots \times \left[\left(A + A' - I + \lambda_t (I - A)'(I - A)\right) \otimes z_t z_t'\right](\theta_t - \bar{\theta}) \\ &\quad + (\theta_t - \bar{\theta})' \left[(2I - 2\lambda_t (I - A)') \otimes z_t\right] w_{t+1} \\ &= V_t + \lambda_t \|w_{t+1}\|^2 + u_t' w_{t+1} - (\theta_t - \bar{\theta})' \left[C_t \otimes z_t z_t'\right](\theta_t - \bar{\theta}) \end{aligned} \tag{6.17}$$

with

$$(6.18)\qquad \begin{aligned} C_t &= I - (A + A') - \lambda_t (I - A)'(I - A), \\ u_t' &= (\theta_t - \bar{\theta})' \left[(2I - 2\lambda_t (I - A)') \otimes z_t \right]. \end{aligned}$$

Define

$$(6.19)\qquad \begin{aligned} \tilde{\eta}_{t+1} &= (\theta_t - \bar{\theta})' \left[C_t \otimes z_t z_t' \right] (\theta_t - \bar{\theta}), \\ \eta_{t+1} &= (\tilde{\eta}_{t+1})^+, \\ \beta_{t+1} &= \lambda_t \|w_{t+1}\|^2 + (-\tilde{\eta}_{t+1})^+. \end{aligned}$$

Then we have

$$(6.20)\qquad V_{t+1} = V_t + \beta_{t+1} - \eta_{t+1} + u_t' w_{t+1}$$

on the event $[t \geq T^*]$.

If $0 \leq t < T^*$ define V_{t+1} by (6.16) and set $\beta_{t+1} = V_{t+1}$, $\eta_{t+1} = V_t$, $u_t' = \mathbf{o}$, and $V_0 = 0$. Then (6.20) holds on the full ω–space.

Next we show that $\tilde{\eta}_{t+1}(\omega) \geq 0$ for all but finitely many $t \geq 0$. This is equivalent to showing that the matrix C_t is non-negative definite for all but finitely many $t \geq 0$. Since

$$(6.21)\qquad \begin{aligned} C_t \geq \mathbf{o} &\iff \lambda_t (I - A)'(I - A) \leq I - (A + A') \\ &\Longleftarrow \lambda_t \lambda_{max} \left[(I - A)'(I - A) \right] \leq \lambda_{min} \left[I - (A + A') \right] \\ &\iff \lambda_t \leq \frac{1 - \lambda_{max}(A + A')}{\lambda_{max}[(I - A)'(I - A)]} \end{aligned}$$

condition (6.12) implies that $C_t \geq \mathbf{o}$ for all but finitely many $t \geq 0$. Hence $\tilde{\eta}_{t+1} \geq 0$ for all but finitely many $t \geq 0$.

Now we can follow the lines of the proof of Theorem 4.3.1 with one modification. Since neither u_t nor w_{t+1} is univariate (although $u_t' w_{t+1}$ is) we cannot directly apply Proposition 4.3.3. A suitable generalization of this result is, however, not difficult to derive. Instead of stating this result as an extra proposition we show it for the special case given by (6.20).

Iteration of (6.20) leads to

$$(6.22)\qquad V_T - V_0 + \sum_{t=1}^{T} \eta_t = \sum_{t=1}^{T} \beta_t + \sum_{t=0}^{T-1} u_t' w_{t+1}.$$

We show that

$$\left|\sum_{t=0}^{T} \boldsymbol{u}_t' \boldsymbol{w}_{t+1}\right| = O\left(\sum_{t=0}^{T} \|\boldsymbol{u}_t\|^2\right)^{\frac{1}{2}+\alpha} \quad \text{a.s.} \tag{6.23}$$

with some $\alpha > 0$. Applying Lemma A.1 in Appendix A we obtain

$$\left|\sum_{t=0}^{T} u_{t,i} w_{t+1,i}\right| = O\left(\sum_{t=0}^{T} u_{t,i}^2\right)^{\frac{1}{2}+\alpha} \quad \text{a.s.} \qquad i = 1, \ldots, k, \tag{6.24}$$

with some $\alpha > 0$. Then (6.23) follows since

$$\max_{1 \le i \le k} u_{t,i}^2 \le \sum_{i=1}^{k} u_{t,i}^2 = \|\boldsymbol{u}_t\|^2 \le k \max_{1 \le i \le k} u_{t,i}^2. \tag{6.25}$$

Hence the analogon to condition (4.14) is shown. Since $\|\boldsymbol{u}_t\|^2 \le C\eta_{t+1}$ with a suitable (pathdependent) positive constant C, as can be shown by the same kind of reasoning as in the proof of Theorem 4.3.1 using (6.12), (6.18), and (6.21), we finally obtain

$$V_T = O\left(\sum_{t=1}^{T} \beta_t\right) = O\left(\frac{\log \lambda_{max}(\boldsymbol{Z}_{t-1})}{\lambda_{min}(\boldsymbol{Z}_{t-1})}\right) \quad \text{a.s.} \tag{6.26}$$

This implies (6.13) and the proof is complete. ■

Notice that the proof uses only one probabilistic result, Lemma A.1 of Appendix A. The remainder is purely algebraic, hence applies pathwise. Since $\|\boldsymbol{u}_t\|^2 \le C\eta_{t+1}$ is the decisive condition for (6.26) to hold, and the former is a consequence of $\boldsymbol{C}_t > \mathbf{o}$ for all but finitely many $t \ge 0$, we may endogenize condition (6.12) in the following sense.

Theorem 6.3.2
Suppose that (A.1)-(A.3) are satisfied. Suppose furthermore that $\boldsymbol{I} - \boldsymbol{A}$ is regular and $\lambda_{max}(\boldsymbol{A} + \boldsymbol{A}') < 1$. Let $\lambda_t = \boldsymbol{z}_t' \boldsymbol{Z}_t^{-1} \boldsymbol{z}_t$. Then

$$\|\boldsymbol{\theta}_{t+1} - \bar{\boldsymbol{\theta}}\|^2 = O\left(\frac{\log \lambda_{max}(\boldsymbol{Z}_t)}{\lambda_{min}(\boldsymbol{Z}_t)}\right) \quad a.s. \tag{6.27}$$

on the event

$$\limsup_{t \to \infty} \lambda_t < \frac{1 - \lambda_{max}(\boldsymbol{A} + \boldsymbol{A}')}{\lambda_{max}((\boldsymbol{I} - \boldsymbol{A})'(\boldsymbol{I} - \boldsymbol{A}))}. \tag{6.28}$$

6.4 Convergence Results

Since the convergence analysis of Chapter 4 carries over, more or less directly, to the multivariate case the following result is immediate.

Theorem 6.4.1
Suppose that (A.1)–(A.3) are satisfied. Suppose furthermore that $\boldsymbol{I}-\boldsymbol{A}$ is regular and $\lambda_{max}(\boldsymbol{A}+\boldsymbol{A}') < 1$.

(i) *If $\lambda_t \to 0$ a.s. and*

$$\text{(6.29)} \qquad \log \lambda_{max}(\boldsymbol{Z}_t) = o(\lambda_{min}(\boldsymbol{Z}_t)) \qquad a.s.,$$

then $\boldsymbol{\theta}_t \to \bar{\boldsymbol{\theta}}$ a.s.

(ii) *If (6.29) holds, then $\boldsymbol{\theta}_t \to \bar{\boldsymbol{\theta}}$ a.s. on the event*

$$\text{(6.30)} \qquad \limsup_{t\to\infty} \lambda_t < \frac{1-\lambda_{max}(\boldsymbol{A}+\boldsymbol{A}')}{\lambda_{max}((\boldsymbol{I}-\boldsymbol{A})'(\boldsymbol{I}-\boldsymbol{A}))} \qquad a.s.$$

As shown in Chapter 4 the condition $\lambda_t \to 0$ a.s. holds for a large class of stochastic processes $\{\boldsymbol{z}_t\}$. To these processes part (i) of Theorem 6.4.1 applies. In particular it applies to the following cases, —

- $\{\boldsymbol{z}_t\}$ is a stationary and ergodic process with a (possibly pathdependent) positive definite variance-covariance matrix,
- $\{\boldsymbol{z}_t\}$ is a stable process in the sense that the PEC holds and $\|\boldsymbol{z}_t\|^2 = o(tr(\boldsymbol{Z}_t))$ a.s.,
- $\{\boldsymbol{z}_t\}$ is an autoregressive process with stable and unit roots,
- $\boldsymbol{z}_t$ contains stationary and ergodic components as above and polynomial trends of distinct order, and
- $\boldsymbol{z}_t$ contains integrated and co-integrated components which satisfy certain restrictions in order to rule out multicollinearities.

In order to conclude this chapter we like to remark that if it were possible to show that the event (6.29) is a.s. if $\boldsymbol{z}_t$ contains also lagged endogenous variables, then Theorem 4.1 would apply. Based on the findings of some computer simulations we conjecture that this holds if $\lambda_{max}(\boldsymbol{A} + \boldsymbol{A}') < 1$ and the characteristic polynomial possesses roots inside or on the unit circle.

In the case of roots outside the unit circle the condition (6.30) is decisive since in that case $\lambda_t \to 0$ does not hold even on $[\boldsymbol{\theta}_t \to \bar{\boldsymbol{\theta}}]$, as shown for the univariate first order autoregressive case in Appendix A. Hence in that case $\lambda_{max}(\boldsymbol{A} + \boldsymbol{A}') < 1$ is not sufficient to ensure convergence and more restrictive parameter conditions are necessary. In particular, these conditions have to ensure that (6.30) holds true on $[\boldsymbol{\theta}_t \to \bar{\boldsymbol{\theta}}]$.

We conjecture that if these parameter conditions are satisfied and, in addition, $||\boldsymbol{A}|| < 1$ holds true, then convergence occurs with probability one. Perhaps, further research will validate this conjecture and close the gap in the analysis of linear models with forecast feedback in the dynamic case.

Appendix A

Univariate Autoregressions with Time-Varying Parameters

In this appendix we consider a univariate first order autoregression

$$y_{t+1} = \xi_t y_t + w_{t+1}, \qquad t \geq 0, \tag{A.1}$$

where $\{w_t\}$ is a martingale difference sequence w.r.t. some filtration $\{\mathcal{F}_t\}$ such that

$$\sup_{t \geq 0} \mathrm{E}[|w_{t+1}|^\alpha | \mathcal{F}_t] < \infty \qquad \text{a.s.} \tag{A.2}$$

for some $\alpha \geq 2$, $\{\xi_t\}_{t \geq 0}$ is a sequence of real valued $\mathcal{F}_t$-adapted random variables, and the initial value y_0 is a real valued $\mathcal{F}_0$-measurable random variable.

We are interested in the following questions: What is the rate of growth of $|y_t|$ and of $\sum_{\tau=0}^t y_\tau^2$ if the process $\{\xi_t\}$ remains bounded above in modulus, for example by one? What can be said about the evolution of $y_t^2 / \sum_{\tau=0}^t y_\tau^2$?

Under the fixed parameter assumption $\xi_t \equiv \xi$ with some constant ξ, thus if $\{y_t\}$ is an ordinary AR(1)–process, these problems are completely solved (see, e.g., LAI/WEI (1983a, 1985)). If the evolution of the parameters is independent of the system dynamics, i.e., if $\{\xi_t\}$ and $\{w_t\}$ are stochastically independent, then some answers are known under additional assumptions on the distribution of $\{\xi_t\}$ (see, e.g., BOUGEROL/PICARD (1992a,b) and TONG (1990)).

But for the feedback case, thus if the evolution of $\{\xi_t\}$ depends on the evolution of $\{y_t\}$, to our knowledge no satisfactory answers exist in the literature. With the following results we give these answers. The technique used in the proofs is partly adapted from LAI/WEI.

Lemma A.1 (WEI (1985))
Let $\{w_t\}$ be a MDS w.r.t. $\{\mathcal{F}_t\}$ such that (A.2) holds with $\alpha > 2$ and let $\{\xi_t\}$ be a sequence of $\mathcal{F}_t$-adapted real valued random variables. Define

$$S_t^2 = \sum_{s=0}^{t} \xi_s^2. \tag{A.3}$$

Then

$$\sum_{t=0}^{T} \xi_t w_{t+1} = O\left(S_T (\log S_T)^\delta\right) \qquad a.s. \tag{A.4}$$

for every $\delta > 1/\min\{\alpha, 4\}$. Furthermore, if

$$\xi_t^2 = o(S_t^{2c}) \qquad \text{for some } 0 < c < 1, \tag{A.5}$$

then

$$\sum_{t=0}^{T} \xi_t w_{t+1} = O\left(S_T (\log\log S_T^2)^{1/2}\right) \qquad a.s. \tag{A.6}$$

Lemma A.2 (WEI (1987))
Let $\{w_t\}$ be a MDS w.r.t. $\{\mathcal{F}_t\}$ such that (A.2) holds with $\alpha \geq 2$ and let $\{\xi_t\}$ be a sequence of $\mathcal{F}_t$-adapted real valued random variables. Define S_t^2 as in Lemma A.1. Let f be a non-decreasing function such that

$$\int_1^\infty (x f^\alpha(x))^{-1}\, dx < \infty. \tag{A.7}$$

Then on the event $[S_t^2 \to \infty]$

$$\sum_{t=0}^{T} \xi_t w_{t+1} = o\left(S_T f(S_T^2)\right) \qquad a.s. \tag{A.8}$$

Lemma A.3 (LAI/WEI (1982a))
Let $\{w_t\}$ be a MDS w.r.t. $\{\mathcal{F}_t\}$ such that (A.2) holds with $\alpha = 2$ and let $\{\xi_t\}$ be a sequence of $\mathcal{F}_t$-adapted real valued random variables. Then

(i) $\sum_{t=0}^{\infty} |\xi_t| w_{t+1}^2 < \infty$ *a.s. on* $\left[\sum_{t=0}^{\infty} |\xi_t| < \infty\right]$,

(ii) $\sum_{t=0}^{T} |\xi_t| w_{t+1}^2 = o\left(\left(\sum_{t=0}^{T} |\xi_t|\right)^{1+\delta}\right)$ *a.s. on* $\left[\sum_{t=0}^{\infty} |\xi_t| = \infty\right]$ $\forall \delta > 0$.

(iii) *If, in addition, (A.2) holds for some $\alpha > 2$, then*

$$\sum_{t=0}^{T} |\xi_t| w_{t+1}^2 = O\left(\sum_{t=0}^{T} |\xi_t|\right) \quad a.s. \tag{A.9}$$

on the event $\left[\sup_{t\geq 0} |\xi_t| < \infty, \sum_{t=0}^{\infty} |\xi_t| = \infty\right]$.

Theorem A.4
Let $\{w_t\}$ be a MDS w.r.t. $\{\mathcal{F}_t\}$ such that (A.2) holds with $\alpha \geq 2$ and let $\{\xi_t\}$ be a sequence of $\mathcal{F}_t$-adapted real valued random variables. Let $\{y_t\}$ be given by (A.1) and let $N = N(\omega)$ be an a.s. finite random time.

(i) *Suppose that $|\xi_t| \leq \rho < 1$ a.s. for all $t \geq N$. Then*

$$|y_t| = o(t^{\beta}) \quad a.s. \tag{A.10}$$

for every $\beta > 1/\alpha$.

(ii) *Suppose that $|\xi_t| \leq 1$ a.s. for all $t \geq N$. Then*

$$|y_t| = O(t) \quad a.s. \tag{A.11}$$

if $\alpha > 2$, and for every $\delta > 0$

$$|y_t| = o\left(t^{1+\delta}\right) \quad a.s. \tag{A.12}$$

if $\alpha = 2$.

(iii) *Suppose that* $|\xi_t| \leq \rho$ *a.s. for all* $t \geq N$ *with some* $\rho > 1$. *Then*

$$\text{(A.13)} \qquad |y_t| = O(\rho^t) \qquad a.s.$$

Proof

Equation (A.1) implies

$$\text{(A.14)} \quad y_t = \left(\prod_{s=N}^{t-1} \xi_s\right) y_N + \sum_{s=N+1}^{t} \left(\prod_{\tau=s}^{t-1} \xi_\tau\right) w_s, \qquad t > N,$$

with the convention $\prod_t^{t-1} \xi_\tau = 1$.

(i) The first term on the right-hand side of (A.14) is finite a.s. because $\rho < 1$. Hence

$$\text{(A.15)} \qquad |y_t| = O\left(\sum_{s=N+1}^{t} \rho^{t-s}|w_s|\right) + O(1) \qquad \text{a.s.}$$

Fix some $\beta > 1/\alpha$. Because for each $\epsilon > 0$

$$\text{(A.16)} \quad \mathrm{P}\left[|w_t|^\alpha > \epsilon t^{\alpha\beta} \middle| \mathcal{F}_{t-1}\right] \leq \frac{1}{\epsilon t^{\alpha\beta}} \mathrm{E}\left[|w_t|^\alpha | \mathcal{F}_{t-1}\right] \qquad \text{a.s.}$$

we can conclude with the aid of the conditional Borel–Cantelli lemma (see, e.g., Stout (1974), p. 55) that

$$\text{(A.17)} \qquad |w_t| = o(t^\beta) \qquad \text{a.s.}$$

This implies

$$\text{(A.18)} \qquad \sum_{s=N+1}^{t} \rho^{t-s}|w_s| = o(t^\beta) \qquad \text{a.s.}$$

and (i) is shown.

(ii) Since $|w_t| \leq 1 + w_t^2$ and $|\prod_{\tau=s}^{t-1} \xi_\tau| \leq 1$ for $s \geq N$ we obtain by Lemma A.3

$$\begin{aligned} \left|\sum_{s=N+1}^{t} \left(\prod_{\tau=s}^{t-1} \xi_\tau\right) w_s\right| &\leq \sum_{s=N+1}^{t} \left|\prod_{\tau=s}^{t-1} \xi_\tau\right| + \sum_{s=N+1}^{t} \left|\prod_{\tau=s}^{t-1} \xi_\tau\right| w_s^2 \\ \text{(A.19)} \qquad &\leq t - N + \sum_{s=1}^{t} w_s^2 \\ &= O(t) \qquad \text{a.s.} \end{aligned}$$

if $\alpha > 2$ where the last line follows from Lemma A.3. Analogously we obtain, for every $\delta > 0$,

$$\left| \sum_{s=N+1}^{t} \left(\prod_{\tau=s}^{t-1} \xi_\tau \right) w_s \right| = o\left(t^{1+\delta}\right) \qquad \text{a.s.} \tag{A.20}$$

if $\alpha = 2$. Hence (ii) is proved.

(iii) Using the same decomposition as above we obtain, again with the aid of Lemma A.3,

$$\left| \sum_{s=N+1}^{t} \left(\prod_{\tau=s}^{t-1} \xi_\tau \right) w_s \right| = O\left(\rho^t\right) + O\left(\rho^t \sum_{s=N+1}^{t} \rho^{-s} w_s^2\right) = O\left(\rho^t\right) \quad \text{a.s.} \tag{A.21}$$

and (iii) is shown. ■

Remark

If the process $\{\xi_t\}$ is deterministic or exogenous in the sense that for all $t \geq 0$, $\sigma(\xi_0, \xi_1, \ldots) \subset \mathcal{F}_t$, then (ii) can be strenghtened to

$$|y_t| = \begin{cases} O\left(t^{\frac{1}{2}}(\log\log t)^{\frac{1}{2}}\right) & \text{a.s. if } \alpha > 2, \text{ and} \\ o\left(t^{\frac{1}{2}}(\log t)^{\delta}\right) & \text{a.s. for every } \delta > 0 \text{ if } \alpha = 2. \end{cases} \tag{A.22}$$

This result is easily obtained applying the second part of Lemma A.1 and Lemma A.2 to the sum in (A.14). Notice that the additional condition on $\{\xi_t\}$ ensures that the necessary measurability conditions are satisfied, i.e., $\prod_{\tau=s}^{t-1} \xi_\tau$ is $\mathcal{F}_{s-1}$-measurable. Without the additional condition the product is only $\mathcal{F}_{t-1}$-measurable so that the lemmata cannot be applied.

Theorem A.5

Let $\{w_t\}$ be a MDS w.r.t. $\{\mathcal{F}_t\}$ such that (A.2) holds with $\alpha \geq 2$ and let $\{\xi_t\}$ be a sequence of $\mathcal{F}_t$-adapted real valued random variables. Let $\{y_t\}$ be given by (A.1) and let $N = N(\omega)$ be an a.s. finite random time.

(i) *Suppose that $|\xi_t| \leq \rho < 1$ a.s. for all $t \geq N$. Then*

$$\sum_{t=0}^{T} y_t^2 = O(T) \qquad a.s. \tag{A.23}$$

if $\alpha > 2$, *and for every* $\delta > 0$

$$\text{(A.24)} \qquad \sum_{t=0}^{T} y_t^2 = o\left(T^{1+\delta}\right) \qquad a.s.$$

if $\alpha = 2$.

(ii) *Suppose that* $|\xi_t| \leq 1$ *a.s. for all* $t \geq N$. *Then*

$$\text{(A.25)} \qquad \sum_{t=0}^{T} y_t^2 = O\left(T^{3}\right) \qquad a.s.$$

if $\alpha > 2$, *and for every* $\delta > 0$

$$\text{(A.26)} \qquad \sum_{t=0}^{T} y_t^2 = O\left(T^{3+\delta}\right) \qquad a.s.$$

if $\alpha = 2$.

(iii) *Suppose that* $|\xi_t| \leq \rho$ *a.s. for all* $t \geq N$ *with some* $\rho > 1$. *Then*

$$\text{(A.27)} \qquad \sum_{t=0}^{T} y_t^2 = O(\rho^{2T}) \qquad a.s.$$

Proof

(ii) and (iii) are immediate consequences of Theorem A.4.
To show (i) notice that (A.14) implies for $t > N$

$$\text{(A.28)} \qquad y_t^2 \leq 2\rho^{2(t-N)} y_N^2 + 2\left(\sum_{s=N+1}^{t} w_s \prod_{\tau=s}^{t-1} \xi_\tau\right)^2,$$

hence

$$\text{(A.29)} \quad \sum_{t=N+1}^{T} y_t^2 \leq 2y_N^2 \sum_{t=1}^{T-N} \rho^{2t} + 2\sum_{t=N+1}^{T}\left(\sum_{s=N+1}^{t} w_s \prod_{\tau=s}^{t-1} \xi_\tau\right)^2 \qquad \text{a.s.}$$

The first sum on the right-hand side converges. For the second sum the Cauchy–Schwarz inequality gives

$$\begin{aligned}
\sum_{t=N+1}^{T}\left(\sum_{s=N+1}^{t} w_s \prod_{\tau=s}^{t-1}\xi_\tau\right)^2 &\leq \sum_{t=N+1}^{T}\left(\sum_{s=N+1}^{t}\prod_{\tau=s}^{t-1}|\xi_\tau| \sum_{s=N+1}^{t} w_s^2 \prod_{\tau=s}^{t-1}|\xi_\tau|\right) \\
&\leq \sum_{t=N+1}^{T}\left(\sum_{s=N+1}^{t}\rho^{t-s}\sum_{s=N+1}^{t}\rho^{t-s}w_s^2\right) \\
&\leq (1-\rho)^{-1}\sum_{t=1}^{T}\sum_{s=1}^{t}\rho^{t-s}w_s^2 \qquad \text{(A.30)} \\
&= (1-\rho)^{-1}\sum_{t=1}^{T}\sum_{s=0}^{T-t}\rho^{s}w_t^2 \\
&\leq (1-\rho)^{-2}\sum_{t=1}^{T} w_t^2 .
\end{aligned}$$

Since Lemma A.3 implies $\sum_{t=1}^{T} w_t^2 = O(T)$ a.s. if $\alpha > 2$ and $\sum_{t=1}^{T} w_t^2 = o(T^{1+\delta})$ a.s. if $\alpha = 2$, (i) is proved. ■

Now we determine the minimum rate of divergence of $\sum_{t=0}^{T} y_t^2$. For the proof we need the following result, a corollary of the local convergence theorem for martingales of CHOW (1965).

Lemma A.6 (CHEN/GUO (1991))
Let $\{w_t\}$ be a MDS w.r.t. $\{\mathcal{F}_t\}$. If either

(A.31) $$\sup_{t\geq 1} \mathrm{E}\left[|w_t|^\alpha \,|\, \mathcal{F}_{t-1}\right] < \infty \quad \textit{a.s.} \quad \textit{or} \quad \sup_{t\geq 1} \mathrm{E}\left[|w_t|^\alpha\right] < \infty$$

for some $\alpha \in [1,2]$, then for any $\beta > 1$

(A.32) $$\sum_{t=1}^{T} w_t = o\left(T^{\frac{\beta}{\alpha}}\right) \qquad \textit{a.s.}$$

Theorem A.7
Let $\{w_t\}$ be a MDS w.r.t. $\{\mathcal{F}_t\}$ such that (A.2) holds with $\alpha > 2$ and

$$\liminf_{T\to\infty} \frac{1}{T}\sum_{t=1}^{T} \mathrm{E}\left[w_t^2 \middle| \mathcal{F}_{t-1}\right] > 0 \qquad a.s. \tag{A.33}$$

Let $\{\xi_t\}$ be a sequence of $\mathcal{F}_t$-adapted random variables and $\{y_t\}$ be given by (A.1). Then

$$\liminf_{T\to\infty} \frac{1}{T}\sum_{t=1}^{T} y_t^2 > 0 \qquad a.s. \tag{A.34}$$

Proof
In view of (A.1) we have

$$\sum_{t=1}^{T} y_t^2 = \sum_{t=1}^{T} \xi_{t-1}^2 y_{t-1}^2 + 2\sum_{t=1}^{T} \xi_{t-1} y_{t-1} w_t + \sum_{t=1}^{T} w_t^2. \tag{A.35}$$

Since by Lemma A.1

$$\sum_{t=1}^{T} \xi_{t-1} y_{t-1} w_t = O\left(\left(\sum_{t=1}^{T} \xi_{t-1}^2 y_{t-1}^2\right)^{\frac{1}{2}+\varepsilon}\right) \qquad \text{a.s.} \tag{A.36}$$

with $0 < \varepsilon < 1/2$ we obtain

$$\sum_{t=1}^{T} y_t^2 = \sum_{t=1}^{T} w_t^2 + \delta_T \tag{A.37}$$

with $\delta_T \geq 0$ for T sufficiently large. Define $\epsilon_t = w_t^2 - \mathrm{E}[w_t^2|\mathcal{F}_{t-1}]$. Then, for T sufficiently large,

$$\frac{1}{T}\sum_{t=1}^{T} y_t^2 \geq \frac{1}{T}\sum_{t=1}^{T} \mathrm{E}[w_t^2|\mathcal{F}_{t-1}] + \frac{1}{T}\sum_{t=1}^{T} \epsilon_t. \tag{A.38}$$

Clearly, $\{\epsilon_t\}$ is a martingale difference sequence w.r.t. $\{\mathcal{F}_t\}$. With the conditional Minkowski inequality it is easy to show that

$$\sup_{t\geq 1} \mathrm{E}\left[|\epsilon_t|^{\alpha/2} \middle| \mathcal{F}_{t-1}\right] < \infty \qquad \text{a.s.} \tag{A.39}$$

Hence we can apply Lemma A.6 and obtain $\sum_{t=1}^{T} \epsilon_t = o(T)$ a.s. Then (A.32) follows from assumption (A.31). ■

Under weaker assumptions on the disturbance terms $\{w_t\}$ we obtain a somewhat weaker result.

Theorem A.8
Let $\{w_t\}$ be a MDS w.r.t. $\{\mathcal{F}_t\}$ such that (A.2) holds with $\alpha \geq 2$. Suppose there exist constants $\epsilon > 0$ and $\delta > 0$ such that

$$\text{(A.40)} \qquad \mathrm{P}\left[w_t^2 > \epsilon \middle| \mathcal{F}_{t-1}\right] > \delta \qquad a.s. \qquad \forall t \geq 1.$$

Then $\sum_{t=1}^{T} y_t^2 = \infty$ a.s.

Proof
In view of (A.37) we have $\sum_{t=1}^{T} y_t^2 = \sum_{t=1}^{T} w_t^2 + \delta_T$ with $\delta_T \geq 0$ for T sufficiently large. From the conditional Borel–Cantelli lemma it follows that $\mathrm{P}[w_t^2 > \epsilon \text{ i.o.}] = 1$. Hence $\sum_{t=1}^{\infty} w_t^2 = \infty$ a.s. and, consequently, $\sum_{t=1}^{\infty} y_t^2 = \infty$ a.s. ∎

Notice that the assumptions of Theorem A.8 are satisfied if $\{w_t\}$ is an i.i.d. sequence with $\mathrm{E}w_t^2 > 0$.

Now we consider the evolution of the quotient $\gamma_t = y_t^2 / \sum_{\tau=0}^{t} y_\tau^2$. The first result is

Theorem A.9
Let $\{w_t\}$ be a MDS w.r.t. $\{\mathcal{F}_t\}$ such that (A.2) holds with $\alpha > 2$. Let $\{\xi_t\}$ be a sequence of $\mathcal{F}_t$-adapted real valued random variables such that $|\xi_t| \leq 1$ for all $t \geq N$ with $N = N(\omega)$ an a.s. finite random time. Let $\{y_t\}$ be given by (A.1) and let

$$\text{(A.41)} \qquad \gamma_t = \frac{y_t^2}{\sum_{\tau=0}^{t} y_\tau^2}.$$

Then $\gamma_t \to 0$ a.s.

For the proof we need the following auxiliary result.

Lemma A.10 (LAI/WEI (1983a))
Let $(a_t)_{t\geq 1}$ *be a sequence of non-negative numbers such that*

$$\sum_{t=1}^{T} a_t = o\left(T^{\delta}\right) \qquad \forall \delta > 0 \tag{A.42}$$

and there exist constants $C > 0$ *and* $\eta > 0$ *such that*

$$a_{t+1} \leq a_t + Ct^{-\eta} \qquad \textit{for all large } t. \tag{A.43}$$

Then $\lim_{t\to\infty} a_t = 0$.

Proof of Theorem A.9
For $t > N$ we have

$$\begin{aligned} \gamma_t = \frac{y_t^2}{\sum_{\tau=0}^{t} y_\tau^2} &= \frac{(\xi_{t-1}y_{t-1} + w_t)^2}{\sum_{\tau=0}^{t} y_\tau^2} \\ &= \xi_{t-1}^2 \frac{y_{t-1}^2}{\sum_{\tau=0}^{t} y_\tau^2} + 2\frac{y_t w_t}{\sum_{\tau=0}^{t} y_\tau^2} - \frac{w_t^2}{\sum_{\tau=0}^{t} y_\tau^2} \\ &\leq \gamma_{t-1} + 2\left|\frac{y_t}{\sum_{\tau=0}^{t} y_\tau^2}\right| |w_t|. \end{aligned} \tag{A.44}$$

Theorem A.7 implies

$$\sqrt{t}\left|\frac{y_t}{\sum_{\tau=0}^{t} y_\tau^2}\right| = \left(\frac{y_t^2}{\sum_{\tau=0}^{t} y_\tau^2}\right)^{\frac{1}{2}} \left(\frac{1}{\frac{1}{t}\sum_{\tau=0}^{t} y_\tau^2}\right)^{\frac{1}{2}} = O(1) \quad \text{a.s.} \tag{A.45}$$

Hence $|y_t|/|\sum_{\tau=0}^{t} y_\tau^2| = O(t^{-1/2})$ a.s. Since $|w_t| = o(t^{\beta})$ a.s. for every $\beta > 1/\alpha$ we can conclude that

$$\left|\frac{y_t}{\sum_{\tau=0}^{t} y_\tau^2}\right| |w_t| = O\left(t^{-\eta}\right) \qquad \text{a.s.} \tag{A.46}$$

with some $\eta > 0$. Since (cf. LAI/WEI (1982a))

$$\sum_{t=0}^{T} \frac{y_t^2}{\sum_{\tau=0}^{t} y_\tau^2} = O\left(\log\left(\sum_{t=0}^{T} y_t^2\right)\right) \tag{A.47}$$

and, by Theorem A.5, $\sum_{t=0}^{T} y_t^2 = O(T^{\delta})$ a.s. with some finite constant $\delta > 0$ we can apply (pathwise) Lemma A.10. This completes the proof.
■

Now we consider the case that the ξ_t's stabilize in some interval $[\rho_1, \rho_2] \subset (1, \infty)$ for $t \to \infty$. It is quite plausible that in this case the process $\{y_t\}$ explodes at approximately a geometrical rate. A rigorous proof of this fact is, however, complicated and involved.

Theorem A.11
Let $\{w_t\}$ be a MDS w.r.t. $\{\mathcal{F}_t\}$ such that (A.2) holds with $\alpha > 2$ and

$$\text{(A.48)} \qquad \liminf_{t\to\infty} \mathrm{E}\left[w_{t+1}^2 \middle| \mathcal{F}_t \right] > 0 \qquad a.s.$$

Let $\{\xi_t\}$ be a sequence of $\mathcal{F}_t$-adapted real valued random variables such that $\xi_t \neq 0$ a.s. for all $t \geq 0$. Furthermore assume that

$$\text{(A.49)}\ \mathrm{P}[\Omega_0] > 0 \quad \textit{with} \quad \Omega_0 = \left[\liminf_{t\to\infty} |\xi_t| > \rho_1 \ , \ \limsup_{t\to\infty} |\xi_t| < \rho_2 \right],$$

where ρ_1, ρ_2 are constants such that $1 < \rho_1 < \rho_2 < \infty$.

Define real valued random variables φ_t, $t \geq 0$, by

$$\text{(A.50)} \qquad \varphi_t = \left(\prod_{s=0}^{t} \xi_s \right)^{-1}$$

with the convention $0^{-1} = 0$. Then

$$\text{(A.51)} \qquad \mathrm{P}[\Omega_1] = 0 \quad \textit{with} \quad \Omega_1 = \left[y_0 + \sum_{t=0}^{\infty} \varphi_t w_{t+1} = 0 \right] \cap \Omega_0$$

and

$$\text{(A.52)} \quad \frac{y_t^2}{\rho_2^{2t}} = O(1) \quad \textit{and} \quad \frac{\rho_1^{2t}}{y_t^2} = O(1) \quad a.s.\ on\ \Omega_0,$$

where $\{y_t\}$ is given by (A.1) with initial value y_0.

The proof of the first part of Theorem A.11 follows roughly the lines of the proof of Corollary 2 in LAI/WEI (1983b) which covers the case that the φ_t's are constants. Since the φ_t's given by (A.50) are random and, moreover, the assertions (A.51) and (A.52) are of a local nature the proof of LAI/WEI has to modified at several points.

Proof

Assume that

$$\text{(A.53)} \qquad P[\Omega_1] = P\left[\left[y_0 + \sum_{t=0}^{\infty} \varphi_t w_{t+1} = 0\right] \cap \Omega_0\right] = 4\eta$$

with $\eta > 0$.

In a first step we define random variables $\tilde{\xi}_t$, $t \geq 0$, by

$$\text{(A.54)} \qquad \tilde{\xi}_t = \begin{cases} \xi_t & \text{if } \ |\xi_t| \in [\rho_1, \rho_2] \\ \rho & \text{if } \ |\xi_t| \notin [\rho_1, \rho_2] \end{cases}$$

with some fixed constant $\rho \in [\rho_1, \rho_2]$. Clearly, $\tilde{\xi}_t$ is $\mathcal{F}_t$-measurable. Since, for all $\omega \in \Omega_0$, $\xi_t(\omega) = \tilde{\xi}_t(\omega)$ for all $t \geq N(\omega)$ with $N(\omega) < \infty$ there exists a constant N_1 and an event $\Omega_2 \subseteq \Omega_1$ such that

$$\text{(A.55)} \qquad P[\Omega_2] \geq 3\eta \qquad \text{and} \qquad \xi_t = \tilde{\xi}_t \quad \forall t \geq N_1 \quad \text{on } \Omega_2.$$

In a second step we define real valued random variables $\varphi(s,t)$, $0 \leq s \leq t$, by

$$\text{(A.56)} \qquad \varphi(s,t) = \left(\prod_{\tau=s+1}^{t} \xi_\tau\right)^{-1}, \qquad s < t,$$

and by $\varphi(s,s) = 1$, $s \geq 0$, again using the convention $0^{-1} = 0$. Analogously, define random variables $\tilde{\varphi}(s,t)$ with ξ_τ replaced by $\tilde{\xi}_\tau$ in (A.56). Finally, define for $t \geq N_1$

$$\text{(A.57)} \qquad \tilde{\varphi}_t = \varphi_{N_1} \tilde{\varphi}(N_1, t).$$

From (A.55) we can conclude that

$$\text{(A.58)} \qquad \varphi_t = \tilde{\varphi}_t \qquad \forall t \geq N_1 \quad \text{on } \Omega_2$$

with $P[\Omega_2] \geq 3\eta$.

Next, it can be shown that there exists a filtration $\{\tilde{\mathcal{F}}_t\}$ with $\mathcal{F}_t \subseteq \tilde{\mathcal{F}}_t$ for all $t \geq 0$, a MDS $\{\tilde{w}_t\}$ w.r.t. $\{\tilde{\mathcal{F}}_t\}$, and positive constants N_2, K_1, and K_2 such that

$$\begin{aligned} & E\left[|\tilde{w}_{t+1}|^\alpha \middle| \tilde{\mathcal{F}}_t\right] && \leq K_1 && \text{a.s.} && \forall t \geq N_2, \\ \text{(A.59)} \qquad & E\left[\tilde{w}_{t+1}^2 \middle| \tilde{\mathcal{F}}_t\right] && \geq K_2 && \text{a.s.} && \forall t \geq N_2, \end{aligned}$$

and

(A.60) $$\mathrm{P}[w_t = \tilde{w}_t \quad \forall t \geq N_2] \geq 1 - \eta.$$

(For details see the proof of Lemma 2 in LAI/WEI (1983b).)

Let $M = \max\{N_1, N_2\}$ and define for $t > M$

(A.61) $$S_t = y_0 + \sum_{\tau=0}^{M-1} \varphi_\tau w_{\tau+1} + \sum_{\tau=M}^{t-1} \tilde{\varphi}_\tau \tilde{w}_{\tau+1}.$$

By construction $\tilde{\varphi}_t$ decreases at approximately a geometrical rate. Hence, in view of Lemma 2.3.2, S_t converges a.s. From Egorov's theorem we can conclude that there exists an event Ω_3 with $\mathrm{P}[\Omega_3] \geq 1 - \eta$ such that

(A.62) $$S_t(\omega) \quad \text{converges uniformly in} \quad \omega \in \Omega_3.$$

From (A.53), (A.58), (A.60), and (A.62) it then follows that there exists an event Ω_4 with $\mathrm{P}[\Omega_4] \geq \eta$ such that

(A.63) $$S_t(\omega) \quad \text{converges uniformly towards 0 in} \quad \omega \in \Omega_4.$$

We now define non-random numbers $M = t_0 < t_1 < \ldots$ inductively as follows. Having defined t_i we can choose t_{i+1} such that

(A.64) $$|S_{t_{i+1}}(\omega)| \leq \rho_2^{-t_i} \frac{1}{i+1} \qquad \forall \omega \in \Omega_4.$$

In view of (A.54) to (A.58) we can conclude that

(A.65) $$\sum_{i=0}^{\infty} \frac{S_{t_{i+1}}^2}{\tilde{\varphi}_{t_i}^2} < \infty \qquad \text{a.s. on } \Omega_4 \quad \text{and} \quad \mathrm{P}[\Omega_4] > 0.$$

In the sequel we shall derive a contradiction to property (A.65). To do so we define a stochastic process $\{u_i\}_{i \geq 1}$ by

(A.66) $$u_i = \sum_{\tau=t_{i-1}}^{t_i - 1} \tilde{\varphi}(t_{i-1}, \tau) \tilde{w}_{\tau+1} = \tilde{\varphi}_{t_{i-1}}^{-1} \sum_{\tau=t_{i-1}}^{t_i - 1} \tilde{\varphi}_\tau \tilde{w}_{\tau+1}$$

and a filtration $\{\mathcal{G}_i\}_{i \geq 0}$ by $\mathcal{G}_i = \tilde{\mathcal{F}}_{t_i}$. Obviously, u_i is $\mathcal{G}_i$-measurable and integrable to order α. Moreover, since

(A.67)
$$\begin{aligned}
\mathrm{E}[u_{i+1} | \mathcal{G}_i] &= \sum_{\tau=t_i}^{t_{i+1}-1} \mathrm{E}\left[\mathrm{E}\left[\tilde{\varphi}(t_i, \tau)\tilde{w}_{\tau+1} \middle| \tilde{\mathcal{F}}_\tau\right] \middle| \tilde{\mathcal{F}}_{t_i}\right] \\
&= \sum_{\tau=t_i}^{t_{i+1}-1} \mathrm{E}\left[\tilde{\varphi}(t_i, \tau)\mathrm{E}\left[\tilde{w}_{\tau+1} \middle| \tilde{\mathcal{F}}_\tau\right] \middle| \tilde{\mathcal{F}}_{t_i}\right] \\
&= 0 \quad \text{a.s.}
\end{aligned}$$

$\{u_i\}$ is a martingale difference sequence w.r.t. $\{\mathcal{G}_i\}$. Furthermore, in view of (A.59),

$$\begin{aligned} \mathrm{E}\left[u_{i+1}^2 \middle| \mathcal{G}_i\right] &= \mathrm{E}\left[\sum_{\tau=t_i}^{t_{i+1}-1} \mathrm{E}\left[\tilde{\varphi}^2(t_i,\tau)\tilde{w}_{\tau+1}^2 \middle| \tilde{\mathcal{F}}_\tau\right] \middle| \tilde{\mathcal{F}}_{t_i}\right] \\ &\leq K_3 \mathrm{E}\left[\sum_{\tau=t_i}^{t_{i+1}-1} \tilde{\varphi}^2(t_i,\tau) \middle| \tilde{\mathcal{F}}_{t_i}\right] \qquad \text{(A.68)} \\ &\leq K_3\left(1-\rho_1^{-2}\right)^{-1} \qquad \text{a.s.} \end{aligned}$$

with some constant K_3 and, since $\tilde{\varphi}^2(t_i, t_i) = 1$,

$$\mathrm{E}\left[u_{i+1}^2 \middle| \mathcal{G}_i\right] \geq \mathrm{E}\left[\tilde{\varphi}^2(t_i,t_i)\tilde{w}_{t_i+1}^2 \middle| \tilde{\mathcal{F}}_{t_i}\right] \geq K_2 \qquad \text{a.s.} \tag{A.69}$$

Finally, with the conditional Minkovski inequality a reasoning analogous to (A.68) shows that

$$\sup_{i\geq 0} \mathrm{E}\left[|u_{i+1}|^\alpha \middle| \mathcal{G}_i\right] < \infty \qquad \text{a.s.} \tag{A.70}$$

Then Theorem A.7 (with u_i playing the role of w_t) implies

$$\liminf_{T\to\infty} \frac{1}{T}\sum_{i=1}^{T} u_i^2 > 0 \qquad \text{a.s.} \tag{A.71}$$

From (A.61) it follows that

$$\frac{S_{t_{i+1}}^2}{\tilde{\varphi}_{t_i}^2} = \frac{S_{t_i}^2}{\tilde{\varphi}_{t_i}^2} + 2\frac{S_{t_i}}{\tilde{\varphi}_{t_i}} u_{i+1} + u_{i+1}^2. \tag{A.72}$$

Since $S_{t_i}/\tilde{\varphi}_{t_i}$ is $\mathcal{G}_i$-measurable and $\{u_i\}$ is a MDS w.r.t. $\{\mathcal{G}_t\}$ such that (A.68) holds true Lemma 2.3.2 (with u_i playing the role of w_t) implies

$$\sum_{i=0}^{T} \frac{S_{t_i}}{\tilde{\varphi}_{t_i}} u_{i+1} = o\left(\sum_{i=0}^{T} \frac{S_{t_i}^2}{\tilde{\varphi}_{t_i}^2}\right) + O(1) \qquad \text{a.s.} \tag{A.73}$$

Summing up (A.72) leads to

$$\sum_{i=0}^{T} \frac{S_{t_{i+1}}^2}{\tilde{\varphi}_{t_i}^2} = \sum_{i=0}^{T} u_{i+1}^2 + \delta_T \tag{A.74}$$

with $\delta_T \geq 0$ a.s. for T sufficiently large. Then (A.65) and (A.71) form a contradiction. Hence (A.53) cannot hold true and (A.51) is shown.

Since

$$
\begin{aligned}
y_{t+1} &= \left(\prod_{s=0}^{t} \xi_s\right) y_0 + \sum_{s=0}^{t} \left(\prod_{\tau=s+1}^{t} \xi_\tau\right) w_{s+1} \\
&= \left(\prod_{s=0}^{t} \xi_s\right) \left[y_0 + \sum_{s=0}^{t} \left(\prod_{\tau=0}^{s} \xi_\tau\right)^{-1} w_{s+1} \right] \\
&= \left(\prod_{s=0}^{t} \xi_s\right) \left[y_0 + \sum_{s=0}^{t} \varphi_s w_{s+1} \right] \qquad \text{a.s.}
\end{aligned}
\tag{A.75}
$$

and the term in square brackets converges a.s. towards an a.s. non-zero limit on the event Ω_0 the assumption (A.51) follows immediately. ■

Theorem A.12

Suppose that the assumptions of Theorem A.11 are satisfied. Define γ_t *by (A.41). Then*

$$
\frac{\rho_1^2 - 1}{\rho_1^2} \leq \liminf_{t\to\infty} \gamma_t \quad \textit{and} \quad \limsup_{t\to\infty} \gamma_t \leq \frac{\rho_2^2 - 1}{\rho_2^2} \quad \textit{a.s. on } \Omega_0 \tag{A.76}
$$

Proof

In a first step we derive a recursive representation of the γ_t's. It is easy to see that

$$
\frac{\gamma_{t+1}}{1-\gamma_{t+1}} = \frac{y_{t+1}^2}{y_t^2}\gamma_t. \tag{A.77}
$$

Let $\pi_t^2 = y_{t+1}^2 / y_t^2$ and define a real valued function $g(\cdot,\cdot)$ on $(0,\infty) \times [0,1]$ by

$$
g(\pi^2, \gamma) = \frac{\pi^2\gamma}{1+\pi^2\gamma}. \tag{A.78}
$$

Then (A.77) implies

$$
\gamma_{t+1} = \frac{\pi_t^2\gamma_t}{1+\pi_t^2\gamma_t} = g(\pi_t^2, \gamma_t). \tag{A.79}
$$

The function g has the following properties (see Figure A.1)

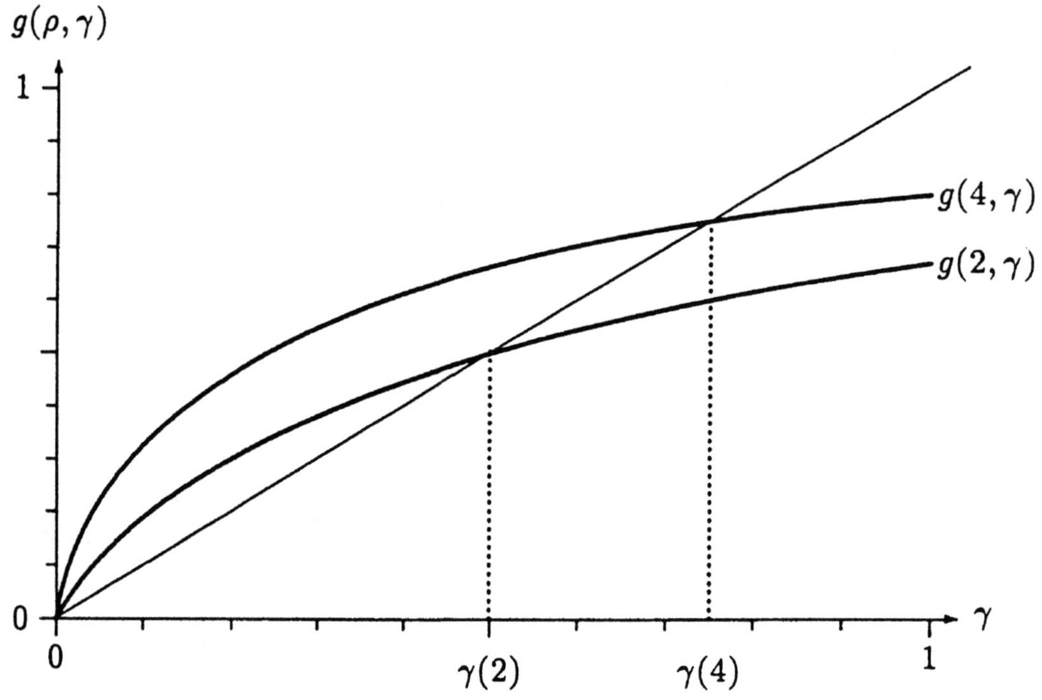

Figure A.1: The function $g(\pi^2, \cdot)$

(i) $\gamma \mapsto g(\pi^2, \gamma)$ is increasing and concave for every $\pi^2 > 0$ and, for every $\pi^2 > 1$, possesses as fixed points 0 and

$$\bar{\gamma} = \bar{\gamma}(\pi^2) = \frac{\pi^2 - 1}{\pi^2}, \tag{A.80}$$

(ii) $\pi^2 \mapsto g(\pi^2, \gamma)$ is increasing for every $\gamma \in (0, 1)$.

Property (i) implies that for every $\pi^2 > 1$ and every initial value $\tilde{\gamma}_0 \in (0, 1)$ the sequence $(\tilde{\gamma}_t)$ recursively defined by $\tilde{\gamma}_{t+1} = g(\pi^2, \tilde{\gamma}_t)$ converges towards $\bar{\gamma}$.

Now Theorem A.11 implies that on the event Ω_0 the process $\{y_t\}$ is 'almost deterministic' in the sense that the influence of the disturbance terms dies out systematically. In particular,

$$\pi_t^2 = \frac{y_{t+1}^2}{y_t^2} = \xi_t^2 + o(1) \qquad \text{a.s. on } \Omega_0 \tag{A.81}$$

This allows us to argue pathwise on the event Ω_0.

Fix some small $\epsilon > 0$. In view of (A.81) and the property (ii) of the function g there exists a (path-dependent) number M such that

$$g\left((\rho_1 - \epsilon)^2, \gamma_t\right) \leq \gamma_{t+1} \leq g\left((\rho_2 + \epsilon)^2, \gamma_t\right) \qquad \forall t \geq M. \tag{A.82}$$

Properties (i) and (ii) of the function g then imply that

$$\frac{(\rho_1 - \epsilon)^2 - 1}{(\rho_1 - \epsilon)^2} \leq \liminf_{t\to\infty} \gamma_t \leq \limsup_{t\to\infty} \gamma_t \leq \frac{(\rho_2 + \epsilon)^2 - 1}{(\rho_2 + \epsilon)^2}. \tag{A.83}$$

Hence (A.76) follows since $\epsilon > 0$ can be chosen arbitrarily. ■

Theorem A.13
Let $\{w_t\}$ be a MDS w.r.t. $\{\mathcal{F}_t\}$ such that (A.2) holds with $\alpha > 2$ and

$$\liminf_{t\to\infty} \mathrm{E}\left[w_{t+1}^2 \middle| \mathcal{F}_t\right] > 0 \qquad a.s. \tag{A.84}$$

Let $\{\xi_t\}$ be a sequence of $\mathcal{F}_t$-adapted real valued random variables such that $\xi_t \neq 0$ a.s. for all $t \geq 0$ and let $\bar{\xi}$ be fixed. Let $\{y_t\}$ and $\{\gamma_t\}$ be given by (A.1), (A.41), resp. Then

$$\gamma_t \to \bar{\gamma} = \begin{cases} 0 & \text{if } |\bar{\xi}| < 1 \\ \dfrac{\bar{\xi}^2 - 1}{\bar{\xi}^2} & \text{if } |\bar{\xi}| > 1 \end{cases} \qquad a.s. \text{ on } [\xi_t \to \bar{\xi}]. \tag{A.85}$$

If $|\bar{\xi}| = 1$, then $\gamma_t \to 0$ a.s. on $[\xi_t \to \bar{\xi}]$ a.s. if on this event

(i) *$|\xi_t| \leq 1$ a.s. for all $t \geq N = N(\omega)$ with $N < \infty$ a.s., or*

(ii) *$\liminf_{t\to\infty} |\prod_0^t \xi_s| > 0$ and $\limsup_{t\to\infty} |\prod_0^t \xi_s| < \infty$ a.s.*

Proof
The assertion for the stable case ($|\bar{\xi}| < 1$) is a generalization of Theorem A.9. It can be shown as in the proof of Theorem A.9 with the exception that all algebraic inequalities are applied (pathwise) on the event $[\xi_t \to \bar{\xi}]$. Without any change in the argumentation we arrive at a local analogon to (A.46). Since also the result (A.47) and Lemma A.10 apply pathwise (cf. LAI/WEI (1982a)) it only remains to show $\sum_0^T y_t^2 = O(T)$ a.s. on $[\xi_t \to \bar{\xi}]$. We thus have to show a local analogon to Theorem A.5. Again, applying all algebraic inequalities on

$[\xi_t \to \bar{\xi}]$ this is easiliy done. (Notice that the probabilistic results used in the proofs of Theorem A.4 and Theorem A.5 are applied exclusively to the disturbance terms w_t.)

The assertion for the explosive case ($|\bar{\xi}| > 1$) follows directly from Theorem A.12 since the event $[\xi_t \to \bar{\xi}]$ is a subset of Ω_0.

The unit root case ($|\bar{\xi}| = 1$) requires some additional considerations. If condition (i) is satisfied on $[\xi_t \to \bar{\xi}]$, the above generalization of Theorem A.9 gives the desired result.

If condition (ii) is satisfied, we consider the evolution of $\tilde{\gamma}_t$ defined by $\tilde{\gamma}_t = \varphi_{t-1}^2 \gamma_t$ with φ_t as in (A.50). The first part of condition (ii) implies $\tilde{\gamma}_t = O(\gamma_t)$ a.s. on $[\xi_t \to \bar{\xi}]$, and the second part of (ii) implies $\gamma_t = O(\tilde{\gamma}_t)$ a.s. on $[\xi_t \to \bar{\xi}]$. Hence $\gamma_t \to 0 \iff \tilde{\gamma}_t \to 0$ a.s. on $[\xi_t \to \bar{\xi}]$.

In view of (A.44) and (A.46) we have

$$\gamma_t = \xi_{t-1}^2 \frac{\sum_{\tau=0}^{t-1} y_\tau^2}{\sum_{\tau=0}^{t} y_\tau^2} \gamma_{t-1} + O\left(t^{-\eta}\right) \qquad \text{a.s.} \tag{A.86}$$

with some $\eta > 0$. This obviously implies

$$\tilde{\gamma}_t \le \tilde{\gamma}_{t-1} + O(t^{-\eta}) \qquad \text{a.s. on } [\xi_t \to \bar{\xi}]. \tag{A.87}$$

In view of (A.19) it is easy to see that condition (ii) implies that $y_t = O(t)$ a.s. on $[\xi_t \to \bar{\xi}]$. Hence $\sum_0^T y_t^2 = O(T^2)$ a.s. on $[\xi_t \to \bar{\xi}]$. Then (A.47) implies that condition (A.42) of Lemma A.10 is satisfied with γ_t playing the role of a_t. Since γ_t and $\tilde{\gamma}_t$ are of the same order it is also satisfied with $\tilde{\gamma}_t$ playing the role of a_t. Then Lemma A.10 gives $\tilde{\gamma}_t \to 0$ a.s., hence $\gamma_t \to 0$ a.s. ■

Remark

Since the unit root case is not covered in its full scope Theorem A.13 is not yet completely satisfactory. Only if $|\xi_t|$ converges from below to $|\bar{\xi}| = 1$ after some finite time (case (i)) or if ξ_t converges sufficiently fast to $\bar{\xi}$ (case (ii)), then we can conclude that $\gamma_t \to 0$ a.s. on $[\xi_t \to \bar{\xi}]$. We believe that $\gamma_t \to 0$ a.s. on $[\xi_t \to \bar{\xi}]$ holds true in general but we are not able to show this.

The situation is very similar to the one in the standard theory of autoregressive processes where the unit root case is the most involved one. The problem we face is, however, much more complicated since the asymptotic behaviour of the process $\{y_t\}$ (which determines the asymptotic behaviour of $\{\gamma_t\}$) depends crucially on the asymptotic behaviour of the parameter process $\{\xi_t\}$. For example, if $|\xi_t|$ converges to 1 from above with a slow rate (e.g., $|\xi_t - \bar{\xi}| = O((\log t)^{-1})$) then $\{y_t\}$ is 'almost deterministic'. In this case a reasoning similar to the one in the proof of Theorem A.12 can show $\gamma_t \to 0$, provided that $|\xi_t - \bar{\xi}|$ possesses a minimum rate of convergence, i.e., $0 < g(t) \leq |\xi_t - \bar{\xi}|$ with some positive function g with $g(t) \to 0$ as $t \to \infty$. (Notice that in view of (A.64) we need the minimum order of convergence to conclude that $\{y_t\}$ is actually 'almost deterministic' and property (A.51) holds true.)

On the other hand, if $|\xi_t|$ converges more rapidly to 1 (e.g., if $|\xi_t - \bar{\xi}| = O(t^{-\eta})$ a.s. with some $0 < \eta \leq 1/2$) then $\{y_t\}$ is not 'almost deterministic'. If it were possible to show that in this case condition (A.42) with $a_t = \gamma_t$ (or a slightly weaker condition) is satisfied, then Lemma A.10 could be applied in order to obtain $\gamma_t \to 0$ a.s. Unfortunately, we see no way in which this can be done. Perhaps, future research will close this gap.

References

BAŞAR, T. (1989)
Some Thoughts on Rational Expectations Models, and Alternate Formulations
Computers Math. Applic., **18**, 591–604

BALASKO, Y. AND D. ROYER (1994)
Stability of Competitive Equilibrium with Respect to Recursive and Learning Processes
Working Paper No. 94.03, University of Geneva

BANERJEE, A., J. DOLADO, J. GALBRAITH AND D. HENDRY (1993)
Co-Integration, Error Correction, and the Econometric Analysis of Non-Stationary Data
Oxford University Press, Oxford

BENASSY, J.-P. (1992)
Are Rational Expectations Really Rational?
Economics Letters, **39**, 49–54

BENVENISTE, A., M. MÉTIVIER, AND P. PRIOURET (1990)
Adaptive Algorithms and Stochastic Approximations
Springer–Verlag, Berlin

BLUME, L. E., M. M. BRAY, AND D. EASLEY (1982)
Introduction to the Stability of Rational Expectations Equilibrium
Journal of Economic Theory, **26**, 313–317

BOUGEROL, P. AND N. PICARD (1992a)
Stationarity of GARCH Processes and some Nonnegative Time Series
Journal of Econometrics, **52**, 115–127

BOUGEROL, P. AND N. PICARD (1992b)
Strict Stationarity of Generalized Autoregressive Processes
The Annals of Probability, **20**, 1714–1730

BRAY, M. (1982)
Learning, Estimation, and the Stability of Rational Expectations
Journal of Economic Theory, **26**, 318–339

BRAY, M. (1983)
Convergence to Rational Expectations Equilibrium; in R. Frydman and E.S. Phelps (eds): *Individual Forecasting and Aggregate Outcomes,* pp. 123–132
Cambridge University Press, Cambridge

BRAY, M. M. AND N. E. SAVIN (1986)
Rational Expectations Equilibria, Learning, and Model Specification
Econometrica, **54**, 1129–1160

BULLARD, J. (1992)
Time-varying Parameters and Nonconvergence to Rational Expectations under Least Squares Learning
Economics Letters, **40**, 159–166

BULLARD, J. (1994)
Learning Equilibria
Journal of Economic Theory, **64**, 468–485

CAGAN, P. (1956)
The Monetary Dynamics of Hyperinflation; in M. Friedman (ed): *Studies in the Quantity Theory of Money,* pp. 25–120
University of Chicago Press, Chicago

CHANG, M. C., C. Y. CYRUS CHU AND K. LIN (1991a)
The Global Stability of Least Square Learning
Discussion Paper, Institute of Economics, Academia Sinica, Taipei

CHANG, M. C., C. Y. CYRUS CHU AND K. LIN (1991b)
A Reformulation of the Least Square Learning Mechanism
Discussion Paper, Institute of Economics, Academia Sinica, Taipei

CHANG, M. C., C. Y. CYRUS CHU AND K. LIN (1991c)
The Recursive Prediction Error Learning: An Alternative to Least Square Learning
Discussion Paper, Institute of Economics, Academia Sinica, Taipei

CHEN, H.-F. AND L. GUO (1991)
Identification and Stochastic Adaptive Control
Birkhäuser, Boston

CHOW, Y. S. (1965)
Local Convergence of Martingales and the Law of Large Numbers
The Annals of Mathematical Statistics, **36**, 552–558

CYERT, R. M. AND M. H. DEGROOT (1974)
Rational Expectations and Bayesian Analysis
Journal of Political Economy, **82**, 521–536

DECANIO, S. J. (1979)
Rational Expectations and Learning from Experience
Quarterly Journal of Economics, **93**, 47–57

DVORETZKY, A. (1956)
On Stochastic Approximation
Proceedings of the Third Berkeley Symposium on Mathematical Statistics and Probability, Vol I, 39–55

EVANS, G. W. (1983)
The Stability of Rational Expectations in Macroeconomic Models; in R. Frydman and E. S. Phelps (eds): *Individual Forecasting and Aggregate Outcomes* pp. 69–94
Cambridge University Press, Cambridge

EVANS, G. W. (1989)
The Fragility of Sunspots and Bubbles
Journal of Monetary Economics, **23**, 297–317

EVANS, G. W. AND S. HONKAPOHJA (1994a)
Learning, Convergence, and Stability with Multiple Rational Expectations Equilibria
European Economic Review, **38**, 1071–1098

EVANS, G. W. AND S. HONKAPOHJA (1994b)
On the Local Stability of Sunspot Equilibria under Adaptive Learning Rules
Journal of Economic Theory, **64**, 142–161

EVANS, G. W. AND S. HONKAPOHJA (1994c)
Convergence of Least Squares Learning to a Non-stationary Equilibrium
Economics Letters, **46**, 131–136

FOURGEAUD, C., C. GOURIEROUX, AND J. PRADEL (1986)
Learning Procedures and Convergence to Rationality
Econometrica, **54**, 845–868

FRIEDMAN, B. M. (1979)
Optimal Expectations and the Extreme Information Assumption of 'Rational Expectations' Macromodels
Journal of Monetary Economics, **5**, 23–41

FRYDMAN, R. (1982)
Towards an Understanding of Market Processes: Individual Expectations, Learning, and Convergence to Rational Expectations Equilibrium
American Economic Review, **72**, 652–668

FRYDMAN, R. (1983)
A Distinction between the Unconditional Expectational Equilibrium and the Rational Expectations Equilibrium; in R. Frydman and E. S. Phelps (eds): *Individual Forecasting and Aggregate Outcomes*, pp. 139–146
Cambridge University Press, Cambridge

FRYDMAN, R. and E.S. PHELPS (1983)
Individual Forecasting and Aggregate Outcomes
Cambridge University Press, Cambridge

GOODWIN, G. C., P. J. RAMADGE, AND P. E. CAINES (1981)
Discrete Time Stochastic Adaptive Control
SIAM Journal of Control and Optimization, **19**, 829–853

GRANDMONT, J.-M. (1985)
On Endogenous Competitive Business Cycles
Econometrica, **53**, 995–1045

GRANDMONT, J.-M. (1992)
Aggregation, Learning and Rationality
Technical Report No. 52, Stanford University

GRAUPE, D. (1984)
Time Series Analysis, Identification and Adaptive Filtering
Robert E. Krieger Publishing Company, Malabar, Florida

GROSSMAN, S. J. AND J. E. STIGLITZ (1980)
On the Impossibility of Informationally Efficient Markets
American Economic Review, **70**, 393–408

HOMMES, C. H. (1991)
Adaptive Learning and Roads to Chaos: The Case of the Cobweb
Economics Letters, **36**, 127–132

HONKAPOHJA, S. (1993)
Adaptive Learning and Bounded Rationality: An Introduction to Basic Concepts
European Economic Review, **37**, 587–594

JORDAN, J. S. (1992)
Convergence to Rational Expectations in a Stationary Linear Game
Review of Economic Studies, **59**, 109–123

KEYNES, J. M. (1936)
The General Theory of Employment, Interest and Money
Macmillan, London

KIRMAN, A. P. (1975)
Learning by Firms about Demand Conditions; in R. H. Day and T. Groves (eds): *Adaptive Economic Models*, pp. 137–156
Academic Press, New York

KIRMAN, A. P. (1983)
On Mistaken Beliefs and Resultant Equilibria; in R. Frydman and E. S. Phelps (eds): *Individual Forecasing and Aggregate Outcomes*, pp. 147–166
Cambridge University Press, Cambridge

KNOPP, K. (1964)
Theorie und Anwendung der unendlichen Reihen
Springer-Verlag, Berlin

KOTTMANN, T. (1990)
Learning Procedures and Rational Expectations in Linear Models with Forecast Feedback
Ph. D. Thesis, Universität Bonn

KOTTMANN, T. AND I. KULIBERDA (1990)
Autoregressive Models with Forecast Feedback: A Monte-Carlo-Study and First Theoretical Results
Discussion Paper B–160, Universität Bonn

KUAN, C.-M. AND H. WHITE (1994)
Adaptive Learning with Nonlinear Dynamics Driven by Dependent Processes
Econometrica, **62**, *1087–1114*

KUSHNER, H. J. AND D. S. CLARK (1978)
Stochastic Approximation Methods for Constrained and Unconstrained Systems
Springer–Verlag, New York

LAI, T. L. (1989)
Extended Stochastic Lyapunov Functions and Recursive Algorithms in Linear Stochastic Systems; in N. Christopeit, K. Helmes and M. Kohlmann (eds): *Stochastic Differential Systems, Lecture Notes in Control and Information Sciences*, **126**, pp. 206–220
Springer–Verlag, Heidelberg

LAI, T. L. AND C. Z. WEI (1982a)
Least Squares Estimates in Stochastic Regression Models with Applications to Identification and Control of Dynamic Systems
The Annals of Statistics, **10**, 154–166

LAI, T. L. AND C. Z. WEI (1982b)
Asymptotic Properties of Projections with Applications to Stochastic Regression Problems
Journal of Multivariate Analysis, **12**, 346–370

LAI, T. L. AND C. Z. WEI (1983a)
Asymptotic Properties of General Autoregressive Models and Strong Consistency of Least-Squares Estimates of Their Parameters
Journal of Multivariate Analysis, **13**, 1–23

LAI, T. L. AND C. Z. WEI (1983b)
A Note on Martingale Difference Sequences Satisfying the Local Marcinkiewicz–Zygmund Condition
Bulletin of the Institute of Mathematics Academia Sinica, **11**, 1–13

LAI, T. L. AND C. Z. WEI (1985)
Asymptotic Properties of Multivariate Weighted Sums with Applications to Stochastic Regression in Linear Dynamic Systems; in P. R. Krishnaiah (ed): *Multivariate Analysis – VI,* pp. 375–393
North-Holland, Amsterdam

LJUNG, L. (1977)
Analysis of Recursive Stochastic Algorithms
IEEE Transactions on Automatic Control, **AC–22**, 551–575

LJUNG, L. AND T. SÖDERSTRÖM (1983)
Theory and Practice of Recursive Identification
MIT Press, Cambridge

LUCAS, R. E. (1972)
Expectations and the Neutrality of Money
Journal of Economic Theory, **4**, 103–124

LUCAS, R. E. (1977)
Understanding Business Cycles; in K. Brunner and A. H. Meltzer (eds): *Stabilization of the Domestic and International Economy, Carnegie–Rochester Conference Series on Public Policy, Vol. 5,* pp. 7–29
North Holland, Amsterdam

MARCET, A. AND T. J. SARGENT (1988)
The Fate of Systems With "Adaptive" Expectations
American Economic Review, Papers and Proceedings, **78**, 168–172

MARCET, A. AND T. J. SARGENT (1989a)
Convergence of Least Squares Learning Mechanisms in Self–Referential Linear Stochastic Models
Journal of Economic Theory, **48**, 337–368

MARCET, A. AND T. J. SARGENT (1989b)
Convergence of Least-Squares Learning in Environments with Hidden State Variables and Private Information
Journal of Political Economy, **97**, 1306–1322

MARCET, A. AND T. J. SARGENT (1989c)
Least–Squares Learning and the Dynamics of Hyperinflation; in W. A. Barnett, J. Geweke, and K. Shell (eds): *Economic Complexity: Chaos, Sunspots, Bubbles, and Nonlinearity*, pp. 119–137
Cambridge University Press, Cambridge

MOHR, M. (1990)
Asymptotic Theory for Ordinary Least Squares Estimators in Regression Models with Forecast Feedback
Ph. D. Thesis, Universität Bonn

MOORE, B. J. (1993)
Least–Squares Learning and the Stability of Equilibria with Externalities
Review of Economic Studies, **60**, 197–208

MUTH, J. F. (1961)
Rational Expectations and the Theory of Price Movements
Econometrica, **29**, 315–335

NERLOVE, M. (1958)
Adaptive Expectations and Cobweb Phenomena
Quarterly Journal of Economics, **73**, 227–240

PESARAN, M. H. (1987)
The Limits to Rational Expectations
Basil Blackwell, Oxford

ROBBINS, H. AND D. SIEGMUND (1971)
A Convergence Theorem for Non Negative Almost Supermartingales and some Applications; in J. S. Rustagi (ed): *Optimizing Methods in Statistics*, pp. 233–257
Academic Press, New York

ROTTER J. B. (1954)
Social Learning and Clinical Psychology
Prentice–Hall, Englewood Cliff

SARGENT, T. J. (1991)
Equilibrium with Signal Extraction from Endogenous Variables
Journal of Economic Dynamics and Control, **15**, 245–273

SARGENT, T. J. AND N. WALLACE (1975)
"Rational" Expectations, the Optimal Monetary Instrument, and the Optimal Money Supply Rule
Journal of Political Economy, **83**, 241–254

STOUT, W. F. (1974)
Almost Sure Convergence
Academic Press, New York

TAYLOR, J. B. (1979)
Estimation and Control of a Macroeconomic Model with Rational Expectations
Econometrica, **47**, *1267–1286*

TAYLOR, J. B. (1981)
Stabilization, Accomodation, and Monetary Rules
American Economic Review, Papers and Proceedings, **71**, *145–149*

TIERNEY, L. (1988)
XLISP-STAT: A Statistical Environment Based on the XLISP Language (Version 2.0)
Technical Report No. 528, University of Minnesota

TONG, H. (1990)
Non-linear Time Series: A Dynamical System Approach
Clarendon Press, Oxford

TOWNSEND, R. M. (1978)
Market Anticipations, Rational Expectations, and Bayesian Analysis
International Economic Review, **19**, 481–494

WALK, H. (1985)
Almost Sure Convergence of Stochastic Approximation Processes
Statistics and Decisions, Supplement Issue No. 2, 137–141

WALK H. (1992)
Foundations of Stochastic Approximation; in L. Ljung, G. Pflug and H. Walk (eds):*Stochastic Approximation and Optimization of Random Systems*
Birkhäuser Verlag, Basel

WALK, H. AND L. ZSIDÓ (1989)
Convergence of the Robbins-Monro Method for Linear Problems in a Banach Space
Journal of Mathematical Analysis and Applications, **139**, 152–177

WEI, C. Z. (1985)
Asymptotic Properties of Least-Squares Estimates in Stochastic Regression Models
The Annals of Statistics, **13**, 1498–1508

WEI, C. Z. (1987)
Adaptive Prediction by Least Squares Predictors in Stochastic Regression Models with Applications to Time Series
The Annals of Statistics, **15**, 1667–1682

WOODFORD, M. (1990)
Learning to Believe in Sunspots
Econometrica, **58**, 277–307

ZENNER, M. (1992a)
Performance of Least Squares Learning in Autoregressive Models with Forecast Feedback - The Deterministic Case
Discussion Paper B–224, Universität Bonn

ZENNER, M. (1992b)
Performance of Least Squares Learning in Autoregressive Models with Forecast Feedback - The Stochastic Case
Discussion Paper B–225, Universität Bonn

ZENNER, M. (1994)
Prediction Error Learning in Univariate Generalized Autoregressive Models
Discussion Paper B–273, Universität Bonn

ZENNER, M. (1995)
OLS–Learning in Non-Stationary Models with Forecast Feedback
Discussion Paper B–315, Universität Bonn

Notational Conventions, Symbols, and Abbreviations

Notational Conventions

The following notational conventions are used throughout the text:

Greek and Roman letters	scalars and sets
Bold lower case letters	vectors
Bold upper case letters	matrices
Calligraphic letters	σ–algebras, probabilistic events
y, $\boldsymbol{y}$	endogenous variables
x, $\boldsymbol{x}$	exogenous variables
$\boldsymbol{z}$	vectors containing possibly both $\boldsymbol{x}$ and $\boldsymbol{y}$
w, $\boldsymbol{w}$	disturbance terms
$(a_t)_{t\geq 0}$	sequences (in an euclidian space)
$\{z_t\}_{t\geq 0}$	stochastic processes

Symbols

■	end of a proof
$\forall$	for all
$\mathcal{A}^c$	complement of the set/event $\mathcal{A}$
$\mathrm{P}[\mathcal{A}]$	probability of the event $\mathcal{A}$
$\mathrm{E}[\boldsymbol{z}]$	expectation of the random variable $\boldsymbol{z}$

$\mathrm{E}[\boldsymbol{z}\|\mathcal{F}]$	conditional expectation of $\boldsymbol{z}$ w.r.t. the σ–algebra $\mathcal{F}$
$\sigma(x_1, \ldots, x_t)$	σ–algebra generated by the random variables $x_1, \ldots, x_t$
$a_t = O(b_t)$	$\sup_t \|a_t/b_t\| < \infty$
$a_t = o(b_t)$	$\lim_t \|a_t/b_t\| = 0$
$(x)^+$	maximum of a real number x and zero
$\Re(\lambda)$	real part of a complex number λ
$\boldsymbol{x}'$	transpose of a column vector $\boldsymbol{x}$
$\\|\boldsymbol{x}\\|$	euclidian norm of $\boldsymbol{x}$, thus $\\|\boldsymbol{x}\\|^2 = \boldsymbol{x}'\boldsymbol{x}$
$\boldsymbol{I}$, $\boldsymbol{I}_k$	identity matrix (of dimension $k \times k$)
$\boldsymbol{A}'$	transpose of the matrix $\boldsymbol{A}$
$tr(\boldsymbol{A})$	trace of $\boldsymbol{A}$
$\|\boldsymbol{A}\|$	determinant of $\boldsymbol{A}$
$\boldsymbol{A}^+$	Moore–Penrose inverse of $\boldsymbol{A}$
$\lambda_{max}(\boldsymbol{A})$	maximum eigenvalue of $\boldsymbol{A}$
$\lambda_{min}(\boldsymbol{A})$	minimum eigenvalue of $\boldsymbol{A}$
$spec(\boldsymbol{A})$	spectrum of $\boldsymbol{A}$
$\\|\boldsymbol{A}\\|$	operator norm of $\boldsymbol{A}$, thus $\\|\boldsymbol{A}\\|^2 = \lambda_{max}(\boldsymbol{A}'\boldsymbol{A})$
$\boldsymbol{A} \otimes \boldsymbol{B}$	Kronecker product of $\boldsymbol{A}$ and $\boldsymbol{B}$
$vec(\boldsymbol{A})$	vectorizing operator applied to $\boldsymbol{A}$

Abbreviations

a.s.	almost sure(ly)
i.i.d.	independently identically distributed
i.o.	infinitely often
l.h.s.	left-hand side
r.h.s.	right-hand side
s.t.	such that
w.r.t.	with respect to
AR	autoregressive
AR(p)	autoregressive of order p
ARMA	autoregressive–moving average
ARX	AR with exogenous inputs
MDS	martingale difference sequence
LEE	limit expectations equilibrium
ODE	ordinary differential equation
OLS	ordinary least squares
PE	prediction error

PEC	persistent excitation condition
RE	rational expectations
REE	rational expectations equilibrium
REH	rational expectations hypothesis
RLS	recursive least squares
RPE	relative prediction error
SG	stochastic gradient

Vol. 344: K. Neumann, Stochastic Project Networks. XI, 237 pages. 1990.

Vol. 345: A. Cambini, E. Castagnoli, L. Martein, P Mazzoleni, S. Schaible (Eds.), Generalized Convexity and Fractional Programming with Economic Applications. Proceedings, 1988. VII, 361 pages. 1990.

Vol. 346: R. von Randow (Ed.), Integer Programming and Related Areas. A Classified Bibliography 1984–1987. XIII, 514 pages. 1990.

Vol. 347: D. Ríos Insua, Sensitivity Analysis in Multiobjective Decision Making. XI, 193 pages. 1990.

Vol. 348: H. Störmer, Binary Functions and their Applications. VIII, 151 pages. 1990.

Vol. 349: G.A. Pfann, Dynamic Modelling of Stochastic Demand for Manufacturing Employment. VI, 158 pages. 1990.

Vol. 350: W.-B. Zhang, Economic Dynamics. X, 232 pages. 1990.

Vol. 351: A. Lewandowski, V. Volkovich (Eds.), Multiobjective Problems of Mathematical Programming. Proceedings, 1988. VII, 315 pages. 1991.

Vol. 352: O. van Hilten, Optimal Firm Behaviour in the Context of Technological Progress and a Business Cycle. XII, 229 pages. 1991.

Vol. 353: G. Ricci (Ed.), Decision Processes in Economics. Proceedings, 1989. III, 209 pages 1991.

Vol. 354: M. Ivaldi, A Structural Analysis of Expectation Formation. XII, 230 pages. 1991.

Vol. 355: M. Salomon. Deterministic Lotsizing Models for Production Planning. VII, 158 pages. 1991.

Vol. 356: P. Korhonen, A. Lewandowski, J . Wallenius (Eds.), Multiple Criteria Decision Support. Proceedings, 1989. XII, 393 pages. 1991.

Vol. 357: P. Zörnig, Degeneracy Graphs and Simplex Cycling. XV, 194 pages. 1991.

Vol. 358: P. Knottnerus, Linear Models with Correlated Disturbances. VIII, 196 pages. 1991.

Vol. 359: E. de Jong, Exchange Rate Determination and Optimal Economic Policy Under Various Exchange Rate Regimes. VII, 270 pages. 1991.

Vol. 360: P. Stalder, Regime Translations, Spillovers and Buffer Stocks. VI, 193 pages . 1991.

Vol. 361: C. F. Daganzo, Logistics Systems Analysis. X, 321 pages. 1991.

Vol. 362: F. Gehrels, Essays In Macroeconomics of an Open Economy. VII, 183 pages. 1991.

Vol. 363: C. Puppe, Distorted Probabilities and Choice under Risk. VIII, 100 pages . 1991

Vol. 364: B. Horvath, Are Policy Variables Exogenous? XII, 162 pages. 1991.

Vol. 365: G. A. Heuer, U. Leopold-Wildburger. Balanced Silverman Games on General Discrete Sets. V, 140 pages. 1991.

Vol. 366: J. Gruber (Ed.), Econometric Decision Models. Proceedings, 1989. VIII, 636 pages. 1991.

Vol. 367: M. Grauer, D. B. Pressmar (Eds.), Parallel Computing and Mathematical Optimization. Proceedings. V, 208 pages. 1991.

Vol. 368: M. Fedrizzi, J. Kacprzyk, M. Roubens (Eds.), Interactive Fuzzy Optimization. VII, 216 pages. 1991.

Vol. 369: R. Koblo, The Visible Hand. VIII, 131 pages. 1991.

Vol. 370: M. J. Beckmann, M. N. Gopalan, R. Subramanian (Eds.), Stochastic Processes and their Applications. Proceedings, 1990. XLI, 292 pages. 1991.

Vol. 371: A. Schmutzler, Flexibility and Adjustment to Information in Sequential Decision Problems. VIII, 198 pages. 1991.

Vol. 372: J. Esteban, The Social Viability of Money. X, 202 pages. 1991.

Vol. 373: A. Billot, Economic Theory of Fuzzy Equilibria. XIII, 164 pages. 1992.

Vol. 374: G. Pflug, U. Dieter (Eds.), Simulation and Optimization. Proceedings, 1990. X, 162 pages. 1992.

Vol. 375: S.-J. Chen, Ch.-L. Hwang, Fuzzy Multiple Attribute Decision Making. XII, 536 pages. 1992.

Vol. 376: K.-H. Jöckel, G. Rothe, W. Sendler (Eds.), Bootstrapping and Related Techniques. Proceedings, 1990. VIII, 247 pages. 1992.

Vol. 377: A. Villar, Operator Theorems with Applications to Distributive Problems and Equilibrium Models. XVI, 160 pages. 1992.

Vol. 378: W. Krabs, J. Zowe (Eds.), Modern Methods of Optimization. Proceedings, 1990. VIII, 348 pages. 1992.

Vol. 379: K. Marti (Ed.), Stochastic Optimization. Proceedings, 1990. VII, 182 pages. 1992.

Vol. 380: J. Odelstad, Invariance and Structural Dependence. XII, 245 pages. 1992.

Vol. 381: C. Giannini, Topics in Structural VAR Econometrics. XI, 131 pages. 1992.

Vol. 382: W. Oettli, D. Pallaschke (Eds.), Advances in Optimization. Proceedings, 1991. X, 527 pages. 1992.

Vol. 383: J. Vartiainen, Capital Accumulation in a Corporatist Economy. VII, 177 pages. 1992.

Vol. 384: A. Martina, Lectures on the Economic Theory of Taxation. XII, 313 pages. 1992.

Vol. 385: J. Gardeazabal, M. Regúlez, The Monetary Model of Exchange Rates and Cointegration. X, 194 pages. 1992.

Vol. 386: M. Desrochers, J.-M. Rousseau (Eds.), Computer-Aided Transit Scheduling. Proceedings, 1990. XIII, 432 pages. 1992.

Vol. 387: W. Gaertner, M. Klemisch-Ahlert, Social Choice and Bargaining Perspectives on Distributive Justice. VIII, 131 pages. 1992.

Vol. 388: D. Bartmann, M. J. Beckmann, Inventory Control. XV, 252 pages. 1992.

Vol. 389: B. Dutta, D. Mookherjee, T. Parthasarathy, T. Raghavan, D. Ray, S. Tijs (Eds.), Game Theory and Economic Applications. Proceedings, 1990. IX, 454 pages. 1992.

Vol. 390: G. Sorger, Minimum Impatience Theorem for Recursive Economic Models. X, 162 pages. 1992.

Vol. 391: C. Keser, Experimental Duopoly Markets with Demand Inertia. X, 150 pages. 1992.

Vol. 392: K. Frauendorfer, Stochastic Two-Stage Programming. VIII, 228 pages. 1992.

Vol. 393: B. Lucke, Price Stabilization on World Agricultural Markets. XI, 274 pages. 1992.

Vol. 394: Y.-J. Lai, C.-L. Hwang, Fuzzy Mathematical Programming. XIII, 301 pages. 1992.

Vol. 395: G. Haag, U. Mueller, K. G. Troitzsch (Eds.), Economic Evolution and Demographic Change. XVI, 409 pages. 1992.

Vol. 396: R. V. V. Vidal (Ed.), Applied Simulated Annealing. VIII, 358 pages. 1992.

Vol. 397: J. Wessels, A. P. Wierzbicki (Eds.), User-Oriented Methodology and Techniques of Decision Analysis and Support. Proceedings, 1991. XII, 295 pages. 1993.

Vol. 398: J.-P. Urbain, Exogeneity in Error Correction Models. XI, 189 pages. 1993.

Vol. 399: F. Gori, L. Geronazzo, M. Galeotti (Eds.), Nonlinear Dynamics in Economics and Social Sciences. Proceedings, 1991. VIII, 367 pages. 1993.

Vol. 400: H. Tanizaki, Nonlinear Filters. XII, 203 pages. 1993.

Vol. 401: K. Mosler, M. Scarsini, Stochastic Orders and Applications. V, 379 pages. 1993.

Vol. 402: A. van den Elzen, Adjustment Processes for Exchange Economies and Noncooperative Games. VII, 146 pages. 1993.

Vol. 403: G. Brennscheidt, Predictive Behavior. VI, 227 pages. 1993.

Vol. 404: Y.-J. Lai, Ch.-L. Hwang, Fuzzy Multiple Objective Decision Making. XIV, 475 pages. 1994.

Vol. 405: S. Komlósi, T. Rapcsák, S. Schaible (Eds.), Generalized Convexity. Proceedings, 1992. VIII, 404 pages. 1994.

Vol. 406: N. M. Hung, N. V. Quyen, Dynamic Timing Decisions Under Uncertainty. X, 194 pages. 1994.

Vol. 407: M. Ooms, Empirical Vector Autoregressive Modeling. XIII, 380 pages. 1994.

Vol. 408: K. Haase, Lotsizing and Scheduling for Production Planning. VIII, 118 pages. 1994.

Vol. 409: A. Sprecher, Resource-Constrained Project Scheduling. XII, 142 pages. 1994.

Vol. 410: R. Winkelmann, Count Data Models. XI, 213 pages. 1994.

Vol. 411: S. Dauzère-Péres, J.-B. Lasserre, An Integrated Approach in Production Planning and Scheduling. XVI, 137 pages. 1994.

Vol. 412: B. Kuon, Two-Person Bargaining Experiments with Incomplete Information. IX, 293 pages. 1994.

Vol. 413: R. Fiorito (Ed.), Inventory, Business Cycles and Monetary Transmission. VI, 287 pages. 1994.

Vol. 414: Y. Crama, A. Oerlemans, F. Spieksma, Production Planning in Automated Manufacturing. X, 210 pages. 1994.

Vol. 415: P. C. Nicola, Imperfect General Equilibrium. XI, 167 pages. 1994.

Vol. 416: H. S. J. Cesar, Control and Game Models of the Greenhouse Effect. XI, 225 pages. 1994.

Vol. 417: B. Ran, D. E. Boyce, Dynamic Urban Transportation Network Models. XV, 391 pages. 1994.

Vol. 418: P. Bogetoft, Non-Cooperative Planning Theory. XI, 309 pages. 1994.

Vol. 419: T. Maruyama, W. Takahashi (Eds.), Nonlinear and Convex Analysis in Economic Theory. VIII, 306 pages. 1995.

Vol. 420: M. Peeters, Time-To-Build. Interrelated Investment and Labour Demand Modelling. With Applications to Six OECD Countries. IX, 204 pages. 1995.

Vol. 421: C. Dang, Triangulations and Simplicial Methods. IX, 196 pages. 1995.

Vol. 422: D. S. Bridges, G. B. Mehta, Representations of Preference Orderings. X, 165 pages. 1995.

Vol. 423: K. Marti, P. Kall (Eds.), Stochastic Programming. Numerical Techniques and Engineering Applications. VIII, 351 pages. 1995.

Vol. 424: G. A. Heuer, U. Leopold-Wildburger, Silverman's Game. X, 283 pages. 1995.

Vol. 425: J. Kohlas, P.-A. Monney, A Mathematical Theory of Hints. XIII, 419 pages, 1995.

Vol. 426: B. Finkenstädt, Nonlinear Dynamics in Economics. IX, 156 pages. 1995.

Vol. 427: F. W. van Tongeren, Microsimulation Modelling of the Corporate Firm. XVII, 275 pages. 1995.

Vol. 428: A. A. Powell, Ch. W. Murphy, Inside a Modern Macroeconometric Model. XVIII, 424 pages. 1995.

Vol. 429: R. Durier, C. Michelot, Recent Developments in Optimization. VIII, 356 pages. 1995.

Vol. 430: J. R. Daduna, I. Branco, J. M. Pinto Paixão (Eds.), Computer-Aided Transit Scheduling. XIV, 374 pages. 1995.

Vol. 431: A. Aulin, Causal and Stochastic Elements in Business Cycles. XI, 116 pages. 1996.

Vol. 432: M. Tamiz (Ed.), Multi-Objective Programming and Goal Programming. VI, 359 pages. 1996.

Vol. 433: J. Menon, Exchange Rates and Prices. XIV, 313 pages. 1996.

Vol. 434: M. W. J. Blok, Dynamic Models of the Firm. VII, 193 pages. 1996.

Vol. 435: L. Chen, Interest Rate Dynamics, Derivatives Pricing, and Risk Management. XII, 149 pages. 1996.

Vol. 436: M. Klemisch-Ahlert, Bargaining in Economic and Ethical Environments. IX, 155 pages. 1996.

Vol. 437: C. Jordan, Batching and Scheduling. IX, 178 pages. 1996.

Vol. 438: A. Villar, General Equilibrium with Increasing Returns. XIII, 164 pages. 1996.

Vol. 439: M. Zenner, Learning to Become Rational. VII, 201 pages. 1996.

Markus Zenner
Kasparstraße 18
50670 Köln

Lebenslauf

14. September 1963	geboren in Marburg/Lahn
1969 - 1972	Grundschule in Dormagen
1972 - 1973	Deutsche Grundschule in Antwerpen/Belgien
1973 - 1976	Europäische Schule in Mol/Belgien
1976 - 1982	Freiherr-vom-Stein-Gymnasium in Leverkusen Abitur am 11. Juni 1982
WS 83/84 - SS 85	Studium der Mathematik mit Nebenfach Betriebswirtschaftslehre an der Universität Marburg/Lahn
WS 85/86 - WS 90/91	Fortführung des Studiums an der Universität Bonn Abschluß als Diplom-Mathematiker am 29. März 1991
4/1991 - 12/1995	Tätigkeit als wissenschaftlicher Mitarbeiter am Institut für Ökonometrie und Operations Research, Abteilung Ökonometrie, der Universität Bonn

GPSR Compliance

The European Union's (EU) General Product Safety Regulation (GPSR) is a set of rules that requires consumer products to be safe and our obligations to ensure this.

If you have any concerns about our products, you can contact us on ProductSafety@springernature.com

In case Publisher is established outside the EU, the EU authorized representative is:

Springer Nature Customer Service Center GmbH
Europaplatz 3
69115 Heidelberg, Germany

Batch number: 10845484

Printed by Printforce, the Netherlands